LANGUAGE!®

The Comprehensive Literacy Curriculum

Jane Fell Greene, Ed.D.

SOPRIS WEST Educational Services
A Cambium Learning Company

BOSTON, MA • NEW YORK, NY • LONGMONT, CO

08 07 06 05   10 9 8 7 6 5 4 3 2

Editorial Director: Nancy Chapel Eberhardt
Word and Phrase Selection: Judy Fell Woods
English Learners: Jennifer Wells Greene
Lesson Development: Sheryl Ferlito, Donna Lutz, Isabel Wesley
Morphology: John Alexander, Mike Minsky, Bruce Rosow
Text Selection: Sara Buckerfield, Jim Cloonan
Decodable and Independent Text: Jenny Hamilton, Steve Harmon

ISBN 1-59318-372-0

Printed in the United States of America

Published and distributed by

SOPRIS
WEST
EDUCATIONAL SERVICES

4093 Specialty Place • Longmont, CO 80504 • (303) 651-2829
www.sopriswest.com

Table of Contents

Check off the activities you complete with each lesson. Evaluate your accomplishments at the end of each lesson. Pay attention to teacher evaluations and comments.

Unit Objectives	Lesson 1 (Date:_____)	Lesson 2 (Date:_____)
STEP 1 **Phonemic Awareness and Phonics** • Say sounds for vowel digraphs <u>ai</u>, <u>ee</u>, <u>oa</u>. • Write the letters for the sounds / $\bar{a}$ /, / $\bar{e}$ /, / $\bar{o}$ / using vowel digraphs. • Identify vowel digraph syllables.	❑ Discover It: Vowel Digraphs ❑ Vowel Chart (T)	❑ Exercise 1: Find It: Vowel Digraphs
STEP 2 **Word Recognition and Spelling** • Read and spell words composed of vowel digraph syllables. • Read and spell the **Essential Words:** *abroad, against, captain, curtain, language, nuisance.* • Read and spell words with prefixes and suffixes.	❑ Exercise 1: Spelling Pretest 1 ❑ Memorize It	❑ Exercise 2: Sort It: Syllable Types ❑ Exercise 3: Write It: Essential Words ❑ Word Fluency 1
STEP 3 **Vocabulary and Morphology** • Identify homophones. • Identify and define noun and adjective suffixes. • Use the meanings of prefixes and suffixes to define words.	❑ Unit Vocabulary ❑ Exercise 2: Word Line: Degrees of Meaning ❑ Draw It: Idioms	❑ Exercise 4: Define It: Suffixes ❑ Exercise 5: Rewrite It: Suffixes ❑ Expression of the Day
STEP 4 **Grammar and Usage** • Identify and use **be** as a linking verb. • Identify irregular verbs. • Write sentences with a predicate nominative.	❑ Exercise 3: Identify It: Nouns Used as Adjectives ❑ Exercise 4: Find It: Nouns Used as Adjectives	❑ Exercise 6: Identify It: Noun Suffixes
STEP 5 **Listening and Reading Comprehension** • Use context-based strategies to define words. • Identify reasons and supporting evidence in informational text. • Identify character traits as part of plot analysis. • Identify and understand signal words for comprehension: **assess**, **justify**.	❑ Independent Text: "Early Olympic Speeders" ❑ Exercise 5: Phrase It ❑ Exercise 6: Use the Clues	❑ Passage Fluency 1 ❑ Exercise 7: Using Visuals: Charts
STEP 6 **Speaking and Writing** • Write responses to sentences using the signal words: **assess**, **justify**. • Organize reasons and supporting evidence from text in a graphic organizer. • Write a paragraph organized by reasons. • Write a description of a character using traits and evidence of traits from the text.	❑ Exercise 7: Rewrite It	❑ Exercise 8: Answer It

Self-Evaluation (5 is the highest)
  Effort = I produced my best work.
  Participation = I was actively involved in tasks.
  Independence = I worked on my own.
	Effort: 1 2 3 4 5
	Participation: 1 2 3 4 5
	Independence: 1 2 3 4 5
		Effort: 1 2 3 4 5
		Participation: 1 2 3 4 5
		Independence: 1 2 3 4 5

Teacher Evaluation	**Effort:** 1 2 3 4 5 **Participation:** 1 2 3 4 5 **Independence:** 1 2 3 4 5	**Effort:** 1 2 3 4 5 **Participation:** 1 2 3 4 5 **Independence:** 1 2 3 4 5

Lesson 3 (Date:_____)	**Lesson 4** (Date:_____)	**Lesson 5** (Date:_____)
❑ Listening for Word Parts: Suffixes	❑ Listening for Word Parts: Suffixes	❑ Content Mastery: Vowel Digraphs
❑ Divide It ❑ Word Fluency 2	❑ Exercise 1: Build It: Words With Suffixes	❑ Content Mastery: Spelling Posttest 1
❑ Vocabulary Focus ❑ Use the Clues ❑ Expression of the Day	❑ Exercise 2: Define It: Suffixes ❑ Exercise 3: Rewrite It: Suffixes	❑ Exercise 1: Define It: Prefixes *fore-, mid-, mis-, over-* ❑ Exercise 2: Rewrite It: Prefixes *fore-, mid-, mis-, over-*
❑ Identify It: Words in Text	❑ Exercise 4: Identify It: Adjective Suffixes ❑ Exercise 5: Find It: Irregular Verb Forms	❑ Masterpiece Sentences: Stages 1–6
❑ Instructional Text: "Fiber Optics: High-Speed Highways for Light"	❑ Take Note: "Fiber Optics: High-Speed Highways for Light"	❑ Map It: Reasons (T)
❑ Exercise 1: Answer It	❑ Map It: Reasons (T) ❑ Challenge Text: "A Slow Take on Fast Food"	❑ Exercise 3: Write It: Reasons Paragraph (T) ❑ Exercise 4: Write It: Conclusion Sentence ❑ Exercise 5: Challenge Writing: A Persuasive Paragraph ❑ Challenge Text: "A Slow Take on Fast Food"
Effort:　　1　2　3　4　5 **Participation:**　1　2　3　4　5 **Independence:**　1　2　3　4　5	**Effort:**　　1　2　3　4　5 **Participation:**　1　2　3　4　5 **Independence:**　1　2　3　4　5	**Effort:**　　1　2　3　4　5 **Participation:**　1　2　3　4　5 **Independence:**　1　2　3　4　5
Effort:　　1　2　3　4　5 **Participation:**　1　2　3　4　5 **Independence:**　1　2　3　4　5	**Effort:**　　1　2　3　4　5 **Participation:**　1　2　3　4　5 **Independence:**　1　2　3　4　5	**Effort:**　　1　2　3　4　5 **Participation:**　1　2　3　4　5 **Independence:**　1　2　3　4　5

Check off the activities you complete with each lesson. Evaluate your accomplishments at the end of each lesson. Pay attention to teacher evaluations and comments.

Unit Objectives	Lesson 6 (Date:_____)	Lesson 7 (Date:_____)
STEP 1 **Phonemic Awareness and Phonics** • Say sounds for vowel digraphs <u>ai</u>, <u>ee</u>, <u>oa</u>. • Write the letters for the sounds / $\bar{a}$ /, / $\bar{e}$ /, / $\bar{o}$ / using vowel digraphs. • Identify vowel digraph syllables.	☐ Content Mastery: Using Student Performance	☐ Listening for Word Parts: Prefixes
STEP 2 **Word Recognition and Spelling** • Read and spell words composed of vowel digraph syllables. • Read and spell the **Essential Words**: *abroad, against, captain, curtain, language, nuisance.* • Read and spell words with prefixes and suffixes.	☐ Exercise 1: Spelling Pretest 2 ☐ Word Fluency 3	☐ Build It: Words With Prefixes ☐ Word Fluency 4
STEP 3 **Vocabulary and Morphology** • Identify homophones. • Identify and define noun and adjective suffixes. • Use the meanings of prefixes and suffixes to define words.	☐ Exercise 2: Word Line: Degrees of Meaning ☐ Expression of the Day	☐ Focus on Vocabulary ☐ Use the Clues ☐ Expression of the Day
STEP 4 **Grammar and Usage** • Identify and use **be** as a linking verb. • Identify irregular verbs. • Write sentences with a predicate nominative.	☐ Exercise 3: Identify It: Linking Verb or Helping Verb ☐ Exercise 4: Code It: Predicate Nominative ☐ Exercise 5: Punctuate It: Commas in a Series	☐ Identify It: Words in Text
STEP 5 **Listening and Reading Comprehension** • Use context-based strategies to define words. • Identify reasons and supporting evidence in informational text. • Identify character traits as part of plot analysis. • Identify and understand signal words for comprehension: **assess, justify.**	☐ Teacher's Edition: "Butterfly's Bet"	☐ Instructional Text: "Raymond's Run" ☐ Text Connection: Identify Character Traits
STEP 6 **Speaking and Writing** • Write responses to sentences using the signal words: **assess, justify.** • Organize reasons and supporting evidence from text in a graphic organizer. • Write a paragraph organized by reasons. • Write a description of a character using traits and evidence of traits from the text.	☐ Map It: Plot (T)	☐ Spotlight on Characters (T)
Self-Evaluation (5 is the highest) **Effort** = I produced my best work. **Participation** = I was actively involved in tasks. **Independence** = I worked on my own.	**Effort:** 1 2 3 4 5 **Participation:** 1 2 3 4 5 **Independence:** 1 2 3 4 5	**Effort:** 1 2 3 4 5 **Participation:** 1 2 3 4 5 **Independence:** 1 2 3 4 5
Teacher Evaluation	**Effort:** 1 2 3 4 5 **Participation:** 1 2 3 4 5 **Independence:** 1 2 3 4 5	**Effort:** 1 2 3 4 5 **Participation:** 1 2 3 4 5 **Independence:** 1 2 3 4 5

Lesson 8 (Date:_____)	Lesson 9 (Date:_____)	Lesson 10 (Date:_____)
❏ Exercise 1: Listening for Stressed Syllables		
❏ Exercise 2: Build It: Words With Affixes	❏ Exercise 1: Sort It: Syllable Types	❏ Content Mastery: Spelling Posttest 2
❏ Exercise 3: Fill In: Words With Affixes ❏ Exercise 4: Fill In: Homophones	❏ Content Mastery: Homophones ❏ Content Mastery: Prefixes and Suffixes	❏ Content Mastery: Using Student Performance ❏ Exercise 1: Define It: Suffixes -dom, -some ❏ Draw It: Idioms
❏ Exercise 5: Identify It: Noun Functions ❏ Exercise 6: Diagram It: Predicate Nominative (T)	❏ Content Mastery	❏ Content Mastery: Using Student Performance
❏ Instructional Text: "Raymond's Run"	❏ Instructional Text: "Raymond's Run" ❏ Exercise 2: Answer It: Multiple Choice	❏ "The Tortoise and the Hare"
❏ Spotlight on Characters (T)	❏ Spotlight on Characters (T) ❏ Write It: Character Summary ❏ Challenge Text: "The Tortoise and the Hare"	❏ Exercise 2: Write It: Character Summary (T) ❏ Challenge Text: "The Tortoise and the Hare"
Effort: 1 2 3 4 5 **Participation:** 1 2 3 4 5 **Independence:** 1 2 3 4 5	**Effort:** 1 2 3 4 5 **Participation:** 1 2 3 4 5 **Independence:** 1 2 3 4 5	**Effort:** 1 2 3 4 5 **Participation:** 1 2 3 4 5 **Independence:** 1 2 3 4 5
Effort: 1 2 3 4 5 **Participation:** 1 2 3 4 5 **Independence:** 1 2 3 4 5	**Effort:** 1 2 3 4 5 **Participation:** 1 2 3 4 5 **Independence:** 1 2 3 4 5	**Effort:** 1 2 3 4 5 **Participation:** 1 2 3 4 5 **Independence:** 1 2 3 4 5

Exercise 1 · Spelling Pretest 1

▶ Write the word your teacher repeats.

1. _____

2. _____

3. _____

4. _____

5. _____

6. _____

7. _____

8. _____

9. _____

10. _____

11. _____

12. _____

13. _____

14. _____

15. _____

Exercise 2 · Word Line: Degrees of Meaning

▸ Read the words in the **Word Bank**.

Word Bank

run	toddle	crawl	scoot
sprint	bolt	jog	walk

▸ Read the topic, or context, above each word line.

▸ Sort and record the words below the word line according to their degree of meaning related to the target word **speed**.

Context: Teen at the Track

slow ———————————————————————————————————— fast

_____ _____ _____ _____ _____

Context: Young Toddler at a Playground

slow ———————————————————————————————————— fast

_____ _____ _____ _____ _____

▸ Create your own word line by choosing a topic from below or creating your own.

▸ Use the dictionary or thesaurus to find and record words relating your topic to the degrees of **speed**.

Possible topics include dancing, skiing, throwing a baseball or football, and driving.

Context: _____

slow ———————————————————————————————————— fast

_____ _____ _____ _____ _____

Exercise 3 · Identify It: Nouns Used as Adjectives

▶ Read the examples with your teacher.

▶ Use the context to decide if the underlined noun is used as a noun or as an adjective.

▶ Put an X in the correct column.

▶ Finish the rest of the sentences independently.

▶ Share your answers with the class.

Examples:	Noun Used as a Noun	Noun Used as an Adjective
<u>Speed</u> matters in some sports.		
<u>Speed</u> skaters are amazingly fast.		

▶ Finish the rest of the sentences independently.

	Noun Used as a Noun	Noun Used as an Adjective
1. Young Betty Robinson became a <u>track</u> star.		
2. The runners race around the <u>track</u>.		
3. <u>Women</u> athletes first competed in Olympic track events in 1928.		
4. Betty Robinson raced against <u>women</u> who were older.		
5. She set the 100-meter <u>record</u>.		
6. Her <u>record</u> time was 12.2 seconds.		
7. Later Betty Robinson survived a <u>plane</u> crash.		
8. She was badly injured, and the <u>plane</u> was destroyed.		
9. The 1936 Olympic Games were held in <u>Berlin</u>.		
10. Betty Robinson was on a relay team in the <u>Berlin</u> games.		

Exercise 4 · Find It: Nouns Used as Adjectives

▶ Read the paragraph below.

▶ Look at the underlined nouns. Find the ones that are used as adjectives.

▶ List those on the line below the paragraph.

---

from "Early Olympic Speeders"

Betty Robinson was that girl. She won the women's 100-meter <u>dash</u>. Robinson had never thought of an Olympic <u>race</u>. One afternoon, she was running to catch a train. A <u>track</u> coach spotted her. Four months later, she won a <u>college</u> championship. Next, she finished second at the Olympic Trials. Then, she won the 100-meter run at the <u>Amsterdam</u> games. She set a <u>record</u> at 12.2 seconds.

Nouns Used as Adjectives: _____

Exercise 5 · Phrase It

▶ Use the penciling strategy to "scoop" the phrases in each sentence.

▶ Read the sentences as you would speak them.

▶ Do the first sentence with your teacher.

---

from "Early Olympic Speeders"

In 1928 an unknown 16-year-old girl won gold. She was a high school junior. She took first place. The event itself was a first. Women's track and field was new. The sport had just been added to the Olympic Games.

Unit 19 · Lesson 1

Exercise 6 · Use the Clues

▸ Read the excerpt below.

▸ Reread the underlined phrase **was born**.

▸ Reread the text before and after the underlined phrase.

▸ Circle the word or words that help to define the phrase **was born**.

---

from "Early Olympic Speeders"

In 1928, an unknown 16-year-old girl won the gold. She was a high school junior. She took first place. The event itself was a first. Women's track and field **was born**. The sport had entered the Olympic Games.

▸ Write a definition for the phrase **was born**, using context clues.

▸ Write a sentence that demonstrates understanding of the context by replacing the phrase **was born** with your definition.

Define It:

was born— _____

Sentence: _____

_____

Exercise 7 · Rewrite It

▶ Read the excerpt below.

▶ Circle the pronouns in the paragraph.

▶ Underline the noun replaced by the pronouns.

▶ Rewrite the paragraph by combining sentences to reduce the number of pronouns.

▶ Replace some of the remaining pronouns to make a more interesting paragraph.

▶ Check that each sentence uses sentence signals—capital letters, commas, and end punctuation.

---

from "Early Olympic Speeders"

Over the next two years, Bleibtrey won every race she entered. She won short races. She won long races. She won freestyle. She won backstroke. She became a celebrated athlete.

Over the next two years, Bleibtrey won every race she entered. _____

_____

_____

Exercise 1 · Find It: Vowel Digraphs

▶ Read the paragraph below.

▶ Underline each word with the vowel digraph **ai, ee,** or **oa**.

▶ Circle the vowel digraph in the word.

▶ Sort and write these words in the columns below according to their long vowel sounds.

---

based on "Fiber Optics: High-Speed Highways for Light"

What happens when you download e-mail from the Internet? What carries the main idea of your message when you shoot the breeze online with a friend? You may be using fiber optics. Fiber optic cables float beneath the streets of many of our cities and towns. These cable roadways contain all kinds of information from around the world.

/ $\bar{a}$ /	/ $\bar{e}$ /	/ $\bar{o}$ /

Exercise 2 · Sort It: Syllable Types

▸ Read each word in the **Word Bank**.

Word Bank

speed	skate	these	coach	polio	try
silo	train	games	three	brain	road

▸ Identify the long vowel syllable type in the word.

▸ Write the word under the correct heading.

Open	Final Silent _e_	Vowel Digraph

Unit 19 · Lesson 2

Exercise 3 · Write It: Essential Words

▶ Review the **Essential Words** in the **Word Bank**.

Word Bank

curtain	against	captain	abroad	nuisance	language

▶ Put the words in alphabetical order and write them on the lines.

▶ Write one sentence for each **Essential Word**.

▶ Check that each sentence uses sentence signals—correct capitalization, commas, and end punctuation.

1. _____

_____

2. _____

_____

3. _____

_____

4. _____

_____

5. _____

_____

6. _____

_____

Exercise 4 · Define It: Suffixes

▸ Read each affixed word.

▸ Underline the base word and circle the suffix in each word.

▸ Write a short definition of the word. Use your **Morphemes for Meaning Cards** for the suffixes **-er, -ist, -ment,** and **-ness** as a resource.

▸ Use a dictionary to check your work.

Example: <u>teach</u>(er)—someone who teaches _____

1. entertainer—_____

_____

2. shipment—_____

_____

3. thickness—_____

_____

4. finalist—_____

_____

5. deeper—_____

_____

Unit 19 · Lesson 2

Exercise 5 · Rewrite It: Suffixes

▸ Read each of the example sentences with your teacher.

▸ Replace the underlined phrase in each with a base word + a suffix.

▸ Reread each sentence to check your work.

▸ Finish the rest of the sentences independently.

▸ Use your **Morphemes for Meaning Cards** for the suffixes **-er, -ist, -ment,** and **-ness** as a resource.

▸ Reread these sentences to check your work.

Sentence with underlined phrase:	Sentence with phrase changed to a single word:
The <u>person who trains</u> others needs to be as dedicated as the athlete.	The _____ needs to be as dedicated as the athlete.
Careful hand washing is helpful in preventing an <u>ill state or condition</u>.	Careful hand washing is helpful in preventing an _____.
1. <u>Someone who waits</u> on tables took our order.	The _____ took our order.
2. My favorite <u>act of entertaining</u> is live music.	My favorite _____ is live music.
3. The weather's <u>state or condition of being damp</u> left us with little to do on our trip to the beach.	The weather's _____ left us with little to do on our trip to the beach.
4. <u>Someone who was driving a motor vehicle</u> drove through a red light.	The _____ drove through a red light.
5. Her <u>state of ailing</u> kept her from going to school and work.	Her _____ kept her from going to school and work.

Exercise 6 · Identify It: Noun Suffixes

▶ Read the text below and underline all the nouns.

▶ Copy only the nouns that have the suffixes **-er**, **-ist**, **-ment**, and **-ness** into the appropriate columns.

---

from "Early Olympic Speeders"

The runner had an agreement with her coach. She would stay back during the preliminary heats. She would hold her fleetness in check and run just fast enough to be one of the finalists. The calmness of this young sprinter was amazing. This race was the fulfillment of her dreams. This young gold medalist was a winner from the moment the starter fired the gun.

-er	-ist	-ment	-ness

Exercise 7 · Using Visuals: Charts

▸ Highlight the headings on the chart.

▸ Put a circle around the sources of the information for the chart.

▸ Use information from **"Early Olympic Speeders"** to complete the chart.

▸ Write a title above the chart.

Title: _____

Sport	Year	Event	Winner	Nation	Winning Time
Swimming	1920	100 m freestyle			
Speed Skating	1924	1500 m			
Sprinting	1928	100 m			

http://www2.sls.lib.il.us/RDS/Community/BettyRobinson/riverdalegirl.html

http://www.hickoksports.com/biograph/bleibtry.shtml

http://www.britannica.com/eb/article?eu=137579&tocid=0&query=ivar%20ballangrud

(continued)

Exercise 7 (continued) · Using Visuals: Charts

Key to Reading Times	Key to Abbreviations
0:00.00 = minutes	m = meters
0:00.00 = seconds	USA =
0:00.00 = tenths of seconds	FIN =
0:00.00 = hundredths of seconds	

▸ Read and discuss the key with your teacher.

▸ Use the key to interpret and record the winning times from the chart on the previous page.

Swimming: _____

Sprinting: _____

Speed Skating: _____

▸ Look for the abbreviations in the chart on the previous page.

▸ Finish the key for the abbreviations.

Exercise 8 · Answer It

▸ Use information from the text and the chart in **"Early Olympic Speeders"** to answer questions using complete sentences.

▸ Circle whether the answer can be found in the text, the chart, or both.

   1. Where were the Olympics held in 1920?   text   chart   both

   _____

   _____

(continued)

Exercise 8 (continued) · Answer It

2. From which country was the winner of the
women's swimming events in the 1920 Olympics?   text   chart both

_____

_____

3. Who was a faster swimmer, Ethelda Bleibtrey
or Jodie Henry?   text   chart   both

_____

_____

4. Which sport is the 100m freestyle event
associated with?   text   chart   both

_____

_____

5. Compare the swimming and sprinting times of early
and current Games. What can you speculate are the
causes for the faster speeds in these three sports?   text   chart both

_____

_____

_____

_____

Exercise 1 · Answer It

▸ Underline the signal word in the question.

▸ Write the answer in complete sentences.

1. Justify using fiber optics rather than electricity.

_____

_____

_____

_____

_____

_____

_____

_____

_____

2. Medical costs are rising. Justify a doctor's request for using fiber optics.

_____

_____

_____

_____

_____

(continued)

3. Imagine you are building a new school. Assess your needs for communication. (television, phone lines, etc.)

_____

_____

_____

_____

_____

4. Summarize ways that fiber optics has changed the way some people work.

_____

_____

_____

_____

5. Do you use fiber optics at school or at home? Predict how fiber optics will affect your life in the future.

_____

_____

_____

_____

Exercise 1 · Build It: Words With Suffixes

▸ Read the base words and suffixes in the **Word Banks**.

Word Banks

art	deep	sleep
help	pave	entertain
contain	humor	pain

-ness	-er	-ist
-less	-ful	-en
-ment		

▸ Combine base words and suffixes to make new words.

▸ Record the words on the lines below.

▸ Check a dictionary to verify that the words you write are real words.

Hint: You can use more than one suffix to make a single word.

_____ _____ _____ _____

_____ _____ _____ _____

_____ _____ _____ _____

_____ _____ _____ _____

_____ _____ _____ _____

_____ _____ _____ _____

Unit 19 · Lesson 4

Exercise 2 · Define It: Suffixes

▸ Read each affixed word.

▸ Underline the base word and circle the suffix.

▸ Write a short definition of the word. Use your **Morphemes for Meaning Cards** for these suffixes as a resource.

▸ Use a dictionary to check your work.

1. sleepless—_____

2. helpful—_____

3. deepen—_____

4. painlessness—_____

5. painfulness—_____

Exercise 3 · Rewrite It: Suffixes

▶ Read each of the example sentences with your teacher.

▶ Replace the underlined phrase with a base word + a suffix.

▶ Reread each sentence to check your work.

▶ Finish the rest of the sentences independently.

▶ Use your **Morphemes for Meaning Cards** for the suffixes **-en, -ful**, and **-less** as a resource.

▶ Reread these sentences to check your work.

Sentence with underlined phrase:	Sentence with phrase changed to a single word:
We felt <u>without hope</u> when the boat drifted down the river.	We felt _____ when the boat drifted down the river.
The sky will <u>become dark</u> just before the storm.	The sky will _____ just before the storm.
1. I'd like to go to the beach on a hot day <u>without a cloud</u>.	I'd like to go to the beach on a hot _____ day.
2. I felt <u>full of cheer</u> when I discovered 20 dollars in my pocket.	I felt _____ when I discovered 20 dollars in my pocket.
3. He could not drive well because of his <u>state of being without care</u> behind the wheel.	He could not drive well because of his _____ behind the wheel.
4. Adding more sugar will cause the lemonade to <u>become sweet</u>.	Adding more sugar will _____ the lemonade.
5. Her <u>state of being full of help</u> was rewarded with a smile and a thank-you.	Her _____ was rewarded with a smile and a thank-you.

Unit 19 · Lesson 4

Exercise 4 · Identify It: Adjective Suffixes

▸ Read each sentence.

▸ Underline all the adjectives with suffixes.

▸ Copy the adjectives that have the suffix -**en**, -**ful**, or -**less** into the appropriate columns.

1. The wooden box contains useless items that should be thrown out.

2. The colorful display of flowers made everyone feel hopeful that spring had arrived.

3. A golden sunset ended a blissful day.

4. The painful broken leg prevented Carlos from playing soccer.

5. Cordless telephones came on the market some years ago.

6. A rainless summer caused the crops to die.

7. The classroom was left in a spotless condition.

8. The judge said the accused was a blameless person.

9. The oaken chest had been in the family for years.

10. The outspoken girl was not helpful in solving the problem.

-en	-ful	-less

Exercise 5 · Find It: Irregular Verb Forms

▸ Read each sentence.

▸ Underline the past tense verb.

▸ Write the past, present, and future forms of the verb in the chart on the next page.

▸ Do the first sentence with your teacher.

1. Some children wept in disappointment after their team's loss.

2. The gash on the athlete's leg bled for a few minutes.

3. The florist kept the flowers in the refrigerator for freshness.

4. Researchers sought new ways of sending information.

5. The large cat crept silently towards the mouse.

6. The baby slept soundly in the quietness of the evening.

7. The racers sped down the track.

8. The scientists met for a discussion of fiber optics.

9. The marathoner felt great tiredness at the end of the race.

10. All the fans saw the athlete's achievement.

(continued)

Unit 19 · Lesson 4

Exercise 5 (continued) · Find It: Irregular Verb Forms

Yesterday	Today	Tomorrow
Past	Present	Future
Irregular Past Tense	Present Tense	Future Tense

▶ Find five nouns with the suffix **-er**, **-ist**, **-ment**, or **-ness** in the sentences on the previous page. Write them on the lines.

_____

_____

_____

Exercise 1 · Define It: Prefixes *fore-, mid-, mis-, over-*

▸ Read each affixed word.

▸ Circle the prefix and underline the base word.

▸ Write a short definition of the word, using your **Morphemes for Meaning Cards** for these prefixes as a resource.

▸ Use a dictionary to check your work.

1. midsummer—_____

2. misfile—_____

3. foresee—_____

4. overdue—_____

5. mismatch—_____

Exercise 2 · Rewrite It: Prefixes *fore-, mid-, mis-, over-*

▸ Read each example sentence with your teacher.

▸ Work together to replace the underlined phrase with a prefix + a base word.

▸ Reread the completed sentences to check your work.

▸ Finish the rest of the sentences independently, using your **Morphemes for Meaning Cards** for these prefixes as a resource.

▸ Reread each completed sentence to check your work.

Sentence with underlined phrase:	Sentence with phrase changed to a single word:
<u>Reading something the wrong way</u> on a test could cause a poor grade.	_____ on a test could cause a poor grade.
My boss <u>paid me too much</u> for the time that I worked.	My boss _____ me for the time that I worked.
1. I <u>spelled a word the wrong way</u> on my test.	I _____ a word on my test.
2. The engine will <u>heat too much</u> if the water pump fails.	The engine will _____ if the water pump fails.
3. Report cards come out <u>in the middle of the year.</u>	Report cards come out _____.
4. They didn't <u>see or hear</u> of any problems <u>before</u> the game.	They didn't _____ any problems at the game.
5. Don't <u>speak the wrong way</u> in class.	Don't _____ in class.

Exercise 3 · Write It: Reasons Paragraph

▸ Use the **Map It: Reasons** template to write a summary.

▸ Write reasons to support this position statement: **Fiber optic technology is being used more and more**.

▸ Include at least three reasons from the text to support your position.

Fiber optic technology is being used more and more.

_____

_____

_____

_____

_____

_____

_____

_____

_____

_____

_____

Exercise 4 · Write It: Conclusion Sentence

▸ Follow these steps to write a conclusion sentence.

1. Read the position statement.

   Fiber optic technology is being utilized more and more.

2. Put a box around two or more words that can be paraphrased.

3. Use a thesaurus to select words for replacement.

   _____

   _____

   _____

   _____

4. Write the conclusion sentence:

   _____

   _____

▸ Transfer your conclusion sentence to the end of your reasons paragraph.

Exercise 5 · Challenge Writing: A Persuasive Paragraph

▶ Write a paragraph that will convince members of the city council to continue to support the fast food ban, or to change their minds about it. Use this page for notes.

1. Begin your paragraph with a strong sentence that states your feelings about the topic.

   _____

   _____

   _____

2. Give three reasons why you feel as you do. Try to include at least one fact. These sentences will make up the body of your paragraph.

   A. _____

   _____

   B. _____

   _____

   C. _____

   _____

3. End with a powerful sentence that gives a call to action.

   _____

   _____

   _____

Writing Tips

DO choose powerful words.

   I firmly believe...

   very unfair...

   negative effect...

DO use language that appeals to your audience.

DON'T repeat ideas.

DO use transition words.

   Finally,...

   I'm sure you'll agree that...

Exercise 1 · Spelling Pretest 2

▶ Write the word your teacher repeats.

1. _____

2. _____

3. _____

4. _____

5. _____

6. _____

7. _____

8. _____

9. _____

10. _____

11. _____

12. _____

13. _____

14. _____

15. _____

Exercise 2 · Word Line: Degrees of Meaning

▶ Read each sentence below.

▶ Read the words in the **Word Bank** under each sentence.

▶ Use a dictionary to define unfamiliar words.

▶ Fill in the blank with the word that makes the best sense according to the context of the sentence.

1. The snail _____ around the tank and then

   _____ back into its shell.

dashed	slithered	popped

2. The deer _____ across the road until he saw headlights.

   Then he _____ across the pavement to safety.

meandered	rolled	dashed

3. The train _____ down the tracks and then

   _____ slowly up the hill.

chugged	rumbled	slithered

4. The jeep _____ across the rugged terrain and then

   _____ along a graded road.

accelerated	meandered	bumped

5. The sailboat _____ through the protected channel and

   then _____ off in high winds.

sped	glided	rolled

Exercise 3 · Identify It: Linking Verb or Helping Verb

▸ Read each sentence.

▸ Decide if the underlined form of the verb **be** is a helping verb or a linking verb.

▸ Fill in the correct bubble.

	Helping Verb	Linking Verb
1. Fiber optics <u>is</u> changing the way information is transmitted.	○	○
2. Fiber optic cables <u>are</u> bundles of long, thin glass tubes.	○	○
3. Each tube <u>is</u> a pathway for digital information.	○	○
4. Before, wires <u>were</u> the way to carry electric pulses.	○	○
5. Fiber optics <u>is</u> used by engineers to channel sunlight into buildings.	○	○
6. My name <u>is</u> Squeaky.	○	○
7. That big boy <u>is</u> my brother.	○	○
8. We <u>were</u> walking together along the sidewalk.	○	○
9. I <u>am</u> a fast runner.	○	○
10. I will <u>be</u> running in the fifty-yard dash.	○	○

Exercise 4 · Code It: Predicate Nominative

▸ Read each sentence.

▸ Decide if the underlined verb is a form of the verb **be**.

▸ Find and label the predicate nominative, if there is one.

1. Squeaky <u>is</u> a racer.

2. Her brother Raymond <u>likes</u> ice cream.

3. In first grade, Squeaky <u>was</u> the fastest runner.

4. Squeaky's family <u>lives</u> in New York City.

5. Squeaky <u>minds</u> Raymond after school.

6. Raymond and Squeaky <u>are</u> siblings.

7. The girl <u>will be</u> a champion.

8. Mr. Pearson <u>brings</u> the clipboards and pencils.

9. Squeaky <u>stands</u> with the other competitors.

10. She <u>is</u> the winner of the race.

Unit 19 · Lesson 6

Exercise 5 · Punctuate It: Commas in a Series

▸ Read each sentence.

▸ Identify the words or word groups in the series in each sentence.

▸ Place a comma between each item in the series.

1. Parents teachers children and officials came to watch the races on May Day.

2. Squeaky put her sneakers t-shirt socks and running shorts in her bag.

3. Squeaky Raymond Cynthia and Gretchen all go to the park.

4. The young girl walked down Broadway Park Avenue Madison and Lexington.

5. Mr. Pearson carries his clipboard cards pencils whistles and safety pins.

6. Raymond can hop skip jump and run.

7. Squeaky has won ribbons medals and awards.

8. Cynthia is good at spelling music and dancing.

9. At the park, parents wear hats corsages and breast-pocket handkerchiefs.

10. Before a race, Squeaky likes to stretch breathe and dream.

Exercise 1 · Listening for Stressed Syllables

▶ Listen for the stressed syllable in each word your teacher says.

▶ Repeat the word to yourself, emphasizing the stressed syllable.

▶ Make an X in the box to mark the position of the stressed syllable.

Word	First Syllable	Second Syllable	Third Syllable
1. mistake			
2. foreword			
3. misgiving			
4. midpoint			
5. forego			
6. foreman			
7. misstep			
8. midriff			
9. misspell			
10. forever			

Unit 19 · Lesson 8

Exercise 2 · Build It: Words With Affixes

▸ Read the base words and affixes in the square.

▸ Combine base words and affixes to build as many real words as possible in five minutes.

▸ Write each word in the correct column in the chart below.

▸ Check a dictionary to verify words.

cast	state	understand
tired	mis- -er over- -ment -ness	fit
drive	interpret	inform

mis-	over-	other

Exercise 3 · Fill In: Words With Affixes

▶ Read each sentence.

▶ Use the words that you built in Exercise 2 to fill in the blanks.

▶ Use a dictionary to verify the meanings of unfamiliar words.

1. The _____ sky may clear this evening.

2. If you _____ the chart, you're likely to disagree with the others.

3. I'm _____ because I haven't slept well for days.

4. An _____ translates conversations and speeches.

5. Your _____ is a problem when you are falling asleep at work!

6. I don't want you to _____ what I'm saying.

7. I put the jeep in _____ to get better gas mileage.

8. The _____ expert gave me tips for a healthy diet.

9. If friends _____ you about the starting time of a movie, you are likely to be late.

10. My bank _____ provides a record of my weekly deposits.

Exercise 4 · Fill In: Homophones

▶ Complete the chart by filling in each blank with a homophone from the **Unit Vocabulary** list in the *Student Text*.

pale	
male	
tale	
waste	
rode	

▶ Now read each sentence below and select a word from the chart that fits the meaning of the sentence.

▶ Use a dictionary for help with word meanings.

1. My pal looked _____ because he didn't feel well.

2. The belt doesn't fit around my _____.

3. Our _____ is delivered late in the afternoon.

4. My little brother is always telling a tall _____.

5. I _____ my bike along trails in the park.

Exercise 5 · Identify It: Noun Functions

▶ Read each sentence.

▶ Decide if the underlined noun is a subject, a direct object, or a predicate nominative.

▶ Put an X in the appropriate box.

	Subject	Direct Object	Predicate Nominative
1. The young boy Raymond has a <u>number</u> of problems.			
2. His sister is his <u>baby sitter</u>.			
3. The <u>children</u> in the neighborhood made fun of Raymond.			
4. Squeaky will defend her <u>brother</u> against everyone.			
5. May Day was the <u>day</u> for the competition.			
6. Squeaky is always the <u>winner</u> in her age group.			
7. The other <u>girls</u> observe her before the race.			
8. Squeaky will be a <u>champion</u> one day.			
9. <u>Raymond</u> races along the fence line.			
10. Squeaky is a self-assured young <u>girl</u>.			

Unit 19 · Lesson 8

Exercise 6 · Diagram It: Predicate Nominative

▶ Do the first example with your teacher.

▶ Read each remaining sentence.

▶ Underline the simple subject.

▶ Draw an arrow from the predicate nominative to the subject.

▶ Diagram the sentence.

1. My nickname is Mercury.

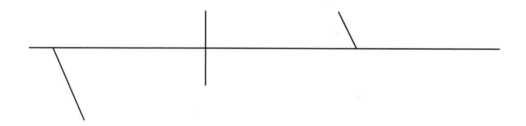

2. Raymond is my older brother.

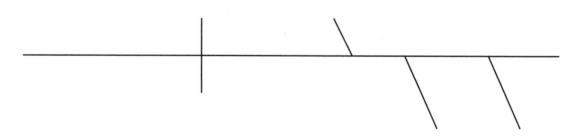

(continued)

Exercise 6 *(continued)* · **Diagram It: Predicate Nominative**

3. I am the fastest runner in my age group.

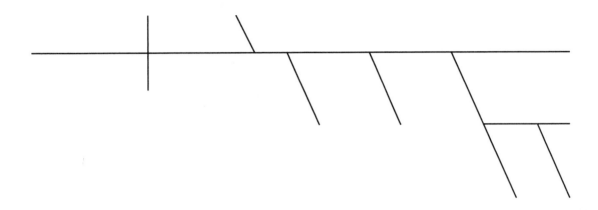

4. Squeaky will be a champion.

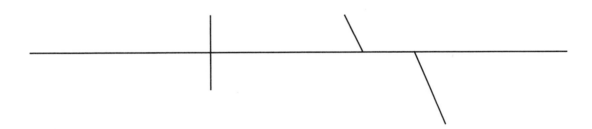

5. Fiber optics is a new technology.

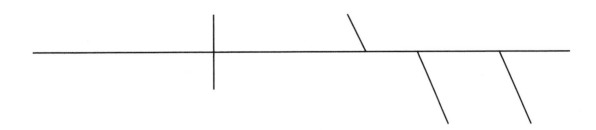

Exercise 1 · Sort It: Syllable Types

▶ Read each word in the **Word Bank**.

Word Bank

cork	subject	standing	fastest	street	third
tale	blur	rain	cuffs	try	home
rodeo	traffic	pony	teeth	coach	scales

▶ Identify the vowel sound in each syllable.

▶ Determine its syllable type.

▶ Write the word under the correct heading.

Open	Final Silent <u>e</u>	Vowel Digraph	<u>r</u>-Controlled	Closed

Exercise 2 · Answer It: Multiple Choice

▶ Follow along as you discuss each question with your teacher.

▶ Underline the correct answer.

1. **"Raymond's Run"** is _____.

    A. fiction

    B. informational text

    C. both

    D. neither

2. The setting of the story is a _____.

    A. beach

    B. city

    C. mountain

    D. farm

3. Squeaky can BEST be described as _____.

    A. fearful

    B. mean

    C. careless

    D. caring

(continued)

Exercise 2 (continued) · Answer It: Multiple Choice

4. Which of the following BEST describes the relationship between Squeaky and Raymond?

   A. Squeaky is Raymond's classmate.

   B. Squeaky is Raymond's sister.

   C. Squeaky is Raymond's pet.

   D. Squeaky and Raymond are best friends.

5. Which of the following BEST describes the author's reason for naming this story **"Raymond's Run"**?

   A. The story is about Raymond running in a race.

   B. The story is about Squeaky running in a race.

   C. The story is about how Squeaky realized that Raymond is a good runner.

   D. The story is about a city park named Raymond's Run.

Unit 19 Lesson 10

Exercise 1 · Define It: Suffixes -dom, -some

▶ Use a dictionary to define each word with an underlined suffix.

▶ Compare definitions of those words to discover the meaning of the suffix.

▶ Define the suffix.

1. boredom—_____

_____

2. freedom—_____

_____

3. kingdom—_____

_____

4. wisdom—_____

_____

5. Words ending with the suffix **-dom** can mean _____

_____

6. threesome—_____

_____

7. fearsome—_____

_____

8. lonesome—_____

_____

9. tiresome—_____

_____

10. Words ending with the suffix **-some** can mean _____

_____

Unit 19 · Lesson 10

Exercise 2 · Write It: Character Summary

▶ Review your **Character Trait** chart for Squeaky.

▶ Use the chart and the text for **"Raymond's Run"** to write a summary proving that Squeaky is **caring**.

▶ Be sure to cite at least three examples from the text.

_____

_____

_____

_____

_____

_____

_____

_____

_____

_____

_____

_____

_____

_____

_____

_____

_____

_____

Check off the activities you complete with each lesson. Evaluate your accomplishments at the end of each lesson. Pay attention to teacher evaluations and comments.

Unit Objectives	Lesson 1 (Date:_____)	Lesson 2 (Date:_____)
STEP 1 — **Phonemic Awareness and Phonics** • Say sounds for vowel digraphs <u>ay</u>, <u>ea</u>, <u>ie</u>, <u>ey</u>, <u>ow</u>, and <u>oe</u>. • Write the letters for the sounds /$\bar{a}$/, /$\bar{e}$/, /$\bar{\iota}$/, and /$\bar{o}$/ using vowel digraphs. • Identify vowel digraph syllables.	☐ Discover It: Vowel Digraphs <u>ay</u> and <u>ai</u> ☐ Memorize It ☐ Vowel Chart	☐ Discover It: Vowel Digraphs <u>oa</u> and <u>ow</u> ☐ Memorize It ☐ Vowel Chart
STEP 2 — **Word Recognition and Spelling** • Read and spell words composed of vowel digraph syllables. • Read and spell the **Essential Words:** *course, friend, guarantee, guard, guess, guest.* • Spell words with prefixes, suffixes, and roots.	☐ Exercise 1: Spelling Pretest 1 ☐ Memorize It	☐ Exercise 1: Sort It: Vowel Digraphs ☐ Exercise 2: Write It: Essential Words ☐ Word Fluency 1
STEP 3 — **Vocabulary and Morphology** • Identify homophones. • Identify and define adjective suffixes. • Use the meanings of prefixes, suffixes, and roots to define words.	☐ Unit Vocabulary ☐ Multiple Meaning Map (T) ☐ Draw It: Idioms	☐ Exercise 3: Write It: Suffixes *-er*, *-est*, and *-y* ☐ Expression of the Day
STEP 4 — **Grammar and Usage** • Identify adjectives. • Identify and use **be** as a linking verb. • Identify irregular verbs. • Identify and write sentences with predicate adjectives.	☐ Exercise 2: Sort It: Adjectives ☐ Exercise 3: Punctuate It: Commas in a Series	☐ Exercise 4: Identify It: Adjective Suffixes ☐ Exercise 5: Punctuate It: Commas in Addresses ☐ Exercise 6: Punctuate It: Commas in Dates
STEP 5 — **Listening and Reading Comprehension** • Use context-based strategies to define words. • Identify components of a business letter. • Identify character traits as part of plot analysis. • Identify and understand signal words for comprehension: **critique, judge.**	☐ Independent Text: "Nash's Bashes: Word Play" ☐ Exercise 4: Phrase It ☐ Exercise 5: Use the Clues	☐ Passage Fluency 1 ☐ Exercise 7: Chart It: Word Play
STEP 6 — **Speaking and Writing** • Write responses to sentences using the signal words: **critique, judge.** • Organize reasons and supporting evidence from text in a graphic organizer. • Write a business letter conveying reasons. • Write a description of a character using traits and evidence of traits from the text.	☐ Exercise 6: Rewrite It	☐ Exercise 8: Answer It
Self-Evaluation (5 is the highest) **Effort** = I produced my best work. **Participation** = I was actively involved in tasks. **Independence** = I worked on my own.	**Effort:** 1 2 3 4 5 **Participation:** 1 2 3 4 5 **Independence:** 1 2 3 4 5	**Effort:** 1 2 3 4 5 **Participation:** 1 2 3 4 5 **Independence:** 1 2 3 4 5
Teacher Evaluation	**Effort:** 1 2 3 4 5 **Participation:** 1 2 3 4 5 **Independence:** 1 2 3 4 5	**Effort:** 1 2 3 4 5 **Participation:** 1 2 3 4 5 **Independence:** 1 2 3 4 5

Lesson 3 (Date:_____)	Lesson 4 (Date:_____)	Lesson 5 (Date:_____)
❑ Discover It: Vowel Digraphs _ea_, _ie_, and _ey_ ❑ Vowel Chart	❑ Discover It: Vowel Digraph _ie_ ❑ Vowel Chart (T)	❑ Content Mastery: Vowel Digraphs
❑ Divide It ❑ Word Fluency 2	❑ Exercise 1: Sort It: Syllable Types ❑ Exercise 2: Build It: Words With Suffixes	❑ Content Mastery: Spelling Posttest 1
❑ Focus on Vocabulary ❑ Use the Clues ❑ Expression of the Day	❑ Exercise 3: Find It: Present Participles and Past Participles	❑ Introduction: Prefix Plus Root
❑ Identify It: Predicate Nominative or Direct Object	❑ Exercise 4: Identify It: Functions of Participles ❑ Exercise 5: Find It: Irregular Verb Forms	❑ Masterpiece Sentences: Stage 4
❑ Instructional Text: "The Marble Champ"	❑ Take Note: "The Marble Champ"	❑ Map It: Business Letter (T)
❑ Exercise 1: Answer It	❑ Map It: Reasons (T) ❑ Challenge Text: "Yo-Yo Ma Plays the World"	❑ Map It: Business Letter (T) ❑ Challenge Text: "Yo-Yo Ma Plays the World"
Effort: 1 2 3 4 5 **Participation:** 1 2 3 4 5 **Independence:** 1 2 3 4 5	**Effort:** 1 2 3 4 5 **Participation:** 1 2 3 4 5 **Independence:** 1 2 3 4 5	**Effort:** 1 2 3 4 5 **Participation:** 1 2 3 4 5 **Independence:** 1 2 3 4 5
Effort: 1 2 3 4 5 **Participation:** 1 2 3 4 5 **Independence:** 1 2 3 4 5	**Effort:** 1 2 3 4 5 **Participation:** 1 2 3 4 5 **Independence:** 1 2 3 4 5	**Effort:** 1 2 3 4 5 **Participation:** 1 2 3 4 5 **Independence:** 1 2 3 4 5

Check off the activities you complete with each lesson. Evaluate your accomplishments at the end of each lesson. Pay attention to teacher evaluations and comments.

	Unit Objectives	Lesson 6 (Date:_____)	Lesson 7 (Date:_____)
STEP 1	**Phonemic Awareness and Phonics** • Say sounds for vowel digraphs <u>ay</u>, <u>ea</u>, <u>ie</u>, <u>ey</u>, <u>ow</u>, and <u>oe</u>. • Write the letters for the sounds /$\bar{a}$/, /$\bar{e}$/, /$\bar{i}$/, and /$\bar{o}$/ using vowel digraphs. • Identify vowel digraph syllables.	❑ Content Mastery: Using Student Performance	❑ Listening for Word Parts: Prefixes
STEP 2	**Word Recognition and Spelling** • Read and spell words composed of vowel digraph syllables. • Read and spell the **Essential Words:** *course, friend, guarantee, guard, guess, guest.* • Spell words with prefixes, suffixes, and roots.	❑ Exercise 1: Spelling Pretest 2 ❑ Word Fluency 3	❑ Build It: Words With Prefixes and Roots ❑ Word Fluency 4
STEP 3	**Vocabulary and Morphology** • Identify homophones. • Identify and define adjective suffixes. • Use the meanings of prefixes, suffixes, and roots to define words.	❑ Exercise 2: Word Line: Degrees of Meaning ❑ Expression of the Day	❑ Focus on Vocabulary ❑ Use the Clues ❑ Expression of the Day
STEP 4	**Grammar and Usage** • Identify adjectives. • Identify and use **be** as a linking verb. • Identify irregular verbs. • Identify and write sentences with predicate adjectives.	❑ Exercise 3: Code It: Predicate Nominative ❑ Exercise 4: Code It: Predicate Adjective ❑ Exercise 5: Punctuate It: Commas in a Series, Date, or Address	❑ Identify It: Functions of Participles
STEP 5	**Listening and Reading Comprehension** • Use context-based strategies to define words. • Identify components of a business letter. • Identify character traits as part of plot analysis. • Identify and understand signal words for comprehension: **critique, judge.**	❑ Teacher's Edition: "The Flute Players" (T)	❑ Instructional Text: "A Game of Catch" (T)
STEP 6	**Speaking and Writing** • Write responses to sentences using the signal words: **critique, judge.** • Organize reasons and supporting evidence from text in a graphic organizer. • Write a business letter conveying reasons. • Write a description of a character using traits and evidence of traits from the text.	❑ Map It: Plot (T)	❑ Spotlight on Characters (T)
	Self-Evaluation (5 is the highest) **Effort** = I produced my best work. **Participation** = I was actively involved in tasks. **Independence** = I worked on my own.	**Effort:** 1 2 3 4 5 **Participation:** 1 2 3 4 5 **Independence:** 1 2 3 4 5	**Effort:** 1 2 3 4 5 **Participation:** 1 2 3 4 5 **Independence:** 1 2 3 4 5
	Teacher Evaluation	**Effort:** 1 2 3 4 5 **Participation:** 1 2 3 4 5 **Independence:** 1 2 3 4 5	**Effort:** 1 2 3 4 5 **Participation:** 1 2 3 4 5 **Independence:** 1 2 3 4 5

Lesson 8 (Date:_____)	**Lesson 9** (Date:_____)	**Lesson 10** (Date:_____)
❏ Exercise 1: Listening for Word Parts: Suffixes		
❏ Exercise 2: Build It: Words With Affixes	❏ Exercise 1: Sort It: Syllable Types	❏ Content Mastery: Spelling Posttest 2
❏ Exercise 3: Fill In: Words With Affixes ❏ Exercise 4: Relate It: Homophones	❏ Content Mastery: Homophones ❏ Content Mastery: Morphology	❏ Content Mastery: Using Student Performance ❏ Exercise 1: Sort It: Root Meanings ❏ Draw It: Idioms
❏ Exercise 5: Code It: Predicate Adjective ❏ Exercise 6: Diagram It: Predicate Adjective	❏ Content Mastery: Irregular Verbs; Predicate Nominative and Predicate Adjective; Commas in a Series, Date, or Address	❏ Content Mastery: Using Student Performance
❏ Instructional Text: "A Game of Catch"	❏ Instructional Text: "A Game of Catch" ❏ Exercise 2: Answer It: Multiple Choice	❏ Instructional Text: "A Game of Catch"
❏ Spotlight on Characters (T)	❏ Spotlight on Characters (T) ❏ Challenge Text: "Young Playwright on Broadway: Lorraine Hansberry's *A Raisin in the Sun*"	❏ Exercise 2: Write It: Character Summary (T) ❏ Challenge Text: "Young Playwright on Broadway: Lorraine Hansberry's *A Raisin in the Sun*"
Effort: 1 2 3 4 5 **Participation:** 1 2 3 4 5 **Independence:** 1 2 3 4 5	**Effort:** 1 2 3 4 5 **Participation:** 1 2 3 4 5 **Independence:** 1 2 3 4 5	**Effort:** 1 2 3 4 5 **Participation:** 1 2 3 4 5 **Independence:** 1 2 3 4 5
Effort: 1 2 3 4 5 **Participation:** 1 2 3 4 5 **Independence:** 1 2 3 4 5	**Effort:** 1 2 3 4 5 **Participation:** 1 2 3 4 5 **Independence:** 1 2 3 4 5	**Effort:** 1 2 3 4 5 **Participation:** 1 2 3 4 5 **Independence:** 1 2 3 4 5

Exercise 1 · Spelling Pretest 1

▶ Write the word your teacher repeats.

1. _____

2. _____

3. _____

4. _____

5. _____

6. _____

7. _____

8. _____

9. _____

10. _____

11. _____

12. _____

13. _____

14. _____

15. _____

Exercise 2 · Sort It: Adjectives

▸ Read each sentence.

▸ Decide whether the underlined adjective tells **which one? what kind?** or **how many?**

▸ Write the adjective in the correct column.

1. Ogden Nash used words in a <u>unique</u> manner.

2. The <u>funny</u> wordsmith provided humor.

3. <u>Many</u> people know his poems.

4. <u>Those</u> poems usually have a strange twist.

5. During the Great Depression <u>some</u> businesses closed.

6. For many people, life offered <u>few</u> moments of joy.

7. *The New Yorker* is a <u>prominent</u> magazine.

8. <u>That</u> magazine published many of Nash's poems.

9. Nash made people laugh during a <u>stressful</u> time.

10. Nash's <u>special</u> word play can be recognized easily.

Which one?	What kind?	How many?

Exercise 3 · Punctuate It: Commas in a Series

▶ Read each sentence.

▶ Identify the words, or word groups, in the series in each sentence.

▶ Place a comma between each item in the series.

1. Some of the poems that Ogden Nash wrote are "The Eel" "The Rhinoceros" "The Cow" and "The Termite."

2. His word play makes us stop pay attention and think.

3. Nash's humor is for sharp quick and wacky people.

4. He uses repetition rhyme and rhythm to play with sounds.

5. We can enjoy celebrate and laugh at Nash's word plays.

6. In 1929, the stock market crashed the Great Depression began and many businesses failed.

7. When poets write, they need ideas a purpose and a focus.

8. Nash's fans read his poems in books magazines and newspapers.

9. Nash knew that words could relieve despair decrease hopelessness provide humor and cause laughter.

10. You, too, can play with words make up rhymes and write funny poems.

Exercise 4 · Phrase It

▸ Use the penciling strategy to "scoop" the phrases in each sentence.

▸ Read the sentences as you would speak them.

▸ Do the first sentence with your teacher.

---

from "Nash's Bashes: Word Play"

Some folks use words to get attention.

Most folks use words to get things done.

Bad folks say words we shouldn't mention.

But Ogden Nash used words for fun.

Exercise 5 · Use the Clues

▶ Read the excerpt below.

▶ Reread each of the underlined pronouns.

▶ Identify and circle the noun or nouns that the pronoun replaces. (You will circle one noun twice.)

---

from "Nash's Bashes: Word Play"

Often, Nash plays with sounds in words. This helps create his word play. He knew what word repetition could do. He knew what rhythm could do. He knew what rhyme could do. They all triggered memory. They all helped him celebrate language.

Exercise 6 · Rewrite It

▶ Reread the excerpt from **"Nash's Bashes: Word Play"** in Exercise 5, **Use the Clues**.

▶ Rewrite the last two sentences in the excerpt in Exercise 5 as one sentence. Replace the first pronoun with the nouns it represents. Use **and** to join the sentences.

▶ Check that the sentence uses sentence signals—capital letters, commas, and end punctuation.

_____

_____

Exercise 1 · Sort It: Vowel Digraphs

▸ Read the paragraph below.

▸ Highlight or underline vowel digraph syllables in words with / $\bar{a}$ / and / $\bar{o}$ /.

▸ Circle the vowel digraphs that represent / $\bar{a}$ / and / $\bar{o}$ /.

▸ Sort the words with vowel digraphs according to their long vowel sound.

▸ Write the words with vowel digraphs under the correct heading.

---

based on: "Nash's Bashes: Word Play"

Ogden Nash became famous. He was known for playing. But his kind of play was unique. He was a 20th century poet. He became famous for playing with words. This fellow knew that words were a great source of laughter when people were feeling low.

Vowel Digraph / $\bar{a}$ /	Vowel Digraph / $\bar{o}$ /

Unit 20 · Lesson 2

Exercise 2 · Write It: Essential Words

▶ Review the **Essential Words** in the **Word Bank**.

Word Bank

guard	friend	course	guarantee	guest	guess

▶ Put the words in alphabetical order and write them on the lines.

▶ Write one sentence for each **Essential Word**.

▶ Check that each sentence uses sentence signals—correct capitalization, commas, and end punctuation.

1. _____

_____

2. _____

_____

3. _____

_____

4. _____

_____

5. _____

_____

6. _____

_____

Exercise 3 · Write It: Suffixes -er, -est, and -y

▶ Read the first sentence with your teacher.

▶ Add the correct suffix to the underlined base word.

▶ Reread the sentence to check to see that it makes sense.

▶ Finish the rest of the sentences independently.

▶ Use your **Morphemes for Meaning Cards** as a resource for suffixes.

1. The morning was <u>snow</u> _____, and school was cancelled.

2. There were three cars parked on the road, and mine was the <u>small</u> _____.

3. The air in the tropics was very <u>steam</u> _____.

4. Have you ever eaten a <u>cream</u> _____ chocolate dessert?

5. My report was <u>brief</u> _____ than yours.

6. Our team was the <u>fast</u> _____ relay team in the event.

7. The <u>sleep</u> _____ child was put to bed.

8. We bought the <u>light</u> _____ backpack the store had.

9. The area nearest the heater was warm and <u>toast</u> _____.

10. This room is <u>neat</u> _____ than that one.

Exercise 4 · Identify It: Adjective Suffixes

▶ Read the paragraph below.

▶ Look at the underlined words.

▶ If an underlined word is an adjective that has the suffix **-er**, **-est**, or **-y**, copy it into the appropriate column.

---

based on "Nash's Bashes: Word Play"

The Great Depression had the <u>biggest</u> effect on <u>society</u> of any economic development in the 20th century. The <u>largest</u> banks closed their doors, and the stock market had its <u>greatest</u> losses. Most <u>wealthier</u> people still had money, but many <u>poorer</u> people were left without income or food. At that time, a <u>young</u> poet began to write his <u>funniest</u> poems. He was <u>lucky</u>, for *The New Yorker* began to publish them. Many of his <u>crazy</u> rhymes made people laugh. People in the <u>deepest</u> despair could smile at his words. <u>Difficult</u> times helped produce a poet who was <u>funny</u> and was also a <u>healer</u>!

-er	-est	-y	

Exercise 5 · Punctuate It: Commas in Addresses

▶ Read each sentence.

▶ Identify the address in the sentence.

▶ Place commas as needed.

1. The President of the United States lives at the White House 1600 Pennsylvania Avenue NW Washington DC 20500.

2. I am going to visit to the zoo at 50 Animal Square Jungleville Arizona.

3. Here is the mailing address for my school: Smith High School 100 Main Street Middletown MN 59222.

4. Send an accident report to this mailing address: Summerburg Police Department 159 Detective Lane Summerburg CA 91111.

▶ Write a sentence using the name and address of someone you know on the lines below.

_____

_____

▶ Write the mailing address of that person on the lines below.

_____

_____

Exercise 6 · Punctuate It: Commas in Dates

▸ Read each sentence.

▸ Identify the date in the sentence.

▸ Place commas where needed.

1. In Congress on July 4 1776 the Declaration of Independence was signed.

2. Paul Revere rode out of Boston on April 18 1776 to warn people in the surrounding area that the British were coming.

3. President Lincoln gave an address at Gettysburg, Pennsylvania on November 19 1863.

4. On May 9 1865 the American Civil War came to an end.

5. Complete the following sentence:

   I was born on _____
             month   day   year

Exercise 7 · Chart It: Word Play

▸ Use the poems from **"Nash's Bashes: Word Play"** to complete the following chart with your teacher.

▸ Use a dictionary to find definitions of actual words.

Poem	Nash's Word	Actual Word		Explanation of Word Play
		Definition		
The Rhinoceros	prepoceros	preposterous		
The Wasp				
The Llama				
The Ostrich				

Exercise 8 · Answer It

▸ Use information from the poems in **"Nash's Bashes: Word Play"** to answer these questions using complete sentences.

▸ Use a dictionary to clarify the meanings of boldface words in the questions.

1. Why isn't a **rhinoceros** a **feast** for human eyes?

_____

2. What did the **termites** do to the **parlor** floor?

_____

3. Explain how a wasp's **hospitality** is a **calamity** for humans.

_____

_____

_____

_____

4. Define **ostrich** using information from the poem.

_____

_____

_____

_____

5. Use a dictionary to add to your definition of **ostrich**.

_____

_____

_____

_____

Exercise 1 · Answer It

▶ Underline the signal word in the question.

▶ Write the answer in complete sentences.

▶ Check for sentence signals—capital letters, commas, and end punctuation.

1. Wanting to win at something, Lupe made a decision to participate in the sport of marbles. Judge Lupe's decision to compete in the sport of marbles.

   _____

   _____

   _____

   _____

2. Explain why Lupe was reluctant to show her thumb to her father.

   _____

   _____

   _____

3. Identify evidence that Lupe's father supported her decision to compete in marbles.

   _____

   _____

   _____

   _____

   _____

(continued)

Exercise 1 *(continued)* · **Answer It**

4. Compare the personality traits of Lupe, the main character in "The Marble Champ," and Squeaky, the main character in "Raymond's Run." Include examples from each story.

_____

_____

_____

_____

5. Pretend you review books and movies for the local newspaper. Critique "The Marble Champ." Be sure to include your opinion about whether this story should appear on the newspaper's recommended reading list.

_____

_____

_____

_____

Exercise 1 · Sort It: Syllable Types

▶ Read the two paragraphs below.

▶ Find each word with a long vowel sound spelled with a vowel digraph, and highlight or underline the word.

▶ Circle the **vowel digraph** in each word you marked.

▶ Sort the words you marked according to their long vowel sound by writing each word under the correct heading on the next page.

from "The Marble Champ"

Lupe Medrano, a shy girl who spoke in whispers, was the school's spelling bee champion, winner of the reading contest at the public library three summers in a row, blue ribbon awardee in the science fair, the top student at her piano recital, and the playground grand champion in chess. She was a straight-A student and—not counting kindergarten, when she had been stung by a wasp—never missed one day of elementary school. She had received a small trophy for this honor and had been congratulated by the mayor.

But though Lupe had a razor-sharp mind, she could not make her body, no matter how much she tried, run as fast as the other girls. She begged her body to move faster, but could never best anyone in the fifty-yard dash.

(continued)

Unit 20 · Lesson 4

Exercise 1 (continued) · Sort It: Syllable Types

e	i	a	o

Exercise 2 · Build It: Words With Suffixes

▶ Read the suffixes and base words in the **Word Banks**.

Word Banks

Base Words

bat	soap	chill
snow	cheap	crab

Suffixes

-y	-er	-est
-ing	-ed	-en

▶ Combine the word parts to make new words.

▶ Use the **Double It** and **Change It** spelling rules when necessary.

▶ Check a dictionary to verify that the words you build are real words.

_____ _____ _____ _____ _____ _____

_____ _____ _____ _____ _____ _____

_____ _____ _____ _____ _____ _____

_____ _____ _____ _____ _____ _____

_____ _____ _____ _____ _____ _____

_____ _____ _____ _____ _____ _____

Exercise 3 · Find It: Present Participles and Past Participles

▸ Read each sentence.

▸ Find and underline the present participle or past participle that describes a noun.

▸ Draw an arrow from the participle to the noun it describes.

▸ Copy the participle under the correct heading.

Sentence	Present Participle	Past Participle
Examples: Ogden Nash wrote <u>amusing</u> poems.	amusing	
The <u>broken</u> string made it hard to play the cello.		broken
The <u>valued</u> player was treated well.		valued
1. Yo-Yo Ma is an honored cellist.		
2. The chosen students were invited to a concert.		
3. Some children were playing with the revolving door.		
4. We were listening to the spoken words of the play.		
5. The towering athlete was a star volleyball player.		
6. A sprained ankle prevented that athlete from playing.		
7. The planning session before the game helped the players immensely.		
8. The blowing wind made it difficult to speak.		
9. The racing car screeched to a stop.		
10. The students were proud of their finished report.		

Unit 20 · Lesson 4

Exercise 4 · Identify It: Functions of Participles

▸ Read each sentence below, identifying and underlining each participle.

▸ Decide whether the underlined participle describes a noun or is the main verb in the simple predicate in the sentence.

▸ If the participle describes a noun, draw an arrow from it to that noun.

▸ If the participle is the main verb, circle it and its helping verb.

> **Example:**
>
> Lupe Medrano was the school's <u>spelling</u> champion.
>
> She was the winner of the <u>reading</u> contest.
>
> She was <u>earning</u> good grades, too.

1. Lupe was not good at sports, even though she always put in a determined effort.

2. Then she thought of marbles, an almost forgotten sport.

3. Soon she was practicing every day.

4. She practiced alone on her smoothed bedspread.

5. Lupe was improving day by day.

6. On the day of the marble contest she was feeling nervous.

7. She won one challenging match after another.

8. Now her success is inspiring other marble players.

Exercise 5 · Find It: Irregular Verb Forms

▶ Read each sentence and underline the past tense verb.

▶ Write the past, present, and future forms of the verb in the chart below the timeline.

1. Lupe Medrano lay in bed dreaming of being a sports champion.

2. Lupe said she would practice marbles every day after school.

3. Lupe read about how to play marbles.

4. Lupe's youngest brother led the way to the playground.

5. Lupe left for the championship in plenty of time.

6. The glassy marbles felt good in her hands.

7. In the end, Lupe swept away all the competition.

8. Competitors paid a small entry fee.

9. After the win, the family ate a victory meal.

10. They even fed their dog a victory bone.

Past	Present	Future
Yesterday	Today	Tomorrow

Exercise 1 · Spelling Pretest 2

▶ Write the word your teacher repeats.

1. _____

2. _____

3. _____

4. _____

5. _____

6. _____

7. _____

8. _____

9. _____

10. _____

11. _____

12. _____

13. _____

14. _____

15. _____

Exercise 2 · Word Line: Degrees of Meaning

▸ Study the words on the word line.

▸ Discuss the meanings of the words **give**, **loan**, and **keep** with your teacher.

▸ Read the words in the **Word Bank**.

Word Bank

share	contribute	deliver	maintain	lend
donate	hold	retain	provide	grasp

▸ Use a dictionary to define unfamiliar words.

▸ Sort and record each word under the word line according to its degree of meaning.

give	loan	keep
_____	_____	_____
_____	_____	_____
_____	_____	_____
_____	_____	_____

(continued)

▸ Read each sentence below.

▸ Fill in the blank with the word that makes the best sense according to the word line on the previous page. Words may be used more than once. There may be more than one correct answer.

1. _____ the ball tightly so that you can _____ possession.

2. I will _____ money for gas if you will _____ me with transportation to the movie theater.

3. Kelvin will _____ his old car to his sister if it can be repaired cheaply, and

   he will _____ it to charity if it cannot.

4. Neva will _____ an important document to you tomorrow, and you must

   _____ possession of it.

5. The twins _____ their toys with one another, but they _____ their own dolls tight all the time.

Exercise 3 · Code It: Predicate Nominative

▶ Read each sentence.

▶ Decide if the form of **be** is the main verb or is a helping verb. Check the correct box to indicate this.

▶ If it is a main verb, find and label the predicate nominative (PN).

▶ Draw an arrow from the predicate nominative to the subject it is renaming.
Note: Not all the sentences have a predicate nominative.

	Main (Linking) Verb	Helping Verb
1. The story of Kokopelli is an old legend.		
2. It was passed from tribe to tribe.		
3. Kokopelli was a maker of music.		
4. Kokopelli's flute was made of wood.		
5. The wood was taken from special trees.		
6. His flute was his only possession.		
7. It was carried by him from village to village.		
8. His shoes were old moccasins.		
9. The flute was a magnificent instrument.		
10. Kokopelli's music was remembered by the ancient people.		

Exercise 4 · Code It: Predicate Adjective

▸ Read each sentence.

▸ Decide if the form of **be** is the main verb or is a helping verb. Check the correct box to indicate this.

▸ If it is a main verb, find and label the predicate adjective (PA).

▸ Draw an arrow from the predicate adjective to the subject it is describing.

▸ Note that not all the sentences have a predicate adjective.

	Main (Linking) Verb	Helping Verb
1. Kokopelli's soothing music was peaceful.		
2. Kokopelli was playing his flute for the whole village.		
3. The villagers were grateful for his music.		
4. The skillful flute player was old.		
5. The children were allowed to follow Kokopelli.		
6. During his visits, the air was softer.		
7. The flute notes were floating in the air.		
8. After a time, tribes were making their own music.		
9. Kokopelli's music was ignored by the people.		
10. Kokopelli was very unhappy.		

Exercise 5 · Punctuate It: Commas in a Series, Date, or Address

▸ Do the examples with your teacher.

▸ Read each of the remaining sentences.

▸ Decide if the sentence contains a series, a date, or an address.

▸ Place commas where needed.

> **Examples:**
>
> Monk Glennie and Scho were seventh graders.
>
> Their friend will move to 40 Mountain Road Hillsville Colorado next spring.
>
> The last championship was won on October 20 2004 in Maryland.

1. Scho climbed up the tree through the fat branches and into the sunlight.

2. Glennie Monk and Scho were involved in a tense drama.

3. Two lower branches broke Scho's rustling crackling tumbling fall.

4. A similar accident happened on September 15 2005 after school.

5. There was a hospital at 270 Accident Street Medville California.

6. School vacation will start on June 7 2007 at 3:00 P.M.

7. Teachers students and principals will leave school behind for a while.

8. During the days weeks and months of summer there will be time to play sports.

9. In August, parents and teachers will buy books pencils erasers and paper.

10. The school at 14 Yard Street Inchton Texas will open for the first time.

Exercise 1 · Listening for Word Parts: Suffixes

▶ Listen to each word your teacher says. Repeat the word.

▶ Mark **Yes** or **No** to tell if you hear a suffix.

▶ If **yes**, write the suffix.

	Do you hear a suffix on the word?		If **Yes**, what is the suffix?
	Yes	**No**	
1.			
2.			
3.			
4.			
5.			
6.			
7.			
8.			
9.			
10.			

Exercise 2 · Build It: Words With Affixes

▶ Combine prefixes, roots, and suffixes to make words.
Example: ex- + port + -er = exporter

▶ Record words in the chart on the next page according to their root.

▶ Use a dictionary to check that you are building real words.

ex-	form	-er
de-	port	-ing
re-	tract	-ed

form	port	tract

Exercise 3 · Fill In: Words With Affixes

▸ Read each sentence.

▸ Use the words that you built in Exercise 2, **Build It: Words With Affixes**, to fill in the blanks.

▸ Use a dictionary to verify the meanings of less familiar words.

1. The _____ president traveled from coast to coast after he left office.

2. Cars get _____ from the United States to many nations overseas.

3. The _____ helped us move our bags into the hotel.

4. The reporter _____ his statement when he gained new facts.

5. Maple syrup is made by _____ sap from maple trees.

6. We are _____ a chess club that will be held on Thursdays.

7. The bird had a _____ beak due to pollution.

8. She _____ the sliver from her hand using tweezers.

9. The witness _____ the events that led to the crash.

10. The coach's bad attitude _____ from the win.

Exercise 4 · Relate It: Homophones

▸ Complete the chart by filling in each blank with a homophone.

brake	
grate	
meet	
reed	
week	

▸ Read each sentence below and select the word in the homophone pair that fits the meaning of the sentence.

▸ Use a dictionary for help with word meanings.

1. I stepped on the _____ hard to prevent a crash.

2. We had a _____ time at the party!

3. Did you _____ her parents?

4. Remember to buy a new _____ for your clarinet.

5. Do you feel _____ after having had the flu?

Exercise 5 · Code It: Predicate Adjective

▸ Read each sentence.

▸ Decide if the form of the verb **be** in the sentence is a linking verb or a helping verb.

▸ If it is a linking verb, write LV above it. If it is a helping verb, write HV above it.

▸ Decide if the sentence has a predicate adjective. If it does, underline the predicate adjective and write PA above it.

1. Monk and Glennie were playing catch by the firehouse.

2. They were really good.

3. Scho was walking along the edge of the field.

4. The autumn day was cloudy.

5. Monk was furious, and his face showed it.

6. Scho was sitting in the tree.

7. Monk was breathing hard.

8. Glennie was standing at the base of the tree.

9. After Scho's fall, the boys were scared.

10. Scho's voice was weak.

Exercise 6 · Diagram It: Predicate Adjective

▶ Do the first example with your teacher.

▶ Read each remaining sentence.

▶ Label the subject (S), the linking verb (LV) and the predicate adjective (PA).

▶ Diagram the sentence.

1. Monk's ball-throwing arm was strong.

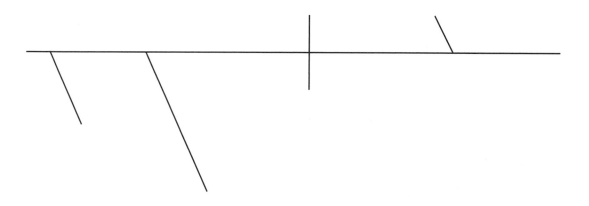

2. The high branches in the tree were willowy.

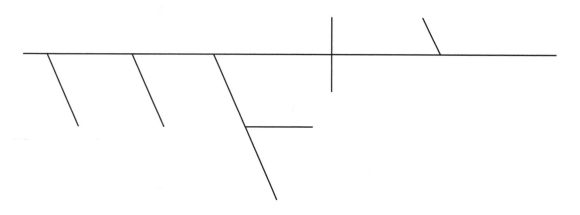

(continued)

Exercise 6 (continued) · Diagram It: Predicate Adjective

3. Scho was panicky in the tree.

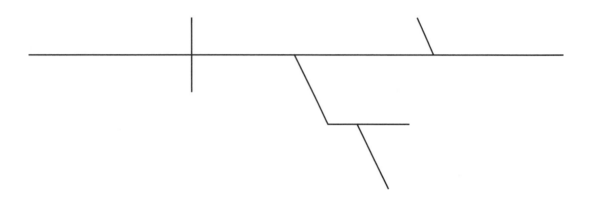

4. Scho was sore after his fall.

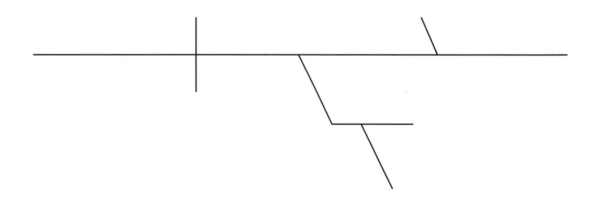

5. The boys will be careful in the future.

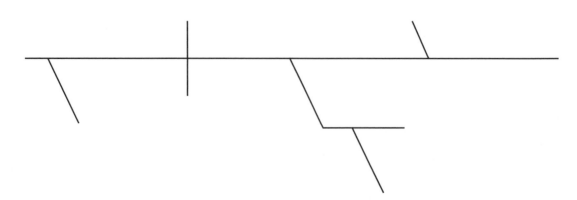

Exercise 1 · Sort It: Syllable Types

▶ Read the words in the **Word Bank**.

Word Bank

game	catch	Scho	cry	shield	street
ferns	burn	throw	forth	chess	spin
pain	time	straight	shade	cross	Yo-ho

▶ Write each word under the correct heading.

Open Syllable	Final Silent _e_ Syllable	Vowel Digraph Syllable	r-Controlled Syllable	Closed Syllable

Exercise 2 · Answer It: Multiple Choice

▸ Follow along as you discuss each question with your teacher.

▸ Underline the correct answer.

1. "A Game of Catch" is

    A. fiction

    B. informational

    C. both

    D. neither

2. The setting of the story is

    A. on a baseball field

    B. on the beach

    C. outside a fire station

    D. on a farm

3. Scho can BEST be described as

    A. afraid

    B. boring

    C. happy

    D. annoying

(continued)

4. In this story, which of the following BEST gives the meaning of the sentence, "Don't burn 'em."

    A. Don't burn anything.

    B. Don't burn the pancakes.

    C. Don't throw a ball too hard.

    D. Don't cheat your friend.

5. Which of the following describes the author's reason for naming this story **"A Game of Catch."**

    A. The story is about playing a game of catch with a baseball.

    B. The story is about how problems can arise when playing a simple game.

    C. The story is about how people include and exclude others from games.

    D. All of the above.

Exercise 1 · Sort It: Root Meanings

▶ Read each word in the **Word Bank**.

Word Bank

compensate	depend	suspense	expend	pensive
dispense	stipend	expense	pendulum	pendant	expensive

▶ Think about its meaning.

▶ Write the word under the heading with the most similar meaning.
Hint: Visit the Web site **www.yourdictionary.com** or use a dictionary if you need help with word meanings or origins.

pend/pens ("hang")	pend/pens ("pay")	pend/pens ("weigh")

Exercise 2 · Write It: Character Summary

▶ Review the **Character Trait** chart for Scho.

▶ Use the chart and the text for **"A Game of Catch"** to write a summary proving that Scho is *assertive* **or** *annoyingly assertive*.

▶ Be sure to cite at least three examples from the text.

_____

_____

_____

_____

_____

_____

_____

_____

_____

_____

_____

_____

_____

_____

_____

_____

_____

(continued)

Exercise 2 (continued) · Write It: Character Summary

_____

_____

_____

_____

_____

_____

_____

_____

_____

_____

_____

_____

_____

_____

_____

_____

_____

_____

_____

_____

Check off the activities you complete with each lesson. Evaluate your accomplishments at the end of each lesson. Pay attention to teacher evaluations and comments.

Unit Objectives	Lesson 1 (Date:_____)	Lesson 2 (Date:_____)
STEP 1 **Phonemic Awareness and Phonics** • Identify stressed and unstressed syllables in multisyllable words. • Recognize the schwa sound in multisyllable words. • Identify conditions when vowels are reduced to schwa.	❑ Discover It: Schwa in Words Beginning or Ending with <u>a</u> ❑ Vowel Chart	❑ Sort It: Schwa in Words Beginning or Ending with <u>a</u>
STEP 2 **Word Recognition and Spelling** • Read and spell words containing syllables reduced to schwa. • Read and spell the **Essential Words:** *beautiful, beauty, business, busy, leopard, women.* • Read and spell words with prefixes, suffixes, and roots.	❑ Exercise 1: Spelling Pretest 1 ❑ Memorize It	❑ Exercise 1: Write It: Essential Words ❑ Word Fluency 1
STEP 3 **Vocabulary and Morphology** • Identify antonyms. • Identify and define noun suffixes. • Use the meanings of prefixes, suffixes, and roots to define words.	❑ Unit Vocabulary ❑ Multiple Meaning Map (T) ❑ Draw It: Idioms	❑ Exercise 2: Rewrite It: Prefix, Root, and Suffix ❑ Expression of the Day
STEP 4 **Grammar and Usage** • Identify nouns and adjectives. • Identify and use the forms of the verb **be**. • Identify and write sentences with predicate nominative and predicate adjectives. • Use quotation marks and commas in a series.	❑ Exercise 2: Identify It: Noun or Adjective ❑ Exercise 3: Punctuate It: Commas in a Series	❑ Identify It: Perfect Tense Verbs ❑ Exercise 3: Identify It: Noun Suffixes
STEP 5 **Listening and Reading Comprehension** • Use context-based strategies to define words. • Identify character traits as part of plot analysis. • Identify and understand signal words for comprehension: **assess, critique, judge, justify.**	❑ Independent Text: "Plant Families" ❑ Exercise 4: Phrase It ❑ Exercise 5: Use the Clues	❑ Passage Fluency 1 ❑ Exercise 4: Using Visuals: Illustrations and Charts
STEP 6 **Speaking and Writing** • Write responses to sentences using the signal words: **assess, critique, judge, justify.** • Organize reasons and supporting evidence from text in a graphic organizer. • Write a description of a character using traits and evidence of traits from the text.	❑ Exercise 6: Rewrite It	❑ Exercise 5: Answer It
Self-Evaluation (5 is the highest) **Effort** = I produced my best work. **Participation** = I was actively involved in tasks. **Independence** = I worked on my own.	**Effort:** 1 2 3 4 5 **Participation:** 1 2 3 4 5 **Independence:** 1 2 3 4 5	**Effort:** 1 2 3 4 5 **Participation:** 1 2 3 4 5 **Independence:** 1 2 3 4 5
Teacher Evaluation	**Effort:** 1 2 3 4 5 **Participation:** 1 2 3 4 5 **Independence:** 1 2 3 4 5	**Effort:** 1 2 3 4 5 **Participation:** 1 2 3 4 5 **Independence:** 1 2 3 4 5

Lesson 3 (Date:_____)	Lesson 4 (Date:_____)	Lesson 5 (Date:_____)
❏ Exercise 1: Listening for Stressed Syllables and Schwa	❏ Exercise 1: Sort It: Schwa	❏ Content Mastery: Schwa
❏ Divide It ❏ Word Fluency 2	❏ Exercise 2: Build It: Words With Prefixes and Suffixes	❏ Content Mastery: Spelling Posttest 1
❏ Vocabulary Focus ❏ Use the Clues ❏ Expression of the Day	❏ Exercise 3: Rewrite It: Prefix Plus Root	❏ Exercise 1: Combine It: Prefixes and Roots ❏ Exercise 2: Define It: Using Prefixes ❏ Exercise 3: Combine It: Noun Suffixes
❏ Identify It: Words in Text ❏ Identify It: Present Perfect Tense Verb or Past Perfect Tense Verb	❏ Exercise 4: Tense Timeline ❏ Exercise 5: Identify It: Functions of Nouns	❏ Masterpiece Sentences: Stage 4
❏ Instructional Text: "A Family in Hiding: Anne Frank's Diary"	❏ Comprehend It ❏ Take Note: Character's Feelings	❏ Take Note: Character's Feelings
❏ Exercise 2: Answer It	❏ Spotlight on Characters (T) ❏ Challenge Text: "Bringing Up Baby: Family Life in the Animal World"	❏ Spotlight on Characters (T) ❏ Challenge Text: "Bringing Up Baby: Family Life in the Animal World" ❏ Exercise 4: Challenge Writing: Write an Animal Story
Effort: 1 2 3 4 5 **Participation:** 1 2 3 4 5 **Independence:** 1 2 3 4 5	**Effort:** 1 2 3 4 5 **Participation:** 1 2 3 4 5 **Independence:** 1 2 3 4 5	**Effort:** 1 2 3 4 5 **Participation:** 1 2 3 4 5 **Independence:** 1 2 3 4 5
Effort: 1 2 3 4 5 **Participation:** 1 2 3 4 5 **Independence:** 1 2 3 4 5	**Effort:** 1 2 3 4 5 **Participation:** 1 2 3 4 5 **Independence:** 1 2 3 4 5	**Effort:** 1 2 3 4 5 **Participation:** 1 2 3 4 5 **Independence:** 1 2 3 4 5

Check off the activities you complete with each lesson. Evaluate your accomplishments at the end of each lesson. Pay attention to teacher evaluations and comments.

Unit Objectives	Lesson 6 (Date:_____)	Lesson 7 (Date:_____)
STEP 1 — **Phonemic Awareness and Phonics** • Identify stressed and unstressed syllables in multisyllable words. • Recognize the schwa sound in multisyllable words. • Identify conditions when vowels are reduced to schwa.	❏ Content Mastery: Using Student Performance	❏ Discover It: Schwa in Unaccented Syllables of Multisyllable Words
STEP 2 — **Word Recognition and Spelling** • Read and spell words containing syllables reduced to schwa. • Read and spell the **Essential Words:** *beautiful, beauty, business, busy, leopard, women.* • Read and spell words with prefixes, suffixes, and roots.	❏ Exercise 1: Spelling Pretest 2 ❏ Word Fluency 3	❏ Build It: Words With Prefixes and Roots ❏ Word Fluency 4
STEP 3 — **Vocabulary and Morphology** • Identify antonyms. • Identify and define noun suffixes. • Use the meanings of prefixes, suffixes, and roots to define words.	❏ Exercise 2: Word Line—Degrees of Meaning ❏ Expression of the Day	❏ Vocabulary Focus ❏ Use the Clues ❏ Expression of the Day
STEP 4 — **Grammar and Usage** • Identify nouns and adjectives. • Identify and use the forms of the verb **be**. • Identify and write sentences with predicate nominative and predicate adjectives. • Use quotation marks and commas in a series.	❏ Exercise 3: Identify It: Predicate Nominative or Predicate Adjective ❏ Punctuate It: Quotation Marks	❏ Identify It: Quotations in Text
STEP 5 — **Listening and Reading Comprehension** • Use context-based strategies to define words. • Identify character traits as part of plot analysis. • Identify and understand signal words for comprehension: **assess, critique, judge, justify.**	❏ "The Marble Champ" (T)	❏ Instructional Text: "My Side of the Story" (T)
STEP 6 — **Speaking and Writing** • Write responses to sentences using the signal words: **assess, critique, judge, justify.** • Organize reasons and supporting evidence from text in a graphic organizer. • Write a description of a character using traits and evidence of traits from the text.	❏ Map It: Plot (T)	❏ Exercise 1: Answer It
Self-Evaluation (5 is the highest) **Effort** = I produced my best work. **Participation** = I was actively involved in tasks. **Independence** = I worked on my own.	**Effort:** 1 2 3 4 5 **Participation:** 1 2 3 4 5 **Independence:** 1 2 3 4 5	**Effort:** 1 2 3 4 5 **Participation:** 1 2 3 4 5 **Independence:** 1 2 3 4 5
Teacher Evaluation	**Effort:** 1 2 3 4 5 **Participation:** 1 2 3 4 5 **Independence:** 1 2 3 4 5	**Effort:** 1 2 3 4 5 **Participation:** 1 2 3 4 5 **Independence:** 1 2 3 4 5

Lesson 8 (Date:_____)	**Lesson 9** (Date:_____)	**Lesson 10** (Date:_____)
❑ Exercise 1: Listening for Stressed Syllables and Schwa		
❑ Exercise 2: Build It: Words With Affixes	❑ Exercise 1: Drop It	❑ Content Mastery: Spelling Posttest 2
❑ Exercise 3: Fill In: Words With Affixes ❑ Draw It: Idioms	❑ Content Mastery: Antonyms ❑ Content Mastery: Morphology	❑ Content Mastery: Using Student Performance ❑ Build It: Words With Prefixes, Roots, and Suffixes
❑ Exercise 4: Punctuate It: Commas in a Series ❑ Exercise 5: Diagram It: Predicate Nominative and Predicate Adjective (T)	❑ Content Mastery	❑ Content Mastery: Using Student Performance
❑ Take Note: Character's Actions	❑ Take Note: Character's Actions	❑ Content Mastery: Answering Questions ❑ Instructional Text: "My Side of the Story" ❑ Exercise 1: Answer It: Multiple Choice
❑ Spotlight on Characters and Plot (T)	❑ Spotlight on Characters and Plot (T) ❑ Challenge Text: "Who Cares About Great-Uncle Edgar?"	❑ Exercise 2: Write It: Problem Summary (T) ❑ Challenge Text: "Who Cares About Great-Uncle Edgar?"
Effort: 1 2 3 4 5 **Participation:** 1 2 3 4 5 **Independence:** 1 2 3 4 5	**Effort:** 1 2 3 4 5 **Participation:** 1 2 3 4 5 **Independence:** 1 2 3 4 5	**Effort:** 1 2 3 4 5 **Participation:** 1 2 3 4 5 **Independence:** 1 2 3 4 5
Effort: 1 2 3 4 5 **Participation:** 1 2 3 4 5 **Independence:** 1 2 3 4 5	**Effort:** 1 2 3 4 5 **Participation:** 1 2 3 4 5 **Independence:** 1 2 3 4 5	**Effort:** 1 2 3 4 5 **Participation:** 1 2 3 4 5 **Independence:** 1 2 3 4 5

Exercise 1 · Spelling Pretest 1

▶ Write the word your teacher repeats.

1. _____

2. _____

3. _____

4. _____

5. _____

6. _____

7. _____

8. _____

9. _____

10. _____

11. _____

12. _____

13. _____

14. _____

15. _____

Exercise 2 · Identify It: Noun or Adjective

▶ Reread the text below.

▶ Look at each underlined word.

▶ Use context to decide if each underlined word is a noun or an adjective.

▶ Put an X in the correct column.

---

from "A Family in Hiding: Anne Frank's Diary"

Anne Frank was born on June 12, 1929, in Frankfurt, <u>Germany</u>. Anne's father, Otto Frank, was a respected <u>businessman</u>. For Anne and her <u>older</u> sister, Margot, the <u>world</u> of <u>early</u> <u>childhood</u> was a <u>secure</u> place inhabited by loving parents and relatives. But beyond this family's <u>comfortable</u> <u>environment</u>, the world around them was not so <u>pleasant</u>.

Word	Noun	Adjective
Germany		
businessman		
older		
world		
early		
childhood		
secure		
comfortable		
environment		
pleasant		

Unit 21 · Lesson 1

Exercise 3 · Punctuate It: Commas in a Series

▶ Read each sentence.

▶ Identify and underline the series of word groups in each sentence.

▶ Place a comma between each word group in the series.

1. In the taxonomy of plant families, roses and apple trees belong together the potato and the chili are in the same family and flowers shaped like crosses go in the same family.

2. While in hiding, Anne Frank observed her brother and sister listened to her parents and wrote her thoughts in her diary.

3. Anne wrote about events in her past happenings in her present situation and imaginary future events.

4. Anne had conflicted feelings about her mother a steady relationship with her father and changeable emotions about her sister.

5. The Frank family hoped that their hiding place would be safe their neighbors would protect their secret and they would survive.

Exercise 4 · Phrase It

▶ Use the penciling strategy to "scoop" the phrases in each sentence.

▶ Read the sentences as you would speak them.

---

from "Plant Families"

Can you tell what plants are related? It isn't always easy to spot relatives. As in human families, they don't always look alike. Think of a rose and an apple. They don't look alike. But roses and apple trees are in the same family. Now, picture that potato again. Next, picture a chili pepper. The potato grows below ground. Its taste is mild. The pepper grows above ground. It tastes spicy. But, you guessed it. Both belong to the same family.

Exercise 5 · Use the Clues

▶ Read the excerpt below.

▶ Reread each of the underlined pronouns.

▶ Identify and circle the noun or nouns that the pronoun replaces. (The word that a pronoun replaces is called its **antecedent**.)

▶ Draw an arrow from the pronoun to the noun or nouns it represents.

> ### from "Plant Families"
>
> Can you tell what plants are related? It isn't always easy to spot relatives. As
>
> in human families, <u>they</u> don't always look alike. Think of a rose and an apple.
>
> <u>They</u> don't look alike. But roses and apple trees are in the same family.

Unit 21 · Lesson 1

Exercise 6 · Rewrite It

▸ Read the excerpt below.

▸ Identify and circle each pronoun.

▸ Identify and underline its antecedent or antecedents—the noun or nouns that the pronoun represents.

▸ Rewrite the last three sentences in the excerpt as one sentence. Replace the first pronoun with the word it replaces. Remove the pronouns that begin the other two sentences. Use **and** to join the sentences.

▸ Check that the sentence uses sentence signals—capital letters, commas, and end punctuation.

---

from "Plant Families"

Scientists called botanists study plants. They consider all parts. They examine the stem. They study the seeds. They inspect the roots.

_____

_____

Exercise 1 · Write It: Essential Words

▶ Review the **Essential Words** in the **Word Bank**.

Word Bank

women	business	beauty	busy	beautiful	leopard

▶ Put the words in alphabetical order and write them on the lines.

▶ Write one sentence for each **Essential Word**.

▶ Check that each sentence uses sentence signals—correct capitalization, commas, and end punctuation.

1. _____

_____

2. _____

_____

3. _____

_____

4. _____

_____

5. _____

_____

6. _____

_____

Unit 21 · Lesson 2

Exercise 2 · Rewrite It: Prefix, Root, and Suffix

▸ Read each example sentence along with your teacher.

▸ Work together to replace each underlined phrase with one word that contains a root and a prefix, suffix, or both.

▸ Write the replacement word in the blank.

▸ Read the completed sentences to check your work.

▸ Read each remaining sentence.

▸ Decide on a one-word replacement for the phrase, and write that word in the blank.

▸ Read the completed sentence to make sure it makes sense.

Note: Use your **Morphemes for Meaning Cards** for **con-, in-, trans-, duc, duct, scrib, script, -ed**, and **-or** as a resource.

Sentence with underlined phrase:	Sentence with phrase changed to a single word:
Example: <u>The person who keeps the band together</u> set a quick tempo for the music.	_____ set a quick tempo for the music.
Example: The monument had the hero's name <u>written into</u> the stone.	The monument had the hero's name _____ in the stone.
1. The student had to <u>write over a copy of</u> her notes into her workbook.	The student had to _____ her notes into her workbook.
2. The student's work was <u>not complete</u>.	The student's work was _____.
3. The characters' parts in the play had to be <u>written in the form for a play</u> carefully.	The characters' parts in the play had to be _____ carefully.
4. The inventor was <u>led into membership</u> in the state's hall of fame.	The inventor was _____ into the state's hall of fame.

Exercise 3 · Identify It: Noun Suffixes

▶ Read each sentence.

▶ Look at the underlined nouns.

▶ Copy only the nouns with the suffixes **-er**, **-ist**, **-ment**, **-ness**, and **-or** into the appropriate columns.

1. As a young <u>child</u>, <u>Anne Frank</u> lived in a comfortable <u>environment</u>.

2. It was a huge <u>adjustment</u> for the <u>family</u> to hide.

3. <u>People</u> in the <u>warehouse</u> became their <u>protectors</u>.

4. Good <u>friends</u> showed <u>kindness</u> by helping the <u>Franks</u>.

5. <u>Anne</u> became an <u>observer</u> of her <u>family</u> and their <u>relationships</u>.

6. At <u>times</u>, she thought her <u>mother</u> was a <u>perfectionist</u>.

7. <u>Anne</u> developed into a fine <u>writer</u> through her frequent writing in her <u>diary</u>.

8. <u>Anne</u> dreamed of being a <u>traveler</u> and visiting <u>Paris</u> and <u>London</u>.

9. A <u>traitor</u> informed the <u>Gestapo</u> of the Franks' hiding <u>place</u>.

10. Today, <u>Anne</u> is famous for her <u>skill</u> as a <u>diarist</u>.

-er	-ist	-ment	-ness	-or

Unit 21 · Lesson 2

Exercise 4 · Using Visuals: Illustrations and Charts

▶ Use the illustration from **"Plant Families"** to complete the following visual with your teacher.

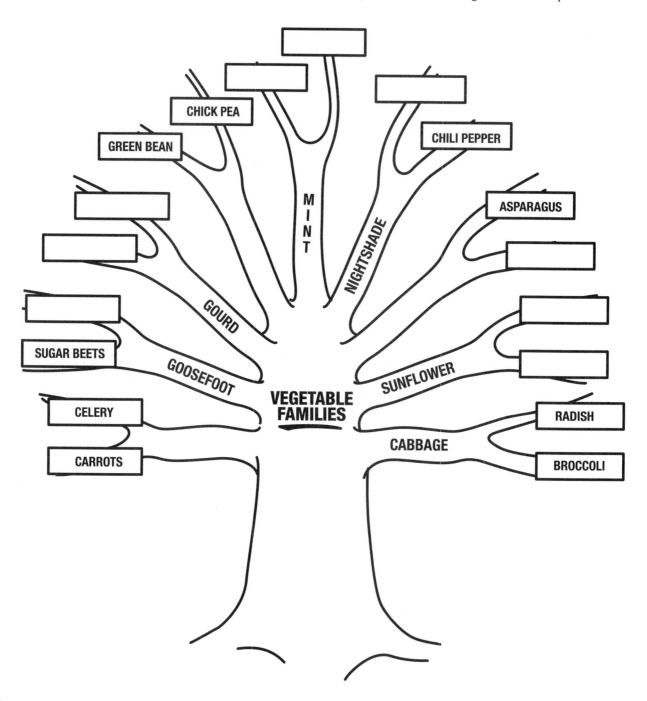

Exercise 5 · Answer It

▸ Use information from the text and the illustration in **"Plant Families"** to answer these
questions. Use complete sentences.

1. What does a botanist do?

_____

_____

2. What happens in taxonomy?

_____

_____

3. What parts of a plant does a botanist study to determine a plant's family?

_____

_____

4. What plant is the chili pepper plant related to?

_____

_____

5. Name two plants that are in the parsley family.

_____

_____

Exercise 1 · Listening for Stressed Syllables and Schwa

▶ Listen to each word your teacher says.

▶ Repeat the word.

▶ Listen for the stressed syllable and underline it.

▶ Listen for the schwa in the unstressed syllable. Circle the vowel that is reduced to schwa.

1. canal

2. suspend

3. subtract

4. support

5. correct

▶ Complete the following sentences:

The stressed syllable in each word above contains a _____.

The unstressed syllable in each word above contains a _____.

Exercise 2 · Answer It

▸ Underline the signal word in each item.

▸ Write the answer in complete sentences.

1. Explain why Anne and her family were forced to hide in the Annex.

_____

_____

_____

_____

_____

_____

2. Assess the challenges that Anne faced in her life. Were they the same challenges that a typical teen faces? Why or why not?

_____

_____

_____

_____

_____

_____

_____

_____

(continued)

3. In her diary, Anne repeatedly voiced her desire to *not* be treated like a child. Explain how she justified this desire.

_____

_____

_____

_____

_____

4. Make a generalization about the kind of person whom Anne admired.

_____

_____

_____

_____

_____

5. Reread lines 222–228. Describe why Anne thought that it was particularly difficult for children to live in the conditions brought on by World War II and the Holocaust.

_____

_____

_____

_____

_____

Exercise 1 · Sort It: Schwa

▶ Listen as your teacher reads the words in the **Word Bank**.

Word Bank

subscribe	subtract	amongst	perform
extra	conform	aside	

▶ Say each word aloud.

▶ Sort and write each word in the proper column according to its schwa condition.

▶ Circle the vowel representing the schwa sound in each word.

▶ Underline the stressed syllable in each word in the second column.

Begin or End with _a_	Unstressed Syllable in a Two-Syllable Word

▶ Fill in the blanks below to review schwa conditions. (Hint: Use information from the chart above.)

One Schwa Condition:

Words beginning or ending with _____ often represent _____.

Examples: _____ _____ _____

(continued)

Unit 21 · Lesson 4

Exercise 1 (continued) · Sort It: Schwa

Another Schwa Condition:

Schwa is often found in the _____ syllable of a two-syllable word.

The stressed syllable contains a _____. (root or prefix)

List the roots that appear in column two above:

_____ _____ _____ _____

The unstressed syllable contains a _____. (root or prefix)

List the prefixes that appear in column two above:

_____ _____ _____ _____

Exercise 2 · Build It: Words With Prefixes and Suffixes

▶ Read the word parts in each table.

▶ Combine two or three word parts in the table to build as many words as you can.

▶ Write the words on the lines below the table.

▶ Apply spelling rules to add endings when necessary.

▶ Check a dictionary to verify that the words you write are real words.

1.

in-	-or	vest	spect
_____	_____	_____	_____

2.

con-	-or	fess	duct
_____	_____	_____	_____

3.

form	-ist	con-	re-
_____	_____	_____	_____

4.

in-	-er	side	quire
_____	_____	_____	_____

5.

spect	in-	-ment	stall
_____	_____	_____	_____

Unit 21 · Lesson 4

Exercise 3 · Rewrite It: Prefix Plus Root

▶ Read each prefix and root or base word.

▶ Underline the last latter of the prefix.

▶ Underline the first letter of the root or base word and write it on the line provided.

▶ Decide if the prefix will change to the first letter of the root or base word.

▶ Combine the prefix and root or base word and write the completed word on the line.

▶ Read the word aloud and place the accent on the root or base word.

Note: The vowels in unaccented syllables are pronounced as schwas.

	Prefix	Root or Base Word	1st Letter of Root or Base Word	Whole Word
1.	con-	+ lect		
2.	in-	+ legal		
3.	in-	+ mediate		
4.	con-	+ mand		
5.	con-	+ rect		
6.	in-	+ regular		
7.	con-	+ lege		
8.	con-	+ mittee		
9.	in-	+ luminate		
10.	con-	+ rupt		

Exercise 4 · Tense Timeline

▶ Complete the first item with your teacher.

▶ Read each remaining sentence.

▶ Look at the underlined verb or verb phrase.

▶ Write that verb or verb phrase in the proper place on the **Tense Timeline**.

▶ Expand the verb to include six forms: past, present, future, past progressive, present progressive, and future progressive.

▶ Refer to the back of the *Student Text* for any irregular verb forms.

1. Anne <u>kept</u> a diary.

2. Anne constantly <u>observed</u> her family.

3. The Frank family <u>was</u> Jewish.

4. The family <u>was hiding</u> from the Gestapo.

5. I <u>am reading</u> *The Diary of a Young Girl*.

	Past	Present	Future
1.			
2.			
3.			
4.			
5.			

Unit 21 · Lesson 4

Exercise 5 · Identify It: Functions of Nouns

▶ Read each sentence below.

▶ Decide whether the underlined nouns name people, places, things, or ideas, or if they are describing other nouns.

▶ If the noun functions like an adjective, draw an arrow from it to the noun it describes.

▶ If the noun names a person, place, thing or idea, circle it.

▶ Put an X in the column to indicate the function of the underlined word.

	Functions as a Noun	Functions as an Adjective
1. We are studying <u>animal</u> life in biology.		
2. Baby elephants live in a <u>group</u>.		
3. The <u>mother</u> elephants and other females look after the young.		
4. The <u>elephant</u> babies are very large.		
5. Some fish build nests from water <u>plants</u>.		
6. The male fish makes a <u>tunnel</u> entrance.		
7. He changes his skin color to attract <u>females</u>.		
8. These babies depend on their <u>parents</u> for everything.		

Exercise 1 · Combine It: Prefixes and Roots

▸ Read the first prefix and root along with your teacher.

▸ Underline the last letter of the prefix.

▸ Underline the first letter of the root and write it on the line provided.

▸ Decide if the last letter of the prefix should change to the first letter of the root, or to the letter <u>m</u>.

▸ Combine the prefix and root, and write the word on the line.

▸ Read the word aloud and place the accent on the root.

▸ Follow the same procedure to complete the rest of the items.

	Prefix	Root or Base Word	1st Letter of Root or Base Word	Whole Word
1.	con- +	pete		
2.	in- +	port		
3.	in- +	perfect		
4.	con- +	plain		
5.	con- +	bine		
6.	in- +	press		
7.	con- +	pose		
8.	con- +	bust		
9.	in- +	bibe		
10.	con- +	bat		

Exercise 2 · Define It: Using Prefixes

▶ Use your knowledge of morphemes and your dictionary to answer the following questions.

▶ Underline the correct answer.

1. If **pete** means "to strive," what does **compete** mean?

    a. to give up   b. to lose   c. to strive together

2. If **bat** means "to beat," what does **combat** mean?

    a. batty   b. to fight   c. to surrender

3. If **pose** means "to put," what does **compose** mean?

    a. to put together   b. to put back   c. to put down

4. If **press** means "to press," what does **impress** mean?

    a. to influence   b. to iron   c. to depress

5. If **port** means "to carry," what does **import** mean?

    a. to carry in   b. to carry out   c. to carry over

Exercise 3 · Combine It: Noun Suffixes

▸ Read the suffixes in the **Word Bank**.

Word Bank

-or	-ness	-er	-ment	-ist

▸ Read the list of words.

▸ Add a suffix from the **Word Bank** to each word to make it into a noun.

▸ Write the complete word on the line.

▸ Refer to your **Morphemes for Meaning Cards** for definitions of each part.

▸ Write a definition for each word.

1. cold + _____ = _____

_____

2. protect + _____ = _____

_____

3. agree + _____ = _____

_____

4. motor + _____ = _____

_____

5. sprint + _____ = _____

_____

Unit 21 • Lesson 5

Exercise 4 • Challenge Writing: Write an Animal Story

The Task: Write a fiction story about an animal. Choose one of the following story ideas, or think of your own:

• a pet that is separated from its owners and has a surprising adventure

• a small wild creature in trouble and the humans who help it

• an unusual animal found by a boy or girl on a city street

• a dangerous rescue in which a pet shows its loyalty to a family

First talk with a partner about the basic parts of your story: characters, setting, and plot. Next fill out the **Story Map** with basic information about characters, setting, events, and plot. Then complete the activity below to work out more specific details for your story.

Story Details

You wrote the basic parts of your story in the **Story Map**. The worksheet below will help you think of interesting details about the characters and setting. Complete it before you start writing.

Characters

    1. What are the names of characters in your story?

    _____

    2. Put a check [√] by the main character. Underline the names of the minor characters.

(continued)

3. What are the traits of the main character? How will you show that the character has these traits?

Trait	Events in the Story That Show the Main Character Has This Trait
1.	
2.	

4. Do the personality traits of the main character change in the story? If so, how will you show this change? Place a star on the **Story Map** by the event where this change occurs. Describe the change on the line below.

_____

Setting

1. Where exactly does the story take place? Inside or outside? Does the location change at all during the story?

_____

_____

2. When does the story take place? What time of day? What season? What year?

_____

_____

▸ Write the word your teacher repeats.

1. _____

2. _____

3. _____

4. _____

5. _____

6. _____

7. _____

8. _____

9. _____

10. _____

11. _____

12. _____

13. _____

14. _____

15. _____

Exercise 2 · Word Line—Degrees of Meaning

▶ Study the words on the word line.

▶ Read the words and phrases in the **Word Bank**.

Word Bank

sometimes	forever	not at all	frequently	at all times
at no time	usually	rarely	occasionally	most of the time

▶ Use a dictionary to define unfamiliar words.

▶ Sort and record on the word line each word and each phrase from the **Word Bank** according to its relationship with the words **never**, **seldom**, **often**, and **always**.

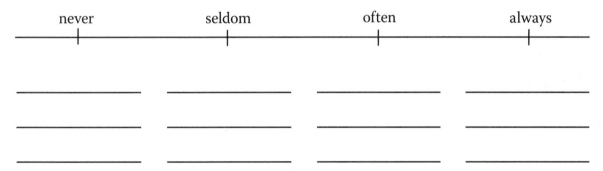

▶ Read each sentence below.

▶ Fill in the blank with the word or phrase from below the word line that makes the best sense in the sentence. There may be more than one correct answer.

    1. You should drive with your seat belt on _____.

    2. School closes _____ due to bad weather.

    3. True best friends last _____!

    4. _____ we see a rainbow after it rains.

    5. It is important to drink water _____ while exercising.

Unit 21 · Lesson 6

Exercise 3 · Identify It: Predicate Nominative or Predicate Adjective

▶ Read each sentence.

▶ Underline the form of **be** that is the main verb in the sentence.

▶ Find and label the predicate nominative (PN) or the predicate adjective (PA).

▶ Draw an arrow from the predicate nominative or predicate adjective to the subject.

1. The boy was outraged.

2. His older brother was being a nuisance.

3. For the young boy, justice was his mother.

4. In fights between the brothers, his mother was the judge.

5. The Scotch tape was the evidence.

6. His startled father was angry at the interruption.

7. He was a big man.

8. The boy was afraid of his father.

9. His brother was more secure.

10. Now the boy is more careful around his brother.

Exercise 1 · Answer It

▶ Underline the signal word in the question.

▶ Write the answer in complete sentences.

1. Explain what the author meant when he wrote, "In those days, justice looked a good deal like my mother."

   _____

   _____

   _____

   _____

   _____

2. Explain why Adam thought he had "the case of a lifetime."

   _____

   _____

   _____

   _____

   _____

3. Describe some of the characteristics of Adam's father.

   _____

   _____

   _____

   _____

   _____

(continued)

Unit 21 · Lesson 7

4. Assess how the story would have been different if the mother had been in the room instead of the father.

_____

_____

_____

_____

_____

5. Make a judgment about which character caused the problem in this story.

_____

_____

_____

_____

_____

Exercise 1 · Listening for Stressed Syllables and Schwa

▶ Listen to each word your teacher says. Repeat the word. Identify the number of syllables in the word by marking a dot above each syllable.

▶ Use the **Count Back Three** method to identify the stressed syllable by counting back three syllables from the end of the word.

▶ Say the word again, listen for the stressed syllable, and underline it.

▶ Listen for the schwa in the unstressed syllable. Circle the vowel that is reduced to schwa.

1. multiply

2. mystery

3. compensate

4. cultivate

5. industry

▶ Complete the following sentences:

Schwa condition:

Schwa often occurs in a (an) _____ syllable of a multisyllable word.
      (stressed or unstressed)

The _____ syllable is often reduced to schwa in multisyllable words.
   (first, second, third)

Exercise 2 · Build It: Words With Affixes

▶ Read the roots, base words, and affixes in the square.

▶ Combine word parts to build as many real words as possible in five minutes.

▶ Write each word in the correct column below the square.

▶ Check a dictionary to verify that the words you have written are real words.

in-	duct	come
con-	-or	script
de-	scrib	quire

in-	con-	-or	other

Exercise 3 · Fill In: Words With Affixes

▶ Use the words that you built in Exercise 2 to fill in the blanks.

1. Before you _____ about a new job, you should prepare a list of questions.

2. How would you _____ the setting of the story?

3. The band _____ motioned to the brass section to play loudly.

4. They will _____ the star athlete into the Hall of Fame today.

5. Please _____ each trophy with the date.

Exercise 4 · Punctuate It: Commas in a Series

▶ Read each sentence.

▶ Identify and underline the word groups in the series in the sentence.

▶ Place a comma between each pair of word groups in the series.

1. People have been searching for their roots constructing family trees and writing family histories for a long time.

2. Family histories were important to establish the rights of rulership to lay claim to land holdings and to keep possessions within a family.

3. Before histories were written, bards sang stories about heroes and their feats about the acts of famous ancestors and about the history of a tribe or clan.

4. *Foxfire* magazine covered traditional crafts and skills of Appalachia enriched the lives of the young people involved and gave rise to many similar projects.

5. The 1976 Bicentennial Year became a year when many Americans looked at their family histories learned where their ancestors had come from and also wondered about the future.

Exercise 5 · Diagram It: Predicate Nominative and Predicate Adjective

▶ Read each sentence.

▶ Identify and label the verb in each sentence as a linking verb (LV) or a helping verb (HV).

▶ Identify what comes after the verb and label it predicate nominative (PN) or predicate adjective (PA).

▶ Diagram the sentence.

  1. The boy was scared of his brother.

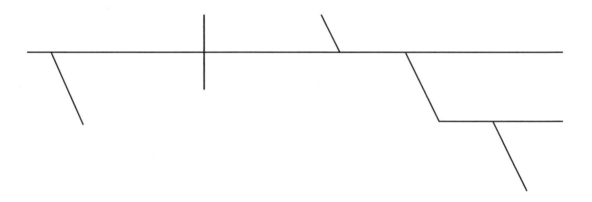

  2. His older brother was a nuisance.

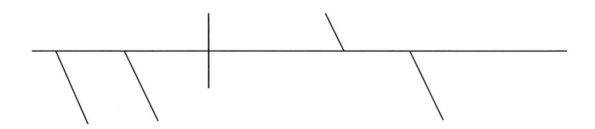

3. The father was very angry.

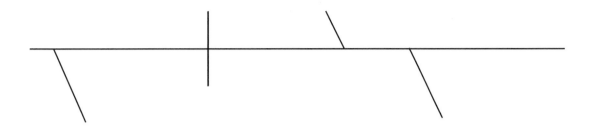

4. The tape was the evidence.

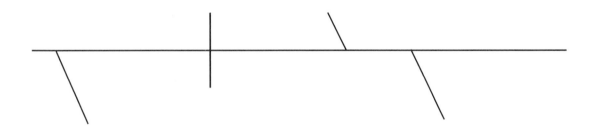

5. The boy is more careful around his brother.

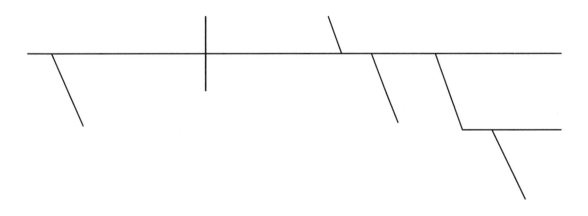

Exercise 1 · Drop It

▸ Read the word in the first column and the suffix in the second column.

▸ Check the box to identify if the **Drop It** spelling rule is needed to add the suffix to the base word.

▸ Combine the word and the suffix to make a new word. Write this word in the **New Word** column.

	Suffix	Drop It	No Rule	New Word
Example transcribe	-er			
1. educate	-or			
2. describe	-ing			
3. conform	-ist			
4. productive	-ly			
5. innovate	-or			
6. elect	-or			
7. incubate	-or			
8. indicate	-or			
9. install	-ment			
10. inside	-er			

Exercise 1 · Answer It: Multiple Choice

▶ Follow along as you discuss each question with your teacher.

▶ Underline the correct answer.

1. Why was Adam convinced that his brother Skip would get into trouble?

    A. Adam had evidence that his brother was guilty.

    B. Skip was always the one to get in trouble.

    C. Their mother was very strict.

    D. Their father was very strict.

2. Why was Adam unable to speak when he opened the door to his mother's room?

    A. He was very angry.

    B. He was shocked.

    C. He didn't want to disturb his father.

    D. He didn't want to disturb his mother.

3. What did Adam's father want for his children?

    A. He wanted them to be independent.

    B. He wanted them to be truthful.

    C. He wanted them to reach their full potential.

    D. all of the above

(continued)

Exercise 1 (continued) · Answer It: Multiple Choice

4. Why did Adam get into trouble?

    A. He had put Scotch tape on Skip's head.

    B. He had burst into a room without knocking.

    C. He had destroyed Skip's baseball trophy.

    D. He had disturbed his mother.

5. Which of the following statements best describes Adam's father?

    A. He was the person to turn to if you were bored.

    B. He was the person to turn to if you had been picked on.

    C. He was the person to turn to if you had any kind of problem.

    D. He was the person to turn to if you had a serious problem.

Exercise 2 · Write It: Problem Summary

▶ Review the **Character Profile** chart you completed for **"My Side of the Story."**

▶ Use the chart and the text for **"My Side of the Story"** to write a summary of how the main character contributed to the problem of the story.

_____

_____

_____

_____

_____

_____

_____

_____

Check off the activities you complete with each lesson. Evaluate your accomplishments at the end of each lesson. Pay attention to teacher evaluations and comments.

Unit Objectives	Lesson 1 (Date:_____)	Lesson 2 (Date:_____)
STEP 1 — **Phonemic Awareness and Phonics** • Identify the final consonant + _le_ syllable type. • Say sounds for vowel digraphs **ou**, **ui**, and **ea**. • Write the letters for the sounds / $\bar{u}$ /, / $\bar{\imath}$ /, and / $\bar{e}$ / using vowel digraphs.	☐ Exercise 1: Sort It: Syllable Types	☐ Discover It: Final Consonant + _le_ ☐ Syllable Awareness: Final Consonant + _le_
STEP 2 — **Word Recognition and Spelling** • Read and spell words containing final consonant + _le_ syllables. • Read and spell the **Essential Words**: _colleague, extraordinary, iron, journal, journey, peculiar_. • Spell words with prefixes, suffixes, and roots.	☐ Exercise 2: Spelling Pretest 1 ☐ Memorize It	☐ Build It: Final Consonant + _le_ Syllables ☐ Exercise 1: Write It: Essential Words ☐ Word Fluency 1
STEP 3 — **Vocabulary and Morphology** • Identify attributes. • Identify and define adjective suffixes. • Use the meanings of prefixes, suffixes, and roots to define words. • Use assimilation to identify words with the prefix **dis-** and assimilated forms.	☐ Unit Vocabulary ☐ Multiple Meaning Map (T) ☐ Draw It: Idioms	☐ Introduction: Prefixes _dis-_, _pro-_; Roots _dict_, _spec_; Suffixes _-able_, _-ous_ ☐ Exercise 2: Divide It: Prefix, Root, Base Word, Suffix ☐ Exercise 3: Define It: Word Parts
STEP 4 — **Grammar and Usage** • Identify phrasal verbs and their meaning. • Write sentences with compound predicate nominatives and adjectives. • Use commas in series, dates, and addresses.	☐ Exercise 3: Identify It: Prepositions and Prepositional Phrases ☐ Exercise 4: Punctuate It: Commas in a Series	☐ Exercise 4: Fill In: Prepositions ☐ Exercise 5: Choose It: Using Adjective Suffixes
STEP 5 — **Listening and Reading Comprehension** • Use context-based strategies to define words. • Identify character traits as part of plot analysis. • Identify and understand signal words for comprehension: **plan**, **design**, **compose**.	☐ Independent Text: "How to Make a Crossword Puzzle" ☐ Exercise 5: Phrase It ☐ Exercise 6: Use the Clues	☐ Passage Fluency 1 ☐ Exercise 6: Using Visuals: Illustrations and Charts
STEP 6 — **Speaking and Writing** • Write responses to sentences using the signal words: **plan**, **design**, **compose**. • Organize descriptive information to write a paragraph. Write a description of a character using traits and evidence of traits from the text.	☐ Exercise 7: Rewrite It	☐ Exercise 7: Answer It
Self-Evaluation (5 is the highest) **Effort** = I produced my best work. **Participation** = I was actively involved in tasks. **Independence** = I worked on my own.	Effort: 1 2 3 4 5 Participation: 1 2 3 4 5 Independence: 1 2 3 4 5	Effort: 1 2 3 4 5 Participation: 1 2 3 4 5 Independence: 1 2 3 4 5
Teacher Evaluation	Effort: 1 2 3 4 5 Participation: 1 2 3 4 5 Independence: 1 2 3 4 5	Effort: 1 2 3 4 5 Participation: 1 2 3 4 5 Independence: 1 2 3 4 5

Lesson 3 (Date:_____)	Lesson 4 (Date:_____)	Lesson 5 (Date:_____)
❏ Discover It: Vowel Digraph Sound-Spelling Patterns ❏ Vowel Chart	❏ Exercise 1: Listening for Syllables	❏ Content Mastery: Final Consonant + *le* and Vowel Digraphs
❏ Divide It: Compound Words ❏ Word Fluency 2	❏ Exercise 2: Sort It: Syllable Types ❏ Drop It: Drop *e* Rule	❏ Content Mastery: Spelling Posttest 1
❏ Vocabulary Focus ❏ Use the Clues ❏ Expression of the Day	❏ Introduction: Assimilation of the Prefix *dis-* ❏ Exercise 3: Add It: Prefixes and Roots ❏ Exercise 4: Define It: Prefix and Root or Base Word	❏ Exercise 1: Define It: Prefixes and Roots ❏ Exercise 2: Rewrite It: Adjective Suffixes
❏ Find It: Prepositional Phrases in Text	❏ Introduction: Phrasal Verbs ❏ Exercise 5: Identify It: Phrasal Verbs	❏ Exercise 3: Define It: Phrasal Verbs ❏ Masterpiece Sentences: Stage 1
❏ Instructional Text: "A Collection of Puzzling Tales" ❏ Comprehend It	❏ Take Note: "A Collection of Puzzling Tales"	❏ Map It: Story Map (Lesson 4) (T)
❏ Exercise 1: Answer It	❏ Map It: Story Map (T) ❏ Challenge Text: "Puzzle People"	❏ Exercise 4: Write It: Plot Summary (T) ❏ Challenge Text: "Puzzle People" ❏ Exercise 5: Challenge Writing: An Evaluative Report
Effort: 1 2 3 4 5 **Participation:** 1 2 3 4 5 **Independence:** 1 2 3 4 5	**Effort:** 1 2 3 4 5 **Participation:** 1 2 3 4 5 **Independence:** 1 2 3 4 5	**Effort:** 1 2 3 4 5 **Participation:** 1 2 3 4 5 **Independence:** 1 2 3 4 5
Effort: 1 2 3 4 5 **Participation:** 1 2 3 4 5 **Independence:** 1 2 3 4 5	**Effort:** 1 2 3 4 5 **Participation:** 1 2 3 4 5 **Independence:** 1 2 3 4 5	**Effort:** 1 2 3 4 5 **Participation:** 1 2 3 4 5 **Independence:** 1 2 3 4 5

Check off the activities you complete with each lesson. Evaluate your accomplishments at the end of each lesson. Pay attention to teacher evaluations and comments.

Unit Objectives	Lesson 6 (Date:_____)	Lesson 7 (Date:_____)
STEP 1 — **Phonemic Awareness and Phonics** • Identify the final consonant + <u>le</u> syllable type. • Say sounds for vowel digraphs <u>ou</u>, <u>ui</u>, and <u>ea</u>. • Write the letters for the sounds / $\bar{u}$ /, / $\bar{\imath}$ /, and / $\bar{e}$ / using vowel digraphs.	❑ Content Mastery: Using Student Performance	❑ Exercise 1: Listening for Stressed Syllables and Prefixes
STEP 2 — **Word Recognition and Spelling** • Read and spell words containing final consonant + <u>le</u> syllables. • Read and spell the **Essential Words**: colleague, extraordinary, iron, journal, journey, peculiar. • Spell words with prefixes, suffixes, and roots.	❑ Exercise 1: Spelling Pretest 2 ❑ Word Fluency 3	❑ Build It: Words With Prefixes and Roots ❑ Word Fluency 4
STEP 3 — **Vocabulary and Morphology** • Identify attributes. • Identify and define adjective suffixes. • Use the meanings of prefixes, suffixes, and roots to define words. • Use assimilation to identify words with the prefix **dis-** and assimilated forms.	❑ Exercise 2: Word Line—Degrees of Meaning ❑ Expression of the Day	❑ Vocabulary Focus ❑ Use the Clues ❑ Expression of the Day
STEP 4 — **Grammar and Usage** • Identify phrasal verbs and their meaning. • Write sentences with compound predicate nominatives and adjectives. • Use commas in series, dates, and addresses.	❑ Introduction: Compound Predicate Nominative and Compound Predicate Adjective ❑ Exercise 3: Combine It: Compound Predicate Nominative, Compound Predicate Adjective, and Compound Direct Object	❑ Identify It: Predicate Nominative, Predicate Adjective, or Direct Object
STEP 5 — **Listening and Reading Comprehension** • Use context-based strategies to define words. • Identify character traits as part of plot analysis. • Identify and understand signal words for comprehension: **plan**, **design**, **compose**.	❑ Instructional Text: "The Disappearing Man"	❑ Text Connection 8
STEP 6 — **Speaking and Writing** • Write responses to sentences using the signal words: **plan**, **design**, **compose**. • Organize descriptive information to write a paragraph. Write a description of a character using traits and evidence of traits from the text.	❑ Exercise 4: Answer It	❑ Spotlight on Plot
Self-Evaluation (5 is the highest) **Effort** = I produced my best work. **Participation** = I was actively involved in tasks. **Independence** = I worked on my own.	**Effort:** 1 2 3 4 5 **Participation:** 1 2 3 4 5 **Independence:** 1 2 3 4 5	**Effort:** 1 2 3 4 5 **Participation:** 1 2 3 4 5 **Independence:** 1 2 3 4 5
Teacher Evaluation	**Effort:** 1 2 3 4 5 **Participation:** 1 2 3 4 5 **Independence:** 1 2 3 4 5	**Effort:** 1 2 3 4 5 **Participation:** 1 2 3 4 5 **Independence:** 1 2 3 4 5

Lesson 8 (Date:_____)	Lesson 9 (Date:_____)	Lesson 10 (Date:_____)
❏ Exercise 1: Listening for Stressed Syllables		
❏ Introduction: Advanced Doubling Rule ❏ Exercise 2: Advanced Double It ❏ Exercise 3: Build It: Words With Prefixes, Suffixes, and Roots	❏ Exercise 1: Identify It: Spelling Rules	❏ Content Mastery: Spelling Posttest 2
❏ Exercise 4: Fill In: Words With Affixes ❏ Exercise 5: Relate It: Attributes	❏ Content Mastery: Attributes ❏ Content Mastery: Word Meanings	❏ Content Mastery: Using Student Performance ❏ Combine It: Prefixes, Roots, and Suffixes
❏ Diagram It: Predicate Nominative, Predicate Adjective, and Direct Object (T) ❏ Exercise 6: Rewrite It: Predicate Nominative, Predicate Adjective, and Direct Object ❏ Exercise 7: Punctuate It: Commas in Dates, Addresses, and a Series	❏ Content Mastery	❏ Content Mastery: Using Student Performance
❏ Exercise 8: Analyzing a Writing Sample	❏ Text Connection 8	❏ Instructional Text: "The Disappearing Man" ❏ Exercise 1: Answer It: Multiple Choice
❏ Exercise 9: Rewrite It	❏ Spotlight on Setting ❏ Challenge Text: "The Rosetta Stone: Key to a Linguistic Puzzle"	❏ Write It: Descriptive Paragraph ❏ Challenge Text: "The Rosetta Stone: Key to a Linguistic Puzzle"
Effort: 1 2 3 4 5 Participation: 1 2 3 4 5 Independence: 1 2 3 4 5	Effort: 1 2 3 4 5 Participation: 1 2 3 4 5 Independence: 1 2 3 4 5	Effort: 1 2 3 4 5 Participation: 1 2 3 4 5 Independence: 1 2 3 4 5
Effort: 1 2 3 4 5 Participation: 1 2 3 4 5 Independence: 1 2 3 4 5	Effort: 1 2 3 4 5 Participation: 1 2 3 4 5 Independence: 1 2 3 4 5	Effort: 1 2 3 4 5 Participation: 1 2 3 4 5 Independence: 1 2 3 4 5

Exercise 1 · Sort It: Syllable Types

▶ Read each word in the **Word Bank**.

Word Bank

cross	try	grid	write	sort
same	short	main	least	silo
blank	so	way	shape	first

▶ Sort the words according to their syllable types.

▶ Label each column.

Exercise 2 · Spelling Pretest 1

▶ Write the word your teacher repeats.

1. _____   6. _____   11. _____

2. _____   7. _____   12. _____

3. _____   8. _____   13. _____

4. _____   9. _____   14. _____

5. _____   10. _____   15. _____

Exercise 3 · Identify It: Prepositions and Prepositional Phrases

▸ Read each sentence with your teacher.

▸ Find, read, and underline the prepositional phrase in the sentence. Then circle the preposition.

▸ Think about the meaning of the preposition.

▸ Decide whether the prepositional phrase functions like an adjective, like an adverb, or like neither. Then underline the correct answer.

1. The clues were hidden within a complex maze.
   The prepositional phrase is functioning like
   a. an adjective   b. an adverb   c. neither

2. She put the last piece onto the puzzle.
   The prepositional phrase is functioning like
   a. an adjective   b. an adverb   c. neither

3. The speeding car was racing towards the tree.
   The prepositional phrase is functioning like
   a. an adjective   b. an adverb   c. neither

4. A cloak upon a ledge was a valuable clue.
   The prepositional phrase is functioning like
   a. an adjective   b. an adverb   c. neither

5. The students completed the puzzle without help.
   The prepositional phrase is functioning like
   a. an adjective   b. an adverb   c. neither

6. A dog amid the crowd began barking.
   The prepositional phrase is functioning like
   a. an adjective   b. an adverb   c. neither

7. The friends waited outside the classroom.
   The prepositional phrase is functioning like
   a. an adjective   b. an adverb   c. neither

(continued)

Unit 22 · Lesson 1

Exercise 3 (continued) · Identify It: Prepositions and Prepositional Phrases

8. The detective discovered a shoe with no laces.
The prepositional phrase is functioning like
a. an adjective　　　b. an adverb　　　c. neither

9. The police hunted among the trash, and they found evidence.
The prepositional phrase is functioning like
a. an adjective　　　b. an adverb　　　c. neither

10. The crime happened behind the factory.
The prepositional phrase is functioning like
a. an adjective　　　b. an adverb　　　c. neither

Exercise 4 · Punctuate It: Commas in a Series

▸ Read each sentence.

▸ Identify and underline the word groups in the series.

▸ Place a comma between each pair of word groups in the series.

▸ Read the sentence with the commas in place.

1. Storytellers were honored for their excellent memories for their ability to recall events from generations past and for their ability to make the stories interesting.

2. When solving a mystery, you must try to visualize the characters imagine the settings and think about the events.

3. You can solve puzzles by reading carefully thinking logically and joining clues together.

4. The store sold difficult crossword puzzles challenging mystery tales and books of cryptic riddles.

5. People love stories that puzzle them make them curious and cause them to think.

Exercise 5 · Phrase It

▸ Use the penciling strategy to "scoop" the phrases in each sentence.

▸ Read the sentences as you would speak them.

> **from "How To Make a Crossword Puzzle"**
>
> The crossword puzzle is based on a game called a word square. In a word square, words of the same length are written both across and down. Each word appears twice. The oldest word squares were found in the ruins of Pompeii, an ancient Roman city.

Exercise 6 · Use the Clues

▸ Read the excerpt below.

▸ Reread the underlined word **ruins**.

▸ Reread the text before and after the underlined word.

▸ Circle the word or words that can help a reader figure out the meaning of the word **ruins** in this sentence.

> **from "How To Make a Crossword Puzzle"**
>
> The crossword puzzle is based on a game called a word square. In a word square, words of the same length are written both across and down. Each word appears twice. The oldest word squares were found in the <u>ruins</u> of Pompeii, an ancient Roman city.

▸ Use the clues to select the best definition for the word **ruins** from the following explanations:
   a) the remains of something that has been destroyed
   b) to spoil something
   c) the books historians write about old places

Unit 22 · Lesson 1

Exercise 7 · Rewrite It

▸ Read the sentences below.

▸ Use arrows to show where you think signal words such as **first**, **then**, **next**, and **finally** could be added to improve the paragraph.

▸ Rewrite the sentences and add signal words such as **first**, **then**, **next**, and **finally** to improve the paragraph.

▸ Check that the sentence uses sentence signals—capital letters, commas, and end punctuation.

Here's how you make a crossword puzzle. You choose 6–8 words and write clues for them. You "cross" the words on grid paper and number them. You number and sort the clues. You make a blank puzzle and rewrite the clues under it.

_____

_____

_____

_____

_____

Exercise 1 · Write It: Essential Words

▸ Review the **Essential Words** in the **Word Bank**.

Word Bank

journey	peculiar	journal	extraordinary	iron	colleague

▸ Put the words in alphabetical order and write them on the lines.

▸ Write one sentence for each **Essential Word**.

▸ Check that each sentence uses sentence signals—correct capitalization, commas, and end punctuation.

1. _____

    _____

2. _____

    _____

3. _____

    _____

4. _____

    _____

5. _____

    _____

6. _____

    _____

Exercise 2 · Divide It: Prefix, Root, Base Word, Suffix

▸ Read each word.

▸ Break the word into its component prefix, root or base word, and suffix.

▸ Write each part in the correct column.

▸ Define each part using your **Morphemes for Meaning** cards.

Word	Prefix	Root or Base Word	Suffix
prospect			
predictable			
disrespectable			
protract			
humorous			

Exercise 3 · Define It: Word Parts

▶ Note that the five words from Exercise 2, **Divide It: Prefix, Root, Base Word, Suffix**, are listed below.

▶ Write a definition for each word using the meaning of each word part above. Remember that Latin roots give clues to the meanings of words. They cannot always be translated directly, however.

▶ Check a dictionary for the meaning of the word and write the definition given there.

▶ Compare the definition of the word with the definition developed from the translation of the word parts.

Word	Definition from Word Parts	Definition from Dictionary
prospect		
predictable		
disrespectable		
protract		
humorous		

Exercise 4 · Fill In: Prepositions

▶ Read each sentence.

▶ Choose a preposition from the **Word Bank** to fill in the blank.

Word Bank

amid	onto	outside	towards	upon
within	beyond	except	among	behind

▶ Reread the sentence to make sure it makes sense.

1. The police officer stepped _____ the ledge very carefully.

2. She spotted a clue _____ the house in the bushes.

3. _____ thirty seconds she was back inside her squad car.

4. She and her partner worked _____ a solution.

5. They later spotted the missing pup _____ a group of leaping, barking dogs at the park.

6. All the dogs _____ one were on leashes.

7. The officers asked the owners to lead their dogs _____ the tennis courts.

8. One officer moved _____ the last dog while the other kneeled in front of it.

9. The friendly dog placed a paw _____ the officer's knee.

10. Not long afterward, the pup was back _____ the people and pets in its own home.

Exercise 5 · Choose It: Using Adjective Suffixes

▸ Read each sentence and the word choices below the sentence.

▸ Use what you know about adjective suffixes to choose the correct word form to go in the blank.

▸ Reread the sentence with the word you chose to make sure it makes sense.

1. The students' graduation was a _____ occasion.

   a. joy

   b. enjoyment

   c. joyous

2. Everyone thought the young star was talented and _____.

   a. adorable

   b. adore

   c. adores

3. A highway worker carefully moved the _____ object out of the roadway.

   a. hazard

   b. hazardous

   c. hazardously

4. After the storm, we had to boil our water, as the tap water was not _____.

   a. drinking

   b. drink

   c. drinkable

5. The _____ situation made us all laugh.

   a. humor

   b. humorous

   c. humorously

Exercise 6 · Using Visuals: Illustrations and Charts

▸ Follow these directions for making your own crossword puzzle. Look back at pages 142–144 in the *Student Text* to reread the steps in detail.

Step 1: Circle 6 to 8 words from the box to include in your puzzle. On the lines below, write a clue for each word. Use a dictionary to help you.

able	flexible	table	guilty	threaten
angle	inevitable	trouble	build	sweat
handle	syllable	uncle	ahead	

Words   **Clues**

_____   _____

_____   _____

_____   _____

_____   _____

_____   _____

_____   _____

_____   _____

_____

Step 2: Make the words "cross." Use the grid on the facing page. Remember to use a pencil.

Step 3: Number the words. Start with the word at the top. Go from top to bottom and from left to right.

(continued)

Exercise 6 (continued) · Using Visuals: Illustrations and Charts

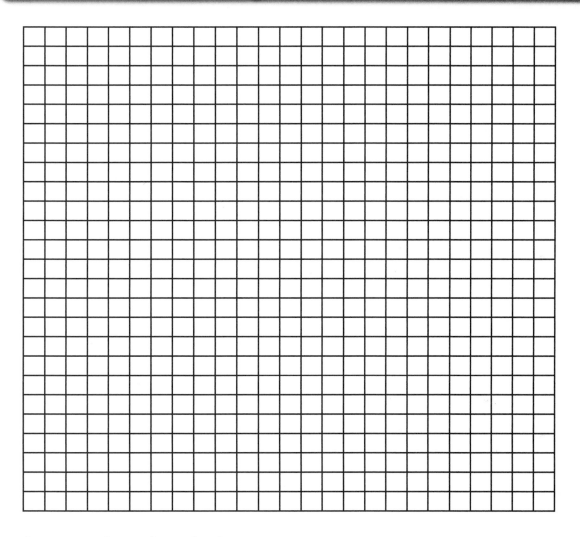

Step 4: Number and sort the clues.

Down		Across	
_____	_____	_____	_____
_____	_____	_____	_____
_____	_____	_____	_____
_____	_____	_____	_____
_____	_____	_____	_____

Step 5: On another section of the grid, trace the shape and make a blank puzzle. (Only the numbers should appear.)

Step 6: Make a final version with the clues in place.

Unit 22 · Lesson 2

Exercise 7 · Answer It

▶ Use information from the text and illustration in **"How To Make a Crossword Puzzle"** to answer these questions using complete sentences.

1. What happens in Step 3?

_____

_____

2. What materials do you need to make a crossword puzzle?

_____

_____

3. What sort of words should you select to make a crossword puzzle?

_____

_____

4. How do you determine whether a clue should be in the **Across** group or the **Down** group?

_____

_____

5. Where should the clues appear on the final chart?

_____

_____

Exercise 1 · Answer It

▸ Underline the signal word in the question.

▸ Write the answer in complete sentences.

1. Describe how the judge found the thief in **"The Sticks of Truth."**

_____

_____

_____

_____

_____

2. Plan a modern-day solution to the problem presented in **"The Cleverest Son."**

_____

_____

_____

3. Summarize the problem in **"The Cleverest Son."**

_____

_____

_____

_____

_____

_____

(continued)

4. Explain how a bee helped King Solomon pass the test in **"Which Flower?"**

_____

_____

_____

_____

_____

_____

5. Compose a different title for the folktale **"Love and Pumpkins."**

_____

_____

_____

Exercise 1 · Listening for Syllables

▶ Listen to each word your teacher says.

▶ Write the last syllable in each word that you hear.

1. _____

2. _____

3. _____

4. _____

5. _____

6. _____

7. _____

8. _____

9. _____

10. _____

11. _____

12. _____

13. _____

14. _____

15. _____

Unit 22 · Lesson 4

Exercise 2 · Sort It: Syllable Types

▶ Read each word in the **Word Bank**.

Word Bank

simple	puzzle	triangle	cattle	gargle
title	table	steeple	example	eagle
couple	guilty	feather	widespread	southern

▶ Divide the word into syllables.

▶ Sort each syllable according to its syllable type.

▶ Write each syllable in the correct column.

Closed Syllable	Open Syllable	r-Controlled Syllable	Final Silent e Syllable	Vowel Digraph Syllable	Final Consonant +le Syllable

Exercise 3 · Add It: Prefixes and Roots

▶ Read each prefix and root.

▶ Underline the first letter of the root.

▶ Decide if the last letter of the prefix **dis-** will change to the first letter of the root, or will be dropped.

▶ Write the changed form of the prefix on the line.

▶ Combine the new form of the prefix and root and write the completed word on the line.

	Prefix	Root	Changed Form of Prefix	Whole Word
1.	dis- +	fer		
2.	dis- +	late		
3.	dis- +	lute		
4.	dis- +	fuse		
5.	dis- +	verge		

Exercise 4 · Define It: Prefix and Root or Base Word

▶ Read the meaning of each word part.

▶ Read each word in heavy black type.

▶ Use the meanings of its word parts to write a definition for the word.

dis- means "absence," "opposite," "to reverse," "to remove," "not," or "apart."
pro- means "forward" or "before."
fract means "to break."
pel means "to drive" or "to push."
ceed means " to go."

1. **Disorder** means _____.

2. **Discharge** means _____.

3. **Propel** means _____.

4. **Proceed** means _____.

5. **Diffract** means _____.

Exercise 5 · Identify It: Phrasal Verbs

▶ Read each sentence.

▶ Locate and underline the phrasal verb.

▶ Copy the phrasal verb into the table.

▶ Write the meaning of the phrasal verb in the table.

▶ Use your dictionary to help with definitions. To find phrasal verbs in the dictionary, look up the verb.

	Phrasal Verb	Definition
1. We stopped and filled up the car with gas.		
2. Please fill out this form.		
3. My sister puzzled out the solution to the problem.		
4. We must hand in our reports before school.		
5. The student made up a story to cover her absence.		
6. We ran into our friend when we were downtown.		
7. The son takes after his mother.		
8. I wake up when the alarm sounds.		
9. The new student catches on quickly to the school rules.		
10. The firefighters put out the fire quickly so it would not spread.		

▶ Read each question.

▶ Locate the word in boldface type. Underline the root and circle the prefix.

▶ Underline the correct meaning of the word.

▶ Use a dictionary if you are unsure of the answer.

1. **tract** means "to pull"; what does **distract** mean?
   a. to pull away from   b. to pull in   c. to pull up

2. **fract** means "to break"; what does **diffract** mean?
   a. to break in   b. to factor   c. to break apart

3. **late** means "wide"; what does **dilate** mean?
   a. wide apart   b. narrow   c. thin

4. **tract** means "to pull"; what does **protract** mean?
   a. to pull out   b. to pull back   c. to pull down

5. **tect** means "to cover"; what does **protect** mean?
   a. to hurt   b. to attack   c. to guard

Exercise 2 · Rewrite It: Adjective Suffixes

▸ Read each of the example sentences with your teacher.

▸ Replace the underlined phrase in each example sentence with an adjective with the suffix **-able** or **-ous**.

▸ Finish the rest of the sentences independently.

▸ Use your **Morphemes for Meaning Cards** for the suffixes **-able** and **-ous** as a resource.

▸ Reread each sentence to check your work.

Sentence with underlined phrase:	Sentence with phrase changed to a single word:
Example: The student was <u>able to be relied on</u>.	The student was _____.
Example: The comic's routine was <u>characterized by humor</u>.	The comic's routine was _____.
1. The puzzle was <u>able to be solved</u>.	The puzzle was _____.
2. The man's income was <u>able to be taxed</u>.	The man's income was _____.
3. The stormy weather was <u>able to be said ahead of time</u>.	The stormy weather was _____.
4. The actor was <u>characterized by fame</u> for his performance in the play.	The actor was _____ for his performance in the play.
5. Fortunately, the stain <u>was able to be removed</u> from her new jacket.	Fortunately, the stain was _____ from her new jacket.
6. The student was <u>characterized by curiosity</u> about many scientific discoveries.	The student was _____ about many scientific discoveries.
7. Before performing on stage, the girl was <u>characterized by nerves</u>.	Before performing on stage, the girl was _____.
8. Although the car was old, it was <u>able to be depended on</u>.	Although the car was old, it was _____.
9. The roads up the snowy mountain were <u>characterized by hazards</u>.	The roads up the snowy mountain were _____.
10. The goods manufactured by the factory were <u>able to be exported</u>.	The goods manufactured by the factory were _____.

Unit 22 · Lesson 5

Exercise 3 · Define It: Phrasal Verbs

▶ Complete this exercise with your teacher.

▶ Read each sentence and underline the phrasal verb.

▶ Read the choices for the meaning of the phrasal verb.

▶ Select the correct meaning, using the context of the sentence to help you.

1. The storm victims got by without heat.
   a. perished   b. survived   c. talked

2. We puzzled over the hints they gave us.
   a. solved   b. played   c. pondered

3. We can pick out our favorite food.
   a. choose   b. eat   c. prepare

4. Please turn down the volume of the radio.
   a. raise   b. lower   c. remove

5. We had the boys look into the disappearance of the puzzle pieces.
   a. find   b. investigate   c. inspect

6. My sister hopes I will give back her new sweater.
   a. return   b. borrow   c. use

7. While running I got exhausted and did not think I could go on.
   a. stop   b. speak   c. continue

8. Our teacher told us to take down notes.
   a. copy   b. write   c. remove

9. The student left out an important detail in his essay.
   a. added   b. described   c. omitted

10. The sports rally was put off because of the snow.
    a. postponed   b. held   c. delayed

Exercise 4 · Write It: Plot Summary

▸ Use the **Story Map** template to write a summary for **"Which Flower?"**

▸ Use the checklist below to revise and check your work.

_____

_____

_____

_____

_____

_____

_____

_____

_____

_____

_____

_____

_____

_____

_____

Check It: Plot Summary Checklist

IDEAS AND CONTENT

☐ Did I include important events?

☐ Did I leave out minor details?

☐ Did I outline the problem?

ORGANIZATION

☐ Did I summarize events in the order in which they occur?

CONVENTIONS

☐ Did I use correct punctuation?

☐ Did I capitalize the right words?

☐ Did I spell everything correctly?

☐ Did I use complete sentences?

Unit 22 · Lesson 5

Exercise 5 · Challenge Writing: An Evaluative Report

Task: Write a report that will inform other students about how to make healthy snack choices. Research the dietary guidelines published by the United States Department of Agriculture. Summarize the information you find that would help people choose good snack foods. Then choose two snack foods to evaluate. One should be a poor snack choice, and the other should be a healthy snack choice. Explain why each snack choice is healthy or not healthy, and analyze the accuracy of the information on its package. In your conclusion, provide recommendations for peers on how to make healthy snack choices.

Notes on USDA Dietary Guidelines

1. What five groups of food are recommended as part of a healthy diet?

   _____   _____   _____

   _____   _____

2. How can you eat healthy snack foods?

   Kinds of snacks that are good to make at home:

   _____

   Kinds of snacks that are good to order when you're out at a restaurant:

   _____

   Kinds of snacks that are good to buy at a store:

   _____

   Ingredients in processed snacks that are best to avoid:

   _____

Summary of the USDA Dietary Guidelines

Write a one-paragraph summary of what you learned from the USDA Web site that might help other kids pick healthier snack foods. Write your summary on a separate sheet of paper.

(continued)

Exercise 5 (continued) · Challenge Writing: An Evaluative Report

Reading Snack Food Labels

Look at the snack food package and the nutrition label below. Then answer the questions.

Nutrition Facts:
Serv. size 1 package (48g)

Amount Per Serving:
Calories 210

	%Daily Value*
Fat Cal. 50	
Total Fat 6g	(8% DV)
Sat. Fat 2g	(10% DV)
Cholest. 0mg	(0% DV)
Sodium 230mg	(10% DV)
Total Carb. 38g	(13% DV)
Fiber Less Than 1 g	(3% DV)
Sugars 22g	
Protein 2g	
Vitamin A	(0% DV)
Vitamin C	(0% DV)
Calcium	(2% DV)
Iron	(4% DV)

*Percent Daily Values (DV) are based on a 2,000 calorie diet.

INGREDIENTS: ENRICHED FLOUR (WHEAT FLOUR, NIACIN, REDUCED IRON, THIAMINE MONONITRATE (VITAMIN B1), RIBOFLAVIN (VITAMIN B2, FOLIC ACID), SUGAR, PARTIALLY HYDROGE-NATED CANOLA, SOYBEAN, AND/OR COTTONSEED OILS, DEXTROSE, GLYCERIN, WHEY (FROM MILK), HIGH FRUCTOSE CORN SYRUP, WHEAT STARCH, LEAVENING (BAKING SODA, CALCIUM PHOSPHATE), EMULSIFIERS (DATEM, MONO- AND DIGLYCERIDES), SALT, CELLULOSE GUM AND GEL, NATURAL AND ARTIFICIAL FLAVOR.

1. How much sodium does one serving of the cookies contain? _____

2. The US Department of Agriculture recommends eating foods low in saturated fat and trans fats. These fats are contained in partially hydrogenated oils. Do the cookies contain partially hydrogenated oils? yes   no

3. The blurb on the front label says that the cookies are a "healthy snack" because they are low in fat. Is it true that the cookies are a healthy snack? Why or why not?

   _____

(continued)

Exercise 5 *(continued)* · Challenge Writing: An Evaluative Report

Evaluating Two Snack Foods

Snack #1: _____	Snack #2: _____
Is it a processed food? yes no	Is it a processed food? yes no
Does it call itself a "healthy snack"? yes no	Does it call itself a "healthy snack"? yes no
How many of these per serving?	How many of these per serving?
Calories _____	Calories _____
Fat/Saturated Fat _____	Fat/Saturated Fat _____
Carbohydrates _____	Carbohydrates _____
Fiber _____	Fiber _____
What healthy nutrients does the snack contain?	What healthy nutrients does the snack contain?
_____	_____
_____	_____
What unhealthy things is the snack high in?	What unhealthy things is the snack high in?
_____	_____
_____	_____

Exercise 1 · Spelling Pretest 2

▶ Write the word your teacher repeats.

1. _____

2. _____

3. _____

4. _____

5. _____

6. _____

7. _____

8. _____

9. _____

10. _____

11. _____

12. _____

13. _____

14. _____

15. _____

Exercise 2 · Word Line—Degrees of Meaning

▶ Discuss the meanings of the words **idle**, **jiggle**, and **tremble** with your teacher.

▶ Study the word line and think about how the three words on it are related.

▶ Read the words in the **Word Bank**.

Word Bank

shake	laze	loaf	vibrate	wiggle
wobble	quake	quiver	shudder	stop

▶ Use a dictionary to find the meanings of unfamiliar words.

▶ Sort and record each word under the word on the word line that has the same degree of meaning.

idle	jiggle	tremble

▶ Read each sentence below.

▶ Fill in the blank with the word that makes the best sense according to the context of the sentence. You may use a word more than once. There may be more than one correct answer.

1. It is dangerous to let the car idle when you _____ to get gas.

2. The jello will _____ once it has set and is ready to eat.

3. I saw her lip _____ when she got nervous.

4. The table will _____ if the legs are not adjusted properly.

5. We saw his whole body _____ with fear when his name was called.

Exercise 3 · Combine It: Compound Predicate Nominative, Compound Predicate Adjective, and Compound Direct Object

▸ Read each pair of sentences.

▸ Label the subject (S) in each sentence.

▸ Underline the verb, and label it linking verb (LV) or action verb (V).

▸ Identify what comes after the verb, and label it direct object (DO), predicate nominative (PN), or predicate adjective (PA).

▸ Combine the sentences and write the combined sentence on the line.

▸ Underline and label the compound part compound direct object (CDO), compound predicate nominative (CPN), or compound predicate adjective (CPA).

▸ Read the combined sentence and adjust the subject and verb as necessary.

Example:

S LV PN
Larry's father was a detective.

S LV PN
Larry's father was an inspector.

CPN
Larry's father was a detective and an inspector.

1. In the lobby, the police were quiet.

   In the lobby, the police were watchful.

   _____

   _____

2. The inspector warned his son to stay away from trouble.

   The inspector warned his son's friend to stay away from trouble.

   _____

   _____

(continued)

Exercise 3 (continued) · Combine It

3. The criminal was the jeweler.

   The criminal was Stockton.

   _____

   _____

4. Stockton committed break-ins.

   Stockton committed burglaries.

   _____

   _____

5. The police were rigorous in their tracking of criminals.

   The police were meticulous in their tracking of criminals.

   _____

   _____

Exercise 4 · Answer It

▶ Underline the signal word in the question.

▶ Write the answer in complete sentences.

1. Summarize what the police knew when they arrived on the scene.

_____

_____

_____

2. The police knew that the thief had run into the building. Design a strategy the police could have used for finding the thief.

_____

_____

_____

3. Explain how Larry identified the thief.

_____

_____

_____

_____

_____

_____

_____

(continued)

Exercise 4 *(continued)* · **Answer It**

  4. Make a generalization about Larry's personality.

  _____

  _____

  _____

  5. Compose a short newspaper article reporting the arrest of Stockton, the jewelry thief.

  _____

  _____

  _____

  _____

  _____

  _____

  _____

  _____

  _____

  _____

Lesson 7

Exercise 1 · Listening for Stressed Syllables and Prefixes

▶ Listen to each word your teacher says.

▶ Repeat the word.

▶ Listen for the stressed syllable and underline it.

▶ Circle the prefix in each word.

1. disarm

2. promote

3. predict

4. inspect

5. regret

▶ Complete the following sentences:

The stressed syllable in each word above contains a _____.

The unstressed syllable in each word above contains a _____.

Exercise 1 · Listening for Stressed Syllables

▶ Listen to each word your teacher says.

▶ Repeat the word.

▶ Count and write the number of syllables in each word.

▶ Write the prefix, root, and suffix in each word.

▶ In the first column, underline the stressed syllable in each word.

	Number of Syllables	Prefix	Root	Suffix
1. inspecting				
2. repulsed				
3. predictable				
4. compelling				
5. expelled				

Exercise 2 · Advanced Double It

▸ Read each word and suffix on chart.

▸ Complete the chart for each word.

Word	Suffix	One Vowel in the Final Syllable of the Word?	One Consonant at the End of the Word?	Final Syllable Stressed?	Double the Final Consonant?	Affixed Word
Example begin	ing					
1. regret	able					
2. embed	ed					
3. profit	ing					
4. depend	able					
5. admit	ed					

Exercise 3 · Build It: Words With Prefixes, Suffixes, and Roots

▶ Read the word parts in each table.

▶ Combine word parts to build as many words as you can.

▶ Write the words on the lines below the table.

▶ Check a dictionary to verify that the words you write are real words.

1.

dis-	tract	fuse	order

_____ _____ _____

2.

in-	re-	spect	-ate

_____ _____ _____

3.

regret	love	depend	-able

_____ _____ _____

4.

humor	rigor	nerve	-ous

_____ _____ _____

5.

pre-	dict	value	-able

_____ _____ _____

Exercise 4 · Fill In: Words With Affixes

▶ Read each sentence.

▶ Use the words from Exercise 3 to fill in the blanks.

▶ Use a dictionary to verify the meanings of unfamiliar words.

1. Security workers will _____ the bags before loading the plane.

2. The outcome of the mystery was _____.

3. _____ jewelry should be locked up in a safe place.

4. The comic was _____ and creative.

5. Many people find pets to be _____.

6. _____ exercise will help you burn calories.

7. Think before you act, so you do not make a _____ mistake.

8. It is important to _____ the substitute teacher.

9. _____ workers are likely to stay employed.

10. Many students get _____ before taking a test.

Exercise 5 · Relate It: Attributes

▶ Complete the chart by filling in each blank with a word from the **Unit Vocabulary List** in the *Student Text*, page 131, that completes the attribute pair.

1. _____:	three sides
2. _____:	peel
3. _____:	wick
4. word:	_____
5. book:	_____

▶ Complete each sentence below with a word from the attribute pairs in the chart.

1. A _____ has three sides.

2. A peel is part of an _____.

3. A wick is part of a _____.

4. A _____ is part of a word.

5. Every book has a _____.

Exercise 6 · Rewrite It: Predicate Nominative, Predicate Adjective, and Direct Object

▶ Read each diagram.

▶ Write the sentence that was diagrammed; do this on line A.

▶ Expand the sentence and write it on line B.

1.

| father | was | detective |

Larry's   a

A. _____

B. _____

_____

2.

| police | were | watchful |

The

A. _____

B. _____

_____

(continued)

Exercise 6 (continued) · Rewrite It: Predicate Nominative, Predicate Adjective, and Direct Object

3.

| Stockton | was | thief |

the

A. _____

B. _____

_____

4.

| Larry | had | interest |

a   great   in   work

police

A. _____

B. _____

_____

5.

| jeweler | was | criminal |

The   a

A. _____

B. _____

_____

Exercise 7 · Punctuate It: Commas in Dates, Addresses, and a Series

▶ Read each sentence.

▶ Add commas where they are needed.

▶ Check the chart to identify the reason for the commas.

	Commas Needed in...		
	Date	Address	Series
1. The game was on Thursday February 23 2006.			
2. The package came from John Smith 100 High Street Coryville MO 99999.			
3. The police will protect the people catch the criminals and watch the safety of the roads.			
4. The beautiful mountains shining lakes and sandy beaches made our trip memorable.			
5. On January 29 2005 my brother was born.			

Unit 22 · Lesson 8

Exercise 8 · Analyzing a Writing Sample

▸ Read **Paragraph 1** and **Paragraph 2** with your teacher.

▸ Compare the paragraphs.

▸ Reread **Paragraph 2** and underline words and images that help you visualize the setting. As you read, consider the following questions:

- What do you see?

- What do you hear?

- What do you feel?

---

adapted from "The Dust Bowl"

Paragraph 1

The day started out nice. Then suddenly it got cold. It became windy and dark. A dust storm hit the town. Everyone hurried home. Soon it was completely dark outside.

Paragraph 2

The day dawned clear and dry across the southern Great Plains. Then, suddenly, in midafternoon, the air turned cooler. Birds began fluttering nervously, and all at once the wind picked up. Suddenly a rolling black cloud of dust darkened the northern horizon. Everyone hurried home. We were trying desperately to beat the overwhelming "black blizzard" before it struck. Within minutes, the sky overhead was dark. Streetlights flickered in the gloom, and drivers turned on their headlights. Soon, the swirling dust storm blotted out our sun.

Exercise 9 · Rewrite It

▶ Read the sentences below with a partner.

▶ Use your imagination to visualize the places discussed in the sentences.

▶ Rewrite the sentences or add sentences to improve the description. Include specific details.

▶ Check that the sentences use sentence signals—capital letters, commas, and end punctuation.

1. It was a cold day.

_____

_____

2. The house looked haunted.

_____

_____

3. We walked through a nice garden.

_____

_____

Lesson 9

Exercise 1 · Identify It: Spelling Rules

▸ Read each word in the first column.

▸ Write its base word and suffix in the next two columns.

▸ Check the box that identifies the spelling rule used to add the word ending.

Affixed Word	Back to the Base	Suffix	Double It	Advanced Double It	Drop It	No Rule
Example 1 deferring						
Example 2 saddled						
1. diffusing						
2. indicated						
3. compelling						
4. swimmable						
5. puzzling						
6. beginning						
7. dependable						
8. expelling						
9. stopped						
10. peddler						

Exercise 1 · Answer It: Multiple Choice

▶ Follow along as you discuss each question with your teacher.

▶ Underline the correct answer.

1. Which of the following statements best describes Larry, the main character in **"The Disappearing Man"**?

   A. He gets into trouble a lot.

   B. He becomes bored easily.

   C. He is afraid of his father.

   D. He would make a good detective.

2. Which of the following pieces of information was most useful to Larry in identifying the thief?

   A. Stockton was a jewelry thief.

   B. No one had seen Stockton go into the building.

   C. There was a costume shop in the building.

   D. Stockton was a loner.

3. Which of the following statements best describes the father's attitude towards Larry's involvement in the search effort?

   A. He was amused.

   B. He was encouraging.

   C. He was annoyed.

   D. He was surprised.

(continued)

4. Why was Larry able to spot Stockton?

    A. Stockton wore a lot of jewelry.

    B. Stockton's pants were too short.

    C. Stockton looked nervous.

    D. Stockton was wearing a mask.

5. **"The Disappearing Man"** is _____.

    A. fiction

    B. informational text

    C. both

    D. neither

Check off the activities you complete with each lesson. Evaluate your accomplishments at the end of each lesson. Pay attention to teacher evaluations and comments.

Unit Objectives	Lesson 1 (Date:_____)	Lesson 2 (Date:_____)
STEP 1 **Phonemic Awareness and Phonics** • Say sounds for vowel diphthongs <u>oi</u>, <u>oy</u>, <u>ou</u>, and <u>ow</u>. • Write the letters for the sounds / oi / and / ou /.	❑ Exercise 1: Identify It: Syllable Types	❑ Discover It: Diphthongs <u>oi</u> and <u>oy</u> ❑ Vowel Chart (T)
STEP 2 **Word Recognition and Spelling** • Read words containing diphthong syllables. • Read and spell the **Essential Words** *courage, debt, herb, honest, honor, hour.* • Read words with prefixes, suffixes, and roots.	❑ Exercise 2: Spelling Pretest 1 ❑ Memorize It	❑ Exercise 1: Write It: Essential Words ❑ Word Fluency 1
STEP 3 **Vocabulary and Morphology** • Identify synonyms. • Identify and define verb suffixes. • Use affixes to define words. • Use assimilation to identify words with the prefix **ex-** and assimilated forms.	❑ Unit Vocabulary ❑ Exercise 3: Using a Thesaurus (T) ❑ Exercise 4: Word Line—Degrees of Meaning ❑ Expression of the Day	❑ Exercise 2: Divide It: Prefix, Root, Base Word, Suffix ❑ Exercise 3: Define It: Word Parts ❑ Draw It: Idioms
STEP 4 **Grammar and Usage** • Identify prepositions and prepositional phrases. • Identify phrasal verbs and their meanings. • Identify and write sentences with compound predicate nominatives, compound predicate adjectives, and compound predicate direct objects. • Identify the use of quotation marks in dialog.	❑ Exercise 5: Identify It: Prepositions and Prepositional Phrases	❑ Exercise 4: Choose It: Verb and Adjective Suffixes ❑ Shifting the Syllable Stress: Grammatical Implications ❑ Exercise 5: Code It: Noun or Verb
STEP 5 **Listening and Reading Comprehension** • Use context-based strategies to define words. • Identify character traits as part of plot analysis. • Identify and understand signal words for comprehension: **hypothesize, revise.**	❑ Independent Text: "Horsepower" ❑ Exercise 6: Phrase It ❑ Exercise 7: Use the Clues	❑ Passage Fluency 1 ❑ Exercise 6: Using Visuals: Illustrations and Charts
STEP 6 **Speaking and Writing** • Write responses to sentences using the signal words: **hypothesize, revise.** • Organize information to write a paragraph. • Write a description of a character using traits and evidence of traits from the text.	❑ Exercise 8: Rewrite It	Exercise 7: Answer It
Self-Evaluation (5 is the highest) **Effort** = I produced my best work. **Participation** = I was actively involved in tasks. **Independence** = I worked on my own.	**Effort:** 1 2 3 4 5 **Participation:** 1 2 3 4 5 **Independence:** 1 2 3 4 5	**Effort:** 1 2 3 4 5 **Participation:** 1 2 3 4 5 **Independence:** 1 2 3 4 5
Teacher Evaluation	**Effort:** 1 2 3 4 5 **Participation:** 1 2 3 4 5 **Independence:** 1 2 3 4 5	**Effort:** 1 2 3 4 5 **Participation:** 1 2 3 4 5 **Independence:** 1 2 3 4 5

Lesson 3 (Date:_____)	**Lesson 4** (Date:_____)	**Lesson 5** (Date:_____)
❑ Discover It: Diphthongs _ou_ and _ow_ ❑ Vowel Chart (T)	❑ Exercise 1: Listening for Diphthong Syllables	❑ Content Mastery: Diphthong Syllables
❑ Divide It ❑ Word Fluency 2	❑ Exercise 2: Sort It: Diphthongs ❑ Exercise 3: Sort It: Sounds for _ow_	❑ Content Mastery: Spelling Posttest 1
❑ Focus on Vocabulary ❑ Use the Clues ❑ Expression of the Day	❑ Exercise 4: Add It: Prefixes and Roots ❑ Exercise 5: Define It	❑ Exercise 1: Add It: Prefixes and Roots ❑ Exercise 2: Rewrite It: Suffixes
❑ Identify It: Quotations in Text	❑ Exercise 6: Identify It: Phrasal Verbs	❑ Masterpiece Sentences
❑ Instructional Text: "Zaaaaaaaap!" ❑ Comprehend It	❑ Take Note: "Zaaaaaaaap!"	❑ Spotlight on Settings
❑ Exercise 1: Answer It	❑ Spotlight on Setting ❑ Challenge Text: "Mohandas Gandhi: Soul Force"	❑ Write It: Descriptive Paragraph ❑ Challenge Text: "Mohandas Gandhi: Soul Force" ❑ Exercise 3: Challenge Writing: A Biographical Essay
Effort: 1 2 3 4 5 **Participation:** 1 2 3 4 5 **Independence:** 1 2 3 4 5	**Effort:** 1 2 3 4 5 **Participation:** 1 2 3 4 5 **Independence:** 1 2 3 4 5	**Effort:** 1 2 3 4 5 **Participation:** 1 2 3 4 5 **Independence:** 1 2 3 4 5
Effort: 1 2 3 4 5 **Participation:** 1 2 3 4 5 **Independence:** 1 2 3 4 5	**Effort:** 1 2 3 4 5 **Participation:** 1 2 3 4 5 **Independence:** 1 2 3 4 5	**Effort:** 1 2 3 4 5 **Participation:** 1 2 3 4 5 **Independence:** 1 2 3 4 5

Check off the activities you complete with each lesson. Evaluate your accomplishments at the end of each lesson. Pay attention to teacher evaluations and comments.

Unit Objectives	Lesson 6 (Date:_____)	Lesson 7 (Date:_____)
STEP 1 — Phonemic Awareness and Phonics • Say sounds for vowel diphthongs **oi**, **oy**, **ou**, and **ow**. • Write the letters for the sounds / *oi* / and / *ou* /.	❑ Content Mastery: Using Student Performance	❑ Exercise 1: Listening for Stressed Syllables and Prefixes
STEP 2 — Word Recognition and Spelling • Read words containing diphthong syllables. • Read and spell the **Essential Words** *courage, debt, herb, honest, honor, hour.* • Read words with prefixes, suffixes, and roots.	❑ Exercise 1: Spelling Pretest 2 ❑ Word Fluency 3	❑ Build It: Words With Affixes and Roots ❑ Word Fluency 4
STEP 3 — Vocabulary and Morphology • Identify synonyms. • Identify and define verb suffixes. • Use affixes to define words. • Use assimilation to identify words with the prefix **ex-** and assimilated forms.	❑ Exercise 2: Word Line—Degrees of Meaning ❑ Expression of the Day	❑ Focus on Vocabulary ❑ Use the Clues ❑ Expression of the Day
STEP 4 — Grammar and Usage • Identify prepositions and prepositional phrases. • Identify phrasal verbs and their meanings. • Identify and write sentences with compound predicate nominatives, compound predicate adjectives, and compound predicate direct objects. • Identify the use of quotation marks in dialog.	❑ Exercise 3: Identify It: Prepositions and Prepositional Phrases ❑ Exercise 4: Identify It: Compound Predicate Nominative, Compound Predicate Adjective, and Compound Direct Object	❑ Identify It: Quotations in Text ❑ Exercise 2: Identify It: Indefinite Pronouns ❑ Introduction: Colons
STEP 5 — Listening and Reading Comprehension • Use context-based strategies to define words. • Identify character traits as part of plot analysis. • Identify and understand signal words for comprehension: **hypothesize, revise.**	❑ Instructional Text: "Satyagraha: Power for Change"	❑ Take Note: "Satyagraha: Power for Change"
STEP 6 — Speaking and Writing • Write responses to sentences using the signal words: **hypothesize, revise.** • Organize information to write a paragraph. • Write a description of a character using traits and evidence of traits from the text.	❑ Exercise 5: Completing an Application	❑ Map It: Story Map (T)
Self-Evaluation (5 is the highest) **Effort** = I produced my best work. **Participation** = I was actively involved in tasks. **Independence** = I worked on my own.	**Effort:** 1 2 3 4 5 **Participation:** 1 2 3 4 5 **Independence:** 1 2 3 4 5	**Effort:** 1 2 3 4 5 **Participation:** 1 2 3 4 5 **Independence:** 1 2 3 4 5
Teacher Evaluation	**Effort:** 1 2 3 4 5 **Participation:** 1 2 3 4 5 **Independence:** 1 2 3 4 5	**Effort:** 1 2 3 4 5 **Participation:** 1 2 3 4 5 **Independence:** 1 2 3 4 5

Lesson 8 (Date:_____)	**Lesson 9** (Date:_____)	**Lesson 10** (Date:_____)
❑ Exercise 1: Listening for Stressed Syllables		
❑ Exercise 2: Sort It: Words With Suffixes ❑ Sort It: Vowel Sounds for -ate	❑ Exercise 1: Build It: Adding Suffixes	❑ Content Mastery: Spelling Posttest 2
❑ Exercise 3: Fill In: Words With -ate ❑ Exercise 4: Replace It: Synonyms	❑ Content Mastery: Synonyms ❑ Content Mastery: Word Meanings	❑ Content Mastery: Using Student Performance ❑ Combine It: Prefixes, Roots, and Suffixes
❑ Exercise 5: Rewrite It: Predicate Nominative, Predicate Adjective, and Direct Object ❑ Exercise 6: Identify It: Indefinite Pronouns	❑ Content Mastery	❑ Content Mastery: Using Student Performance
❑ Take Note: "Satyagraha: Power for Change"	❑ Instructional Text: "Satyagraha: Power for Change" ❑ Exercise 2: Answer It: Multiple Choice	Share It: Descriptive Paragraph
❑ Map It: Story Map ❑ Exercise 7: Answer It	❑ Write It: Descriptive Paragraph ❑ Challenge Text: "Blackout"	❑ Write It: Descriptive Paragraph ❑ Challenge Text: "Blackout"
Effort: 1 2 3 4 5 **Participation:** 1 2 3 4 5 **Independence:** 1 2 3 4 5	**Effort:** 1 2 3 4 5 **Participation:** 1 2 3 4 5 **Independence:** 1 2 3 4 5	**Effort:** 1 2 3 4 5 **Participation:** 1 2 3 4 5 **Independence:** 1 2 3 4 5
Effort: 1 2 3 4 5 **Participation:** 1 2 3 4 5 **Independence:** 1 2 3 4 5	**Effort:** 1 2 3 4 5 **Participation:** 1 2 3 4 5 **Independence:** 1 2 3 4 5	**Effort:** 1 2 3 4 5 **Participation:** 1 2 3 4 5 **Independence:** 1 2 3 4 5

Exercise 1 · Identify It: Syllable Types

▶ Read the words in the first column.

▶ Identify the syllables in each word.

▶ Say each syllable in the word and write it in the correct column.

	Closed Syllable	r-Controlled Syllable	Open Syllable	Final Silent *e* Syllable	Vowel Digraph Syllable	Final Consonant + *le* Syllable
Example 1 number						
Example 2 funny						
1. Thursday						
2. safety						
3. turkey						
4. eagle						
5. middle						
6. namely						
7. steeple						
8. lifesize						
9. marble						
10. unit						

Exercise 2 · Spelling Pretest 1

▶ Write the word your teacher repeats.

1. _____

2. _____

3. _____

4. _____

5. _____

6. _____

7. _____

8. _____

9. _____

10. _____

11. _____

12. _____

13. _____

14. _____

15. _____

Unit 23 · Lesson 1

Exercise 3 · Using a Thesaurus

▸ Read the thesaurus entry for the target word, **power**.

▸ Underline each of the meanings of **power**, which appear in bold print.

▸ Highlight each synonym for **power** that you are familiar with.

▸ Write one sentence for each meaning of the word **power**. Use a synonym that you highlighted from the thesaurus entry.

Source: yourdictionary.com

power
noun

1. **Capacity or power for work or vigorous activity:**
   animation, energy, force, might, potency, puissance, sprightliness, steam, strength.

2. **The state or quality of being physically strong:**
   brawn, might, muscle, potence, potency, powerfulness, puissance, sinew, strength, thew (often used in plural).

3. **The right and power to command, decide, rule, or judge:**
   authority, command, control, domination, dominion, jurisdiction, mastery, might, prerogative, sovereignty, sway.

---

1. _____

   _____

2. _____

   _____

3. _____

   _____

Exercise 4 · Word Line—Degrees of Meaning

▶ With your teacher, read each word in the **Word Bank** and discuss its meaning.

Word Bank

forceful	fragile	strong	weak	insecure	neutral

▶ Write each word under the word on the word line which has the same degree of meaning.

▶ Look up the words **powerless**, **neutral**, and **powerful** in the thesaurus. Locate another word to add under each of these words on the word line.

powerless   powerful

_____   _____   _____

_____   _____   _____

_____   _____   _____

_____   _____   _____

_____   _____   _____

_____   _____   _____

_____   _____   _____

▶ Read each sentence below.

▶ Fill in the blank with the word or phrase from above that makes the best sense in the sentence. There may be more than one correct answer.

1. The _____ flowers were not able to weather the storm.

2. The _____ jury put aside their personal feelings in reaching a verdict.

3. _____ winds made travel almost impossible.

4. _____ board members convinced the rest to vote to approve the proposal.

5. When my brother was treated rudely, he felt _____ and did not stand up for himself.

Exercise 5 · Identify It: Prepositions and Prepositional Phrases

▸ Read each preposition in the **Word Bank**.

Word Bank

towards	unlike	with	except	against
within	besides	without	beneath	despite

▸ Discuss its meaning with your teacher.

▸ Read each sentence.

▸ Look in the sentence for one of the prepositions from the **Word Bank**. When you find one, underline it.

▸ Discuss the meaning of the prepositional phrase with your teacher.

▸ Circle the object of the preposition.

1. Maitn climbed the tree despite the danger.

2. Everyone except Josha was present.

3. The boy had no other homework besides math.

4. The pear tasted unlike any other fruit.

5. The mother leaned the trike against the tree.

6. The corral looked like a spider web without the spider.

7. Josha improved with the pear treatment.

8. The batteries were kept within the huge plant.

9. The areas beneath the clouds became dark.

10. The storm clouds raced towards the land.

Exercise 6 · Phrase It

▶ Use the penciling strategy to "scoop" the phrases in each sentence.

▶ Read the sentences as you would speak them.

> ### from "Horsepower"
>
> We can measure length by using a ruler. We can measure heat and cold with a thermometer. We can measure how fast a car is going with a speedometer. But what if we want to measure a car's power? What would we use? Believe it or not, we would use horses.

Exercise 7 · Use the Clues

▶ Read the excerpt below.

▶ Reread each of the underlined pronouns.

▶ Identify and circle the noun or nouns that the pronoun replaces. (Remember that the word that a pronoun replaces is called its **antecedent**.)

▶ Draw an arrow from the pronoun to the noun or nouns it represents.

> ### from "Horsepower"
>
> For centuries, people have used horses to move things. They used them for war. They used them for travel. Horses were used to pull plows. They were used to pull mills. These mills ground grain into flour.

Unit 23 · Lesson 1

▶ Read the sentences below.

▶ Rewrite the two sentences in the excerpt as one sentence. Remove the pronoun that begins the second sentence. Replace the word **horses** in the second sentence with a pronoun. Use **and** to join the sentences.

▶ Check that the sentence uses sentence signals—capital letters, commas, and end punctuation.

---

from "Horsepower"

When early humans started farming, they tamed horses. They used horses for riding.

_____

_____

Exercise 1 · Write It: Essential Words

▸ Review the **Essential Words** in the **Word Bank**.

Word Bank

honest	herb	honor	hour	debt	courage

▸ Put the words in alphabetical order and write them on the lines.

▸ Write one sentence for each **Essential Word**.

▸ Check that each sentence uses sentence signals—correct capitalization, commas, and end punctuation.

1. _____

   _____

2. _____

   _____

3. _____

   _____

4. _____

   _____

5. _____

   _____

6. _____

   _____

Exercise 2 · Divide It: Prefix, Root, Base Word, Suffix

▶ Read each word.

▶ Break each word into its prefix, root or base word, and suffix components.

▶ Write each word part in the correct column.

▶ Define each word part, using your **Morphemes for Meaning Cards** as a resource.

Word	Prefix	Root or Base Word	Suffix
imperfect			
factor			
dejected			
dictator			
idolize			

Exercise 3 · Define It: Word Parts

▸ Read each sentence with your teacher.

▸ Note that the five words from Exercise 2, **Divide It: Prefix, Root, Base Word, Suffix**, are written in bold type in the sentences.

▸ Write a definition for the word in bold type on line A, using the context of the sentence and the meaning of each word part.

▸ Write the dictionary definition of the word on line B.

▸ Compare the dictionary definition of the word with the translation of the word parts.

1. The **imperfect** batteries were discarded, as they did not work.

   A. _____

   B. _____

2. The rainy weather was an important **factor** in our decision to postpone the baseball game.

   A. _____

   B. _____

3. The students felt sad and **dejected** when their team failed to make the playoffs.

   A. _____

   B. _____

4. The **dictator** would not allow people to have any freedom when he was ruling the country.

   A. _____

   B. _____

5. The fans adore and **idolize** the pop star.

   A. _____

   B. _____

Unit 23 · Lesson 2

Exercise 4 · Choose It: Verb and Adjective Suffixes

▸ Read the words in the **Word Bank**.

Word Bank

dictate	desperate	approximate	hesitates	private
illustrate	operates	considerate	immediate	estimate

▸ Read each sentence.

▸ Choose the correct word to go in the blank.

▸ Write **V** (verb) or **ADJ** (adjective) above the word.

▸ Reread the sentence to make sure it makes sense.

1. Mriel is a _____ boy who helps tend to Josha.

2. The girls must _____ the distance from the pear tree to the power plant.

3. Maitn is _____ to find a cure for Josha.

4. Maitn's mother _____ a machine at the power plant.

5. Josha and Mriel _____ their journal entries with pictures.

6. When the warning siren sounds, there must be an _____ response.

7. The rules _____ what the workers must do.

8. Josha did not go to a public hospital, but to a _____ clinic.

9. Maitn _____ a moment before grabbing the pear.

10. Josha guesses the _____ number of people present.

Exercise 5 · Code It: Noun or Verb

▸ Read each sentence.

▸ Write **N** if the underlined word is a noun. Write **V** if it is a verb.

▸ Write the word on the line, placing a mark (') on the stressed syllable.

1. The students <u>protest</u> the shortened lunchtime.   _____

2. The <u>protest</u> does not stop the work in the power plant.   _____

3. The <u>object</u> of the corral is to provide electricity to towns.   _____

4. The agents <u>object</u> to the complex plans.   _____

5. The doctors <u>present</u> their findings to Josha's mother.   _____

6. The gift is a surprise <u>present</u>.   _____

7. There has been some <u>progress</u> made in harnessing
   lightning for electricity.   _____

8. The laden trucks <u>progress</u> slowly towards the power plant.   _____

9. Maitn's mother has a <u>contract</u> to work at the power plant.   _____

10. The pupils of the boy's eyes <u>contract</u> in the bright light.   _____

Exercise 6 · Using Visuals: Illustrations and Charts

▸ Examine the illustration from **"Horsepower,"** which is included below.

▸ Estimate how much horsepower a school bus has.

▸ Draw a bar on the chart to represent your estimate.

▸ Estimate how much horsepower a golf cart has.

▸ Draw a bar on the chart to represent your estimate.

Horsepower Produced

	0	500	1000	1500	2000
Horse	(1 hp)				
Typical Lawnmower	(5 hp)				
Chevrolet Corvette	(345 hp)				
Electric Train					(6,000 hp)
Golf Cart					
School Bus					

Exercise 7 · Answer It

▶ Use information from the text and the illustration in **"Horsepower"** to answer these questions. Use complete sentences.

1. How do we measure the power of cars?

_____

_____

2. When did humans first tame the horse?

_____

_____

3. Why did James Watt coin the term **horsepower**?

_____

_____

4. What is the definition for horsepower?

_____

_____

5. What does a dynamometer do?

_____

_____

Exercise 1 · Answer It

▸ Underline the signal word in each question.

▸ Write the answer in complete sentences.

▸ Check for sentence signals—capital letters, commas, and end punctuation.

1. Make a hypothesis about how Maitn and Josha know each other.

_____

_____

_____

2. Revise the prediction you made earlier of how the story would end.

_____

_____

_____

3. Summarize the factors that contributed to the energy crisis during the era of "The Dark."

_____

_____

_____

_____

(continued)

4. Assess the level of danger that Josha and Maitn are exposed to during the storm.

_____

_____

_____

_____

_____

_____

_____

5. Paraphrase Maitn's explanation of how a pear can help Josha.

_____

_____

_____

_____

_____

_____

_____

Exercise 1 · Listening for Diphthong Syllables

▸ Listen to each word your teacher says.

▸ Repeat the word.

▸ Identify the position of the / *oi* / sound in each word.

▸ Write each word in the column for the correct spelling pattern: **oi** or **oy**.

	oi spelling pattern	**oy** spelling pattern
1.		
2.		
3.		

▸ Complete the following sentences:

4. _____ is found at the beginning or middle of words or syllables.

5. _____ is found at the end of words or syllables.

(continued)

Exercise 1 (continued) · Listening for Diphthong Syllables

▶ Listen to each word your teacher says.

▶ Repeat the word.

▶ Identify the position of the / *ou* / sound in each word.

▶ Write each word in the column for the correct spelling pattern: **ou** or **ow**.

	ou spelling pattern	**ow** spelling pattern
6.		
7.		
8.		

▶ Complete the following sentences:

9. _____ is found at the beginning or middle of words or syllables.

10. _____ is found at the end of words or syllables.

▶ In words with / *ou* / followed by **l** or **n**, the / *ou* / spelling is **ow**. Write 5 examples on the lines below.

11. _____ 12. _____ 13. _____ 14. _____ 15. _____

Unit 23 · Lesson 4

Exercise 2 · Sort It: Diphthongs

▸ Read each word in the **Word Bank**.

Word Bank

spoil	bound	brown	broil	joy
cloud	moist	crowd	ploy	proud

▸ Identify the diphthong in each syllable.

▸ Write the word under the correct heading.

/ oi /	/ ou /

Exercise 3 · Sort It: Sounds for <u>ow</u>

▸ Listen to each word your teacher says.

▸ Identify the sound represented by the <u>**ow**</u> in each word.

▸ Write the word in the column based on the sound for <u>**ow**</u>.

<u>ow</u> as in **show**	<u>ow</u> as in **cow**

Unit 23 · Lesson 4

Exercise 4 · Add It: Prefixes and Roots

▸ Recall that **ex-** changes to **ef-** before a root starting with **f**, and changes to **e** before roots starting with **j**, **l**, **m**, **n**, **r**, and **v**.

▸ Read each prefix and root.

▸ Underline the first letter of the root.

▸ Decide if the last letter of the prefix **ex-** will change to the first letter of the root, or will the **x** be dropped.

▸ Write the changed form of the prefix on the line.

▸ Combine the correct form of the prefix and root and write the completed word on the line.

	Prefix	Root	Changed Form of Prefix	Whole Word
1.	ex- +	fect		
2.	ex- +	lect		
3.	ex- +	laborate		
4.	ex- +	fort		
5.	ex- +	rupt		

Exercise 5 · Define It

▶ Read each sentence.

▶ Use your knowledge of morphemes to select the correct meaning of the word in bold type.

▶ Use your **Morphemes for Meaning Cards** and a dictionary as references.

1. If the root **meate** means "to pass," what does **permeate** mean?
   ○ to pass over   ○ to pass through   ○ to pass down

2. If the root **pare** means "to make ready," what does **prepare** mean?
   ○ unready   ○ to sit through   ○ to get ready

3. If the root **vade** means "to go," what does **pervade** mean?
   ○ to go in   ○ to go out   ○ to go through

4. If the root **colate** means "to filter," what does **percolate** mean?
   ○ to filter through   ○ to filter out   ○ to filter over

5. If the root **dict** means "to say," what does **predict** mean?
   ○ to say through   ○ to say before   ○ to say after

6. If the root **lapse** means "to slip," what does **elapse** mean?
   ○ to slip on   ○ elastic   ○ to slip by

7. If the root **lect** means "to choose," what does **elect** mean?
   ○ to reject   ○ to pick from   ○ to defeat

8. If the root **rupt** means "to break," what does **erupt** mean?
   ○ to explode   ○ mistake   ○ to contain

9. If the root **laborate** means "a state of being worked," what does **elaborate** mean?
   ○ to make simple   ○ to make up   ○ to add details

10. If the root **fort** means "strong," what does **effort** mean?
    ○ simple work   ○ easy work   ○ hard work

Unit 23 · Lesson 4

Exercise 6 · Identify It: Phrasal Verbs

▶ Complete this exercise with your teacher.

▶ Read each sentence.

▶ Locate and underline the phrasal verb.

▶ Copy the phrasal verb into the table.

▶ Write the meaning of the phrasal verb in the table.

▶ Use your dictionary to help with definitions. To find phrasal verbs in the dictionary, look up the verb.

1. I pointed the new house out to my friends.

2. His mother told him to throw his old sneakers away.

3. I remembered an important fact, and then left it out of my answer.

4. To attract customers, the store gave free samples away.

5. Every day the official takes the flag down at sunset.

6. In order to improve his grades, the student did his report over.

7. The girl was offered an after school job, but she turned it down.

8. The drama department set the stage up just as they wanted it.

9. It was cold, so I put a sweater on.

10. To rebuild the old bridge, the workmen blew the foundation up.

Exercise 6 (continued) · Identify It: Phrasal Verbs

Phrasal Verb	Definition

Exercise 1 · Add It: Prefixes and Roots

▸ Recall that **ex-** changes to **ef-** before a root starting with **f**, and changes to **e-** before roots starting with **j**, **l**, **m**, **n**, **r**, and **v**.

▸ Read each prefix and root

▸ Underline the first letter of the root.

▸ Decide if the last letter of the prefix **ex-** will change to the first letter of the root, or will be dropped.

▸ Write the correct form of the prefix on the line.

▸ Combine the correct form of the prefix and the root, and write the completed word on the line.

	Prefix	Root	Changed Form of Prefix	Whole Word
1.	ex- +	rase		
2.	ex- +	lapse		
3.	ex- +	normous		
4.	ex- +	ject		

▸ Using a dictionary and your knowledge of morphemes, write a definition of each of the following words:

erase _____

eject _____

▸ Write a sentence with each of these words:

elapse _____

enormous _____

Exercise 2 · Rewrite It: Suffixes

▶ Read the words in the **Word Bank**.

Word Bank

stimulated	memorize	humanized	minimized
standardized	indeterminate	speculated	legalized
pulsates	impersonate	idolized	verbalize

▶ Read each of the example sentences with your teacher.

▶ Replace the underlined phrase in each sentence with a word from the **Word Bank** that has the suffix **-ate** or **-ize**.

▶ Finish the rest of the sentences independently.

▶ Use your **Morphemes for Meaning Cards** for the suffixes **-ate** and **-ize** as a resource.

▶ Reread each sentence to check your work.

(continued)

Exercise 2 (continued) · Rewrite It: Suffixes

Sentence with underlined phrase:	Sentence with phrase changed to a single word:
Example: The scientist <u>used a stimulus to cause</u> the chemical elements to interact.	The scientist _____ the chemical elements to interact.
Example: The student had to <u>put into memory</u> the speech.	The student had to _____ the speech.
1. The fan <u>made into an idol</u> the pop star.	The fan _____ the pop star.
2. When the heart beats, it <u>has a pulse</u>.	When the heart beats, it _____.
3. The mother's story <u>made human</u> the enormous tragedy.	The mother's story _____ the enormous tragedy.
4. The boys <u>looked into the future</u> about the length of the final exam.	The boys _____ about the length of the final exam.
5. There are <u>not a determined</u> number of stars in the sky.	There are an _____ number of stars in the sky.
6. The state has <u>caused to be legal</u> the use of express lanes by fuel-efficient cars.	The state has _____ the use of express lanes by fuel-efficient cars.
7. The actor could <u>become the person of</u> many different people.	The actor could _____ many different people.
8. Sometimes it is hard to <u>put into to words or make verbal</u> our feelings.	Sometimes it is hard to _____ our feelings.
9. Some rules of the road have been <u>made standard</u> throughout the country.	Some rules of the road have been _____ throughout the country.
10. I <u>made the minimum size of</u> the picture to fit the small page.	I _____ the picture to fit the small page.

Exercise 3 · Challenge Writing: A Biographical Essay

The Task: Mohandas Gandhi was described as using the "powers of courage, nonviolence, and truth" to overcome difficulties and lead the people of India to independence. Research and then write a biographical essay about a person who has overcome odds to achieve great things.

Use the model below to help you organize information for writing as you research. Copy the model onto 5x8 lined note cards. Follow the steps on the **Writer's Checklist**.

Using Note Cards

▸ Copy the notes from the board onto the sample card below.

▸ Use this format as you create note cards for your research on the person you have chosen to write a biography about.

How to Research for a Biographical Essay

*Write sources for notes on the other side of the card.	**Question:**
	NOTES:
	Answer:

How to Write a Bibliography

A bibliography comes at the end of a research report. It lets readers know what sources of information the writer used in preparing the report. You should prepare a bibliography for any research report you write. The models below show bibliography entries for three kinds of sources: a nonfiction book, an encyclopedia article, and an article from an Internet site.

▸ Study each model.

▸ Use these models as guides when you prepare your own bibliography.

(continued)

Exercise 3 (continued) · Challenge Writing: A Biographical Essay

Nonfiction Book:
Maloof, George. <u>Vegetarian Animals</u>. New York: Savannah Press, 2002.

AUTHOR	TITLE	CITY OF PUBLISHER	PUBLISHER AND YEAR PUBLISHED

Note: You can look on the copyright page of a book to find this information.

Encyclopedia Article:
"Lynx." <u>Big Book Encyclopedia</u>. 2003 ed.

TITLE OF ARTICLE	NAME OF ENCYCLOPEDIA	EDITION

Article from an Internet Site:
"Endangered Animals in the United States." <u>Animal Updates Online</u>. 27 March 2004. <http://www.animalupdate.com/article/endangered.html>.

TITLE OF ARTICLE	WEBSITE ADDRESS	NAME OF WEBSITE	DATE ARTICLE VIEWED

▸ Read the information about each research source below, and then write a bibliography entry for it.

An article about France in the 2001 *Encyclopedia of Everything*.

_____

A book called *Our Flying Friends*, written by Delia Felton in 2003 and published by Animal Experts Press, located in San Francisco, California.

_____

_____

An Internet article called "Hanging Out in the Rainforest Canopy" viewed on February 18, 2005, at the following web address: http://www.rainforesttop.com/hangingout.html.

_____

_____

In a bibliography, entries are organized alphabetically by author's last name or by the title of the work if the author's name is not known.

▸ Place a 1, 2, or 3 by each entry you created to show the order in which they would appear in a bibliography.

Exercise 1 · Spelling Pretest 2

▶ Write the word your teacher repeats.

1. _____

2. _____

3. _____

4. _____

5. _____

6. _____

7. _____

8. _____

9. _____

10. _____

11. _____

12. _____

13. _____

14. _____

15. _____

Unit 23 · Lesson 6

Exercise 2 · Word Line—Degrees of Meaning

▸ Study the words on the word line.

▸ Read the words and phrases in the **Word Bank**.

Word Bank

put up with	decline	disagree with	agree	consent	disapprove
refuse	allow	concur	disallow	protest	permit

▸ Use a dictionary and what you know about prefixes, roots, and suffixes to define unfamiliar words.

▸ Sort and record on the word line each word and each phrase from the **Word Bank** according to its relationship with the words **accept**, **tolerate**, **object**, and **reject**.

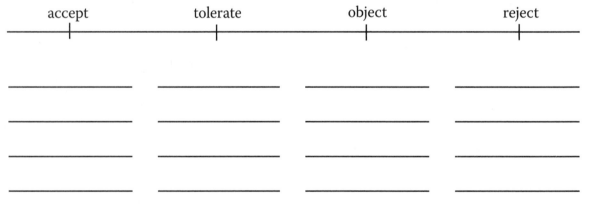

(continued)

Exercise 2 *(continued)* · Word Line—Degrees of Meaning

▶ Read each sentence below.

▶ Fill in the blank with the word or phrase from the word line that makes the best sense in the sentence. There may be more than one correct answer.

1. A substitute teacher should not have to _____ poor behavior from students.

2. Your parents can _____ with the conditions of the contract by checking the NO box.

3. If you _____ with what you have read, sign your name at the bottom of the form.

4. The principal may _____ to the gym being used for that purpose, because it might ruin the floor.

5. It is wise for young people to _____ offers for free credit cards.

▶ Locate the words **accept**, **tolerate**, **object**, and **reject** in the thesaurus.

▶ Select another example for each word and add them to the columns above.

Unit 23 · Lesson 6

Exercise 3 · Identify It: Prepositions and Prepositional Phrases

▶ Do this exercise with your teacher.

▶ Read each sentence.

▶ Circle the preposition and underline the prepositional phrase.

▶ Identify the object of the preposition. Write OP over that word.

▶ Answer the questions at the end of the exercise.

1. Ramdas practiced *satyagraha* despite Bill Patchett.

2. Everyone except Ramdas was sad the team lost.

3. Ramdas had a calmness unlike the other boys.

4. Kenneth, with his honesty and kindness, made a good friend.

5. All the team members besides Patchet knew Kenneth's plan.

6. Argyle High played against Midland High.

7. Bill Patchet stood on the sideline without his helmet.

8. Kenneth found the strength within himself.

9. The enormous football player rushed towards Kenneth.

10. Kenneth found himself beneath a very heavy player.

▶ Look at sentence 5. Is the prepositional phrase acting as an adverb or an adjective? Underline the correct answer.
   a. adverb   b. adjective

▶ Look at sentence 9. Is the prepositional phrase acting as an adverb or an adjective? Underline the correct answer.
   a. adverb   b. adjective

Exercise 4 · Identify It: Compound Predicate Nominative, Compound Predicate Adjective, and Compound Direct Object

▶ Read each sentence

▶ Label the subject (S) in each sentence.

▶ Underline the verb. If it is a linking verb, label it LV. If it is an action verb, label it V.

▶ Identify and underline each part of the compound predicate nominative (PN), compound predicate adjective (PA), or compound direct object (DO).

▶ Circle the conjunction joining the compound parts.

1. Rollin Acres was my best buddy and the team's fullback.

2. Ramdas used a bandage and a splint on my finger.

3. Kenneth's finger was swollen and sore.

4. Bill Patchet hit his head and fists on the locker.

5. Sarah was a friend and a fellow student.

6. Ramdas was brave and strong.

7. Mahatma Gandhi preached peaceful resistance and nonviolence.

8. Gandhi's followers were resolute and peaceful.

9. These Indians protested the law and the salt tax at Dharasana Salt Works.

10. Martin Luther King was a believer and follower of Gandhi's teachings.

Unit 23 · Lesson 6

Exercise 5 · Completing an Application

▶ Review and complete the application below.

Football Team Application

Part I Athlete Information

Last Name: _____ First Name: _____

Address: _____

City: _____ State: _____ Zip: _____

Home Phone: (   ) _____ Mobile Phone: (   ) _____

E-mail address: _____

Current Grade: _____

Total years of football experience: _____ List other teams played for in the past:

1. Name of Team _____ When: _____ Where: _____

2. Name of Team _____ When: _____ Where: _____

In Case of Emergency, Please Notify the Following Parent or Guardian:

Name: _____ Relationship: _____ Phone: _____

Part II Personal Statement

In a few sentences, please explain what strengths you would bring to the team.

_____

_____

_____

_____

Exercise 1 · Listening for Stressed Syllables and Prefixes

▶ Listen to each word your teacher says. Repeat the word.

▶ Listen for the stressed syllable and underline it.

▶ Circle the prefix in each word.

1. deject

2. inspect

3. perform

4. infect

5. deduct

6. distract

7. retract

8. induct

9. detract

10. disinfect

▶ Complete the following sentences:

The stressed syllable in each word above contains a _____.

The unstressed syllable in each word above contains a _____.

Which word contains two prefixes? _____

Unit 23 · Lesson 7

Exercise 2 · Identify It: Indefinite Pronouns

▸ Read each sentence.

▸ Identify and circle the indefinite pronoun in it.

1. Everyone on the team played hard.

2. Did anyone suffer a severe injury?

3. Some have minor sprains or bruises.

4. A few will miss practice on Monday.

5. Ken leaves nothing of value in his locker.

Exercise 1 · Listening for Stressed Syllables

▸ Listen to each word your teacher says.

▸ Repeat the word.

▸ Count and write the number of syllables in each word.

▸ Write each prefix, root or base word, and suffix in each word.

▸ In the first column, underline the stressed syllable in each word.

	Number of Syllables	Prefix	Base Word	Root	Suffix
Example: <u>joy</u>ous	2		joy		ous
Example: in<u>ject</u>ed	3	in		ject	ed
1. disjointed					
2. cloudy					
3. disinfected					
4. rejoining					
5. dismounted					
6. dejected					
7. interjecting					
8. loudly					
9. projected					
10. pointedly					

Unit 23 · Lesson 8

Exercise 2 · Sort It: Words With Suffixes

▶ Read each word and suffix in the **Word Bank**.

Word Bank

verbal + ize	fertile + ize	colony + ize	consider + ate	determine + ate
pulse + ate	economy + ize	formal +ize	scrutiny + ize	idol + ize

▶ Combine the suffix and the base word to create a new word.

▶ Sort each new word according to the spelling pattern followed when adding **-ize** or **-ate**.

Hint: Use the *At a Glance* in the *Student Text* for help with spelling.

Drop y, Then Add Suffix	Drop e, Then Add Suffix	Add Suffix

Exercise 3 · Fill In: Words With -ate

▶ Read each sentence with your teacher.

▶ Consider whether the missing word functions as a verb or as an adjective.

▶ Use a word from the **Word Bank** to fill in the blank.

Word Bank

ultimate	appropriate	dedicate	hesitate	desperate
separate	alternate	relate	estimate	private

▶ Recall what you know about how the function of a word ending in **-ate** affects its pronunciation. Use this knowledge to decide how to pronounce the word in the bank.

▶ Read the completed sentence aloud with your teacher.

Hint: Some words will be used twice with different pronunciations.

1. Our school will _____ the library to the former mayor.

2. Will you _____ the mail into _____ folders?

3. One alternative is to _____ drivers on _____ hours.

4. Conferences will be held in a _____ area.

5. My friend was so _____ for a ticket to the new movie that she got in line four hours early.

6. The treasurer will _____ the _____ funds for the event.

7. Can you _____ the time it will take to fix my car?

8. Don't _____ when merging onto the expressway.

9. My vacation was an _____ experience.

10. Her counselor is able to _____ to teens and their issues.

Unit 23 · Lesson 8

Exercise 4 · Replace It: Synonyms

▶ Read the passage below.

▶ Use a thesaurus to find a synonym for **move** as it is used in each sentence with a blank.

▶ Write the synonym in the blank.

▶ Try not to use the same word twice. You may use the word **move** once.

▶ Use a thesaurus or a dictionary to help you with shades of meaning.

---

adapted from "Horsepower"

How would you measure the power used to _____ something? For many centuries, people used horses to _____ things. People asked, "How far could a horse _____ a load of coal? How far could it _____ in one minute?" The distance moved multiplied by the weight carried is the formula still used to determine horsepower. Horsepower measures the power needed to _____ things.

Exercise 5 · Rewrite It: Predicate Nominative, Predicate Adjective, and Direct Object

▸ Read each diagram.

▸ Write the complete sentence below on line A.

▸ Expand the sentence and write it on line B.

▸ Use your **Masterpiece Sentence Cue Chart** to help you expand the sentences.

1.

Ramdas	pulled	finger

Kenneth's

A. _____

B. _____

_____

2.

protestors	were	defenseless

The

A. _____

B. _____

_____

(continued)

Exercise 5 *(continued)* · **Rewrite It: Predicate Nominative, Predicate Adjective, and Direct Object**

3.

| Sarah | was | friend |

Kenneth's

A. _____

B. _____

_____

4.

| Kenneth | tried | nonviolence |

on / field / the / football

A. _____

B. _____

_____

5.

| Bill | laid | hand |

on / shoulder / Ramdas's / a

A. _____

B. _____

_____

Exercise 6 · Identify It: Indefinite Pronouns

▶ Read each sentence.

▶ Identify and circle each indefinite pronoun.

> Did anyone leave a mouth guard on the bench by the coach's office? Nobody claimed it on Friday. Everyone must keep track of personal items. Several have been left out in the locker room recently. All are now in the lost-and-found.

Exercise 7 · Answer It

▶ Underline the signal word in the question.

▶ Write the answer in complete sentences.

1. Make a generalization about Bill Patchett.

_____

_____

_____

2. Explain Ramdas's response to Bill Patchett.

_____

_____

_____

_____

_____

_____

_____

(continued)

3. Hypothesize why Kenneth changes his mind about the best way to deal with Bill Patchett.

_____

_____

_____

_____

_____

4. Summarize Kenneth's approach to using *satyagraha* on the football field.

_____

_____

_____

_____

_____

_____

_____

_____

5. Compose an alternate ending to the story.

_____

_____

_____

_____

_____

_____

Exercise 1 · Build It: Adding Suffixes

▶ Review the spelling rules for adding suffixes in the Appendix of the *Student Text*.

▶ Read the words and suffixes in each table below.

▶ Combine parts to build words.

▶ Spell the words on the lines below the table.

▶ Code each word with the spelling rule you used to add the suffix:

(a) The Doubling Rule (b) Drop **e** (c) Change **y** (d) no rule

1.

drowsy	loud	proud	-est

_____   _____   _____

2.

adequate	moderate	separate	-ly

_____   _____   _____

3.

operate	illustrate	estimate	-ing

_____   _____   _____

4.

colony	memory	fertile	-ize

_____   _____   _____

5.

permit	emit	expire	-ed

_____   _____   _____

Exercise 2 · Answer It: Multiple Choice

▶ Work independently to identify the correct answer to each question below.

▶ Underline the correct answer.

▶ Discuss the correct answers with your teacher.

1. Why was Kenneth pulled from the game?

    A. He got into an argument.

    B. He was not playing well.

    C. He was injured.

    D. He did not want to play.

2. Which of the following statements best describes Ramdas?

    A. He is idealistic.

    B. He picks fights.

    C. He only cares about winning.

    D. He is timid.

3. Which of the following statements best summarizes the message of *satyagraha*?

    A. You should not stand up for yourself.

    B. You should try to bring about change with your soul, not your fist.

    C. You should not care if people hit you.

    D. You should avoid conflict.

(continued)

Exercise 2 *(continued)* · **Answer It: Multiple Choice**

4. How did Kenneth change over the course of the story?

   A. He became someone who is determined to do the right thing.

   B. He went from being good at football to being great at football.

   C. He started to dislike Ramdas.

   D. He started to imitate Bill Patchett.

5. **"Satyagraha: Power for Change"** is _____.

   A. fiction

   B. informational text

   C. both

   D. neither

Check off the activities you complete with each lesson. Evaluate your accomplishments at the end of each lesson. Pay attention to teacher evaluations and comments.

Unit Objectives	Lesson 1 (Date:_____)	Lesson 2 (Date:_____)
STEP 1 **Phonemic Awareness and Phonics** • Segment syllables from multisyllable words. • Identify syllable types: closed, r-controlled, open, final silent e, vowel digraph, final consonant + le, and diphthong. • Identify stress patterns.	❑ Exercise 1: Sort It: Syllable Types	❑ Exercise 1: Sort It: Syllable Types
STEP 2 **Word Recognition and Spelling** • Read and spell multisyllable words. • Read and spell the **Essential Words:** *half, limousine, listen, pour, tambourine, villain.* • Read and spell words with prefixes, suffixes, and roots.	❑ Exercise 2: Spelling Pretest 1 ❑ Memorize It	❑ Exercise 2: Build It ❑ Exercise 3: Write It: Essential Words ❑ Word Fluency 1
STEP 3 **Vocabulary and Morphology** • Identify antonyms and synonyms. • Identify and define adjective and verb suffixes. • Use the meanings of prefixes, suffixes, and roots to define words.	❑ Unit Vocabulary ❑ Multiple Meaning Map (T) ❑ Draw It: Idioms	❑ Exercise 4: Divide It: Prefix, Root, Base Word, Suffix ❑ Exercise 5: Define It: Word Parts ❑ Expression of the Day
STEP 4 **Grammar and Usage** • Identify adjectives and nouns. • Identify irregular verbs. • Identify predicate adjectives, predicate nominatives, and direct objects.	❑ Exercise 3: Identify It: Noun Categories ❑ Exercise 4: Punctuate It: Commas in a Series	❑ Exercise 6: Identify It: Adjective Suffixes
STEP 5 **Listening and Reading Comprehension** • Use context-based strategies to define words. • Identify topic, main ideas, and details. • Identify character traits as part of plot analysis. • Identify, understand, and answer questions that use different types of signal words.	❑ Independent Text: "Dream While You Sleep" ❑ Exercise 5: Phrase It ❑ Exercise 6: Use the Clues	❑ Passage Fluency 1 ❑ Exercise 7: Using Visuals: Charts
STEP 6 **Speaking and Writing** • Write responses to sentences using the signal words: **explain, justify, hypothesize.** • Organize reasons and supporting evidence from text in a graphic organizer. • Write a character trait summary paragraph.	❑ Exercise 7: Rewrite It	❑ Exercise 8: Answer It
Self-Evaluation (5 is the highest) **Effort** = I produced my best work. **Participation** = I was actively involved in tasks. **Independence** = I worked on my own.	**Effort:**　　1　2　3　4　5 **Participation:**　1　2　3　4　5 **Independence:**　1　2　3　4　5	**Effort:**　　1　2　3　4　5 **Participation:**　1　2　3　4　5 **Independence:**　1　2　3　4　5
Teacher Evaluation	**Effort:**　　1　2　3　4　5 **Participation:**　1　2　3　4　5 **Independence:**　1　2　3　4　5	**Effort:**　　1　2　3　4　5 **Participation:**　1　2　3　4　5 **Independence:**　1　2　3　4　5

Lesson 3 (Date:_____)	Lesson 4 (Date:_____)	Lesson 5 (Date:_____)
❑ Exercise 1: Sort It: Syllable Types	❑ Exercise 1: Identify It: Syllable Types	❑ Sort It: Syllable Types
❑ Divide It ❑ Word Fluency 2	❑ Exercise 2: Identify It: Spelling Rules ❑ Exercise 3: Build It: Using Prefixes and Suffixes	❑ Content Mastery: Spelling Posttest 1
❑ Vocabulary Focus ❑ Use the Clues ❑ Expression of the Day	❑ Exercise 4: Define It: Prefixes, Roots, Base Words, and Suffixes ❑ Exercise 5: Rewrite It: Prefix, Root, Base Word, and Suffix	❑ Exercise 1: Add It: Verb Suffixes
❑ Identify It: Noun, Verb, or Adjective	❑ Exercise 6: Find It: Irregular Verb Forms ❑ Exercise 7: Punctuate It: Commas in Dates and Addresses	❑ Masterpiece Sentences: Stage 2
❑ Instructional Text: "Dreaming the Night Away"	❑ Take Note: "Dreaming the Night Away"	❑ Map It: Main Ideas (T)
❑ Exercise 2: Answer It	❑ Map It: Main Ideas (T) ❑ Challenge Text: "Pursuit of a Dream"	❑ Exercise 2: Write It: Main Ideas Paragraph (T) ❑ Exercise 3: Write It: Conclusion Sentence ❑ Challenge Text: "Pursuit of a Dream" ❑ Exercise 4: Challenge Writing: A Compare and Contrast Essay
Effort: 1 2 3 4 5 **Participation:** 1 2 3 4 5 **Independence:** 1 2 3 4 5	**Effort:** 1 2 3 4 5 **Participation:** 1 2 3 4 5 **Independence:** 1 2 3 4 5	**Effort:** 1 2 3 4 5 **Participation:** 1 2 3 4 5 **Independence:** 1 2 3 4 5
Effort: 1 2 3 4 5 **Participation:** 1 2 3 4 5 **Independence:** 1 2 3 4 5	**Effort:** 1 2 3 4 5 **Participation:** 1 2 3 4 5 **Independence:** 1 2 3 4 5	**Effort:** 1 2 3 4 5 **Participation:** 1 2 3 4 5 **Independence:** 1 2 3 4 5

Check off the activities you complete with each lesson. Evaluate your accomplishments at the end of each lesson. Pay attention to teacher evaluations and comments.

	Unit Objectives	Lesson 6 (Date:_____)	Lesson 7 (Date:_____)
STEP 1	**Phonemic Awareness and Phonics** • Segment syllables from multisyllable words. • Identify syllable types: closed, r-controlled, open, final silent e, vowel digraph, final consonant + le, and diphthong. • Identify stress patterns.	❏ Sort It: Syllable Types	❏ Listening for Word Parts: Prefixes and Suffixes
STEP 2	**Word Recognition and Spelling** • Read and spell multisyllable words. • Read and spell the **Essential Words:** *half, limousine, listen, pour, tambourine, villain.* • Read and spell words with prefixes, suffixes, and roots.	❏ Exercise 1: Spelling Pretest 2 ❏ Word Fluency 3	❏ Exercise 1: Build It: Words With Roots and Affixes ❏ Word Fluency 4
STEP 3	**Vocabulary and Morphology** • Identify antonyms and synonyms. • Identify and define adjective and verb suffixes. • Use the meaning of prefixes, suffixes, and roots to define words.	❏ Exercise 2: Word Line—Degrees of Meaning ❏ Expression of the Day	❏ Vocabulary Focus ❏ Use the Clues ❏ Expression of the Day
STEP 4	**Grammar and Usage** • Identify adjectives and nouns. • Identify irregular verbs. • Identify predicate adjectives, predicate nominatives, and direct objects.	❏ Exercise 3: Identify It: Predicate Nominative or Predicate Adjective	❏ Identify It: Predicate Nominative, Predicate Adjective, or Direct Object
STEP 5	**Listening and Reading Comprehension** • Use context-based strategies to define words. • Identify topic, main ideas, and details. • Identify character traits as part of plot analysis. • Identify, understand, and answer questions that use different types of signal words.	❏ Instructional Text: "Dream Team"	❏ Instructional Text: "Dream Team"
STEP 6	**Speaking and Writing** • Write responses to sentences using the signal words: **explain**, **justify**, **hypothesize**. • Organize reasons and supporting evidence from text in a graphic organizer. • Write a character trait summary paragraph.	❏ Character Analysis ❏ Spotlight on Characters ❏ Reader Response	❏ Spotlight on Characters ❏ Challenge Text: "Martin Luther King, Jr.: The Freedom Dreamer"
	Self-Evaluation (5 is the highest) **Effort** = I produced my best work. **Participation** = I was actively involved in tasks. **Independence** = I worked on my own.	**Effort:** 1 2 3 4 5 **Participation:** 1 2 3 4 5 **Independence:** 1 2 3 4 5	**Effort:** 1 2 3 4 5 **Participation:** 1 2 3 4 5 **Independence:** 1 2 3 4 5
	Teacher Evaluation	**Effort:** 1 2 3 4 5 **Participation:** 1 2 3 4 5 **Independence:** 1 2 3 4 5	**Effort:** 1 2 3 4 5 **Participation:** 1 2 3 4 5 **Independence:** 1 2 3 4 5

Lesson 8 (Date:_____)	Lesson 9 (Date:_____)	Lesson 10 (Date:_____)
		❑ Summative Test: Phonemic Awareness and Phonics
❑ Progress Indicators: Test of Silent Word Reading Fluency (TOSWRF)	❑ Progress Indicators: Spelling Inventory	❑ Content Mastery: Spelling Posttest 2
❑ Exercise 1: Fill In: Words With Roots and Affixes ❑ Draw It: Idioms		❑ Summative Test: Vocabulary and Morphology
❑ Exercise 2: Diagram It: Predicate Nominative, Predicate Adjective, and Direct Object (T)	❑ Exercise 1: Rewrite It: Predicate Nominative, Predicate Adjective, and Direct Object	❑ Summative Test: Grammar and Usage
❑ Instructional Text: "Dream Team" ❑ Exercise 3: Answer It: Multiple Choice	(There are no instructional activities in this step in order to allow time for the Summative Test: Composition in Step 6.)	❑ Progress Indicator: Degrees of Reading Power (DRP)
❑ Spotlight on Characters: Character Analysis (T) ❑ Exercise 4: Write It: Character Summary ❑ Challenge Text: "Martin Luther King, Jr.: The Freedom Dreamer"	❑ Summative Test: Composition	(There are no instructional activities in this step in order to allow time for the Degrees of Reading Power (DRP) test in Step 5.)
Effort: 1 2 3 4 5 Participation: 1 2 3 4 5 Independence: 1 2 3 4 5	Effort: 1 2 3 4 5 Participation: 1 2 3 4 5 Independence: 1 2 3 4 5	Effort: 1 2 3 4 5 Participation: 1 2 3 4 5 Independence: 1 2 3 4 5
Effort: 1 2 3 4 5 Participation: 1 2 3 4 5 Independence: 1 2 3 4 5	Effort: 1 2 3 4 5 Participation: 1 2 3 4 5 Independence: 1 2 3 4 5	Effort: 1 2 3 4 5 Participation: 1 2 3 4 5 Independence: 1 2 3 4 5

Exercise 1 · Sort It: Syllable Types

▸ Read each word in the **Word Bank**.

Word Bank

drift	dart	forth	time	when
stage	turn	wake	back	stretch
prime	her	skirt	rule	thorn

▸ Look at the sound-spelling pattern for each vowel sound.

▸ Sort the words according to syllable type.

▸ Label each column with its syllable type.

Exercise 2 · Spelling Pretest 1

▶ Write the word your teacher repeats.

1. _____

2. _____

3. _____

4. _____

5. _____

6. _____

7. _____

8. _____

9. _____

10. _____

11. _____

12. _____

13. _____

14. _____

15. _____

Exercise 3 · Identify It: Noun Categories

▶ Reread the paragraph below.

▶ Look at each of the underlined nouns.

▶ Decide if the noun names a person, a place, a thing, or an idea.

▶ Copy each word into the correct column.

---

from "Dreaming the Night Away"

This is the <u>dance</u> of REM. Somewhere deep inside your <u>mind</u> you are creating a little drama for an audience of one. Your <u>story</u>, though, can hardly be called one of the year's ten best. It's almost impossible to follow. The <u>events</u> are confusing and disconnected. The <u>characters</u> come and go for no apparent <u>reason</u>. The dialogue doesn't make any sense. It's a <u>mess</u>, all right, but you don't seem to notice it. On and on you dream, accepting even the most ridiculous <u>situations</u> without question, thoroughly convinced that it's all really happening. Furthermore, you are not just a sleepy member of the audience, you're a <u>participant</u>, and you react to everything that goes on. A frightening dream in particular catches you like a <u>hook</u>, and you actually experience fear.

Person	Place	Thing	Idea

Exercise 4 · Punctuate It: Commas in a Series

▶ Read each sentence.

▶ Identify the words or word groups in the series.

▶ Place a comma between each item in the series.

1. There is a calm angelic and peaceful look on your face when you sleep.

2. Suddenly your eyes are rolling back and forth back and forth and back and forth.

3. Your breath is coming in quick shallow and rapid bursts.

4. Your blood pressure has shot up your heart is pumping and beads of perspiration break out.

5. When we sleep we toss turn and roll around quite a bit.

6. Sleepwalkers will open their eyes swing their legs over the side of the bed and head off on some errand.

7. Sleepwalkers can steer around furniture walk the dog and even drive a car.

8. It is a myth that a sleepwalker will get lockjaw die of a heart attack or become paralyzed if woken.

9. Sleepwalking is as strange mysterious and otherworldly as dreaming.

10. Scientists are studying observing and documenting incidences of sleepwalking.

Exercise 5 · Phrase It

▶ Use the penciling strategy to "scoop" the phrases in each sentence.

▶ Read the sentences as you would speak them.

---

from "Dream While You Sleep"

Benjamin Franklin warned it could be a waste of time. Shakespeare disagreed. He called sleep the bath that heals the pains of work. He said that sleep soothes troubled minds. He called it the most nourishing food in life's feast.

Exercise 6 · Use the Clues

▶ Read the excerpt from **"Dream While You Sleep"** below.

▶ Reread the underlined phrase **waste of time**.

▶ Reread the text before and after the underlined phrase.

▶ Circle the word or words that help to define the phrase **waste of time**.

▶ Write a definition for the phrase **waste of time**, using context clues.

▶ Write a sentence that demonstrates understanding of the context by writing a sentence using the phrase **waste of time**, and then rewriting the sentence using your definition in place of **waste of time**.

---

from "Dream While You Sleep"

It looks like Shakespeare was on the right track. Sleep is definitely not a waste of time. It's essential. We can't live without it. But it's not so much the body that needs it. It's the brain!

Define It:

waste of time—_____

Sentence:

_____

_____

_____

_____

Exercise 7 · Rewrite It

▶ Read the following groups of sentences.

▶ Rewrite each group by combining sentences and adding a conjunction to contrast the ideas.

▶ Check that each sentence uses sentence signals—capital letters, commas, and end punctuation.

1. Some people remember their dreams. Other people say they never remember their dreams.

   _____

   _____

2. The body doesn't really need to sleep. The brain does.

   _____

   _____

3. Our dreams often don't make sense. We don't mind.

   _____

   _____

4. During REM, our logic center does not operate. Our limbic system does.

   _____

   _____

5. During REM, our eyelids are closed. Our eyes are very active, darting back and forth beneath our eyelids.

   _____

   _____

   _____

Exercise 1 · Sort It: Syllable Types

▶ Read each syllable in the **Word Bank**.

Word Bank

male	ble	bi	dle	mise
zle	grid	et	driz	crum
pro	can	com	fe	po

▶ Look at the sound-spelling pattern for each vowel sound.

▶ Sort the syllables according to syllable type.

▶ Label each column with its syllable type.

Exercise 2 · Build It

▸ Combine syllables from Exercise 1, **Sort It: Syllable Types**, to build new words.

▸ Record the words on the lines below.
   Hint: Write syllables on small paper squares to make building easier.

_____   _____   _____

_____   _____   _____

_____   _____   _____

_____   _____   _____

Exercise 3 · Write It: Essential Words

▶ Review the **Essential Words** in the **Word Bank**.

Word Bank

listen	villain	pour	half	limousine	tambourine

▶ Put the words in alphabetical order and write them on the lines.

▶ Write one sentence for each **Essential Word**.

▶ Check that each sentence uses sentence signals—correct capitalization, commas, and end punctuation.

1. _____

2. _____

3. _____

4. _____

5. _____

6. _____

Exercise 4 · Divide It: Prefix, Root, Base Word, Suffix

▸ Read each word.

▸ Break the word into its parts: prefix, root or base word, and suffix.

▸ Write each word part in the correct column.

▸ Define each word part using your **Morphemes for Meaning Cards**.

Word	Prefix	Root or Base Word	Suffix
inspector			
reformer			
exporter			
cleverness			
conformist			

Exercise 5 · Define It: Word Parts

▸ Note that the five words from the previous exercise, **Divide It: Prefix, Root, Base Word, Suffix**, are listed below.

▸ Write a definition for each word using the meaning of each of its word parts in Exercise 4. **Hint**: Remember, Latin roots give a clue to the meaning. They cannot always be translated directly. Your **Morphemes for Meaning Cards** can help you write the definitions.

Word	Definition
inspector	
reformer	
exporter	
cleverness	
conformist	

Exercise 6 · Identify It: Adjective Suffixes

▶ Reread the paragraph.

▶ Look at the underlined words.

▶ Copy the underlined adjectives with the suffixes **-able**, **-ed**, **-ful**, **-ing**, **-less**, **-ous**, and **-y** onto the lines below.

▶ Underline the base word and circle the suffix in each.

After a <u>demanding</u> day of <u>endless</u> tests and a <u>vigorous</u> game of football, the teenager fell into a <u>deep</u> sleep. But to the <u>careful</u> observer it was not a <u>restful</u> sleep. The boy's <u>twitchy</u> legs and <u>jerky</u> arms were in <u>constant</u> motion. After a <u>reasonable</u> number of hours, however, the boy did fall into a <u>peaceful</u> and <u>undisturbed</u> sleep.

---

1. _____   6. _____

2. _____   7. _____

3. _____   8. _____

4. _____   9. _____

5. _____   10. _____

Exercise 7 · Using Visuals: Charts

▸ Highlight all of the headings on the chart.

▸ Put a √ mark next to the source of the information.

▸ Circle the asterisks.

▸ Read and discuss the note indicated by an asterisk with your teacher.

▸ Use information from **"Dream While You Sleep"** and the **"Cycles of Sleep"** graph to complete the chart.

▸ Write a title above the chart.

Title: _____

	Frequency per Night *	Characteristics of Stage
First Stage	2	We're in and out of sleep.
Second Stage	9	
Third Stage	6	We've begun to sleep deeply.
Fourth Stage	2	
REM Stage		

http://faculty.washington.edu/chudler/sleep.html

*This column indicates the number of times we pass through each stage of sleep in a typical night.

Exercise 8 · Answer It

▸ Use information from the text and the chart in **"Dream While You Sleep"** to answer each of these questions. Write complete sentences.

▸ Circle whether the answer can be found in the text, the chart, or both.

1. What does REM stand for?   text   chart   both

_____

2. During which stage of sleep do we usually dream?   text   chart   both

_____

3. During which stage of sleep do we spend the most time?   text   chart   both

_____

4. Which stage are we in directly before REM occurs?   text   chart   both

_____

5. What happens during REM?   text   chart   both

_____

_____

_____

_____

Exercise 1 · Sort It: Syllable Types

▶ Read each word in the **Word Bank**.

Word Bank

sweat	hours	join	ploy	sleep
play	shout	health	plains	coil
fowl	shown	tread	dream	tails

▶ Look at the sound-spelling pattern for each vowel sound.

▶ Sort the words according to syllable type.

▶ Label each column.

Unit 24 · Lesson 3

Exercise 2 · Answer It

▶ Underline the signal word in each question.

▶ Write the answer in complete sentences.

1. The author compares dreams to stories. Explain why dreams are like unusual stories.

_____

_____

_____

_____

2. Summarize what happens to our bodies when we dream.

_____

_____

_____

3. Justify the author's concern about sleepwalking.

_____

_____

_____

4. Assess why lucid dreaming is not necessarily a good thing.

_____

_____

_____

5. Hypothesize why our muscles are immovable when we dream.

_____

_____

_____

_____

Exercise 1 · Identify It: Syllable Types

▶ Read each word in the first column.

▶ Identify the syllables in it.

▶ Spell each syllable found in the word and write it in the correct column.

	Closed Syllable	r-Controlled Syllable	Open Syllable	Final Silent e Syllable	Vowel Digraph Syllable	Final Consonant + le Syllable	Diphthong Syllable
Example 1 copper							
Example 2 details							
1. flowers							
2. preamble							
3. tidy							
4. slowly							
5. painful							
6. deafness							
7. winterize							
8. beagle							
9. foreground							
10. overpower							

Unit 24 · Lesson 4

Exercise 2 · Identify It: Spelling Rules

▸ Read the word in the first column.

▸ Write its base word and suffix in the next two columns.

▸ Check each box that identifies the spelling rule used to add the word ending.

	Back to the Base	Suffix	Double It	Drop It	Change It	No Rule
Example 1 cried						
Example 2 beginning						
1. famous						
2. advisable						
3. friskiness						
4. joined						
5. theorize						
6. scandalous						
7. stirring						
8. agonize						
9. inquiring						
10. shimmering						

Exercise 3 · Build It: Using Prefixes and Suffixes

▸ Read the word parts in each table.

▸ Combine word parts to build new words.

▸ Check the dictionary to verify that you are building real words.

1.

dis-	-able	pose	flam

_____   _____   _____

2.

over-	load	-ful	play

_____   _____   _____

3.

mis-	-less	count	job

_____   _____   _____

4.

see	fore-	print	-able

_____   _____   _____

5.

colony	bar	-ize	de-

_____   _____   _____

Unit 24 · Lesson 4

Exercise 4 · Define It: Prefixes, Roots, Base Words, and Suffixes

▸ Read each affixed word.

▸ Circle the prefix, underline the base word or root, and circle the suffix.

▸ Write a short definition of the word, using your **Morphemes for Meaning Cards** as a resource.

▸ Use a dictionary to check your work.

1. conformed—_____

2. unhealthy—_____

3. inscribed—_____

4. discountable—_____

5. exporting—_____

Exercise 5 · Rewrite It: Prefix, Root, Base Word, and Suffix

▶ Read each sentence.

▶ Find the underlined phrase and decide what single word could replace it.

▶ Use your **Morphemes for Meaning Cards** as a resource for meanings of word parts.

▶ Write the replacement word in the blank.

▶ Reread the sentence to check your work.

1. The skater's movements were <u>without effort</u>.	The skater's movements were _____.
2. The photo was not able to be <u>produced again</u>.	The photo was not able to be _____.
3. The news item was <u>able to be carried back</u>.	The news item was _____.
4. The landing gear on a plane is <u>able to be pulled back</u>.	The landing gear on a plane is _____.
5. The book had a page that had been <u>written on</u>.	The book had a page that had been _____.

Exercise 6 · Find It: Irregular Verb Forms

▸ Read each sentence and underline the irregular past tense verb.

▸ Write the past, present, and future forms of that verb in the chart below the timeline.

1. The young man dreamt he inherited a lot of money.

2. He bought a brand new racing car.

3. While driving down the highway, he wove in and out of the traffic.

4. He left the car with a flat tire on the road.

5. During the night, someone stole the car.

6. The young man threw on his clothes so he could go to find the thief.

7. He met a police officer as he was looking for the thief.

8. He wept while telling his sad tale.

9. The police officer taught the thief a lesson by arresting him.

10. But wait! This was just a dream!

Past	Present	Future
Yesterday	Today	Tomorrow

Exercise 7 · Punctuate It: Commas in Dates and Addresses

▸ Read each sentence.

▸ Identify the address or date in each sentence.

▸ Place commas as needed.

1. Next year, we are moving to 9 Sweet Lane Candyville Colorado 44444.

2. July 5 2010 is our projected moving date.

3. Our school address is Brown High School 10 Book Street Upton Georgia 22222.

4. The nearest library is at 25 Book Avenue Readville Texas 11111.

5. My mother was born on February 28 1978.

6. A new ball field is being built at 300 Bat Road Diamond Park Florida 66666.

7. We are going to plant trees at 900 Garden Row Flowerville Michigan 33333.

8. My younger brother was born on January 1 2005.

▸ Write a sentence that includes the date of birth of someone you know on the line below.

_____

▸ Write a sentence that includes the address of someone you know on the line below.

_____

Exercise 1 · Add It: Verb Suffixes

Each of the sentences has an underlined base word or root that requires a suffix.
Do the following:

▶ Read each sentence.

▶ Add the correct suffix. Use your **Morphemes for Meaning Cards** as a resource for suffixes and their meanings.

▶ Reread the sentence to check that it makes sense.

1. Teachers love to <u>educ</u> _____ children.

2. I was <u>dream</u> _____ as I sat at my desk.

3. The photographer will <u>dark</u> _____ the room.

4. The actors <u>fantas</u> _____ about being on Broadway.

5. When the snow came, they <u>plow</u> _____ the street.

6. At holiday times, people <u>don</u> _____ gifts.

7. Last year I <u>subscrib</u> _____ to the magazine.

8. The company was <u>export</u> _____ computers.

9. The weather man <u>predict</u> _____ the wind storm.

10. The mathematician will <u>calcul</u> _____ the possible cost.

Exercise 2 · Write It: Main Ideas Paragraph

▶ Use your **Map It: Main Ideas** template to write a summary.

▶ Write reasons to support this topic statement: A dream is like a story. However, dreams are very strange stories.

▶ Include at least three reasons from the text to support your position.

_____

_____

_____

_____

_____

Exercise 3 · Write It: Conclusion Sentence

▶ Follow these steps to write a conclusion sentence.

1. Read the topic sentence.

   However, dreams are very strange stories.

2. Put a box around two or more words that can be paraphrased.

3. Use a thesaurus to select words for replacement.

_____

_____

_____

4. Write the conclusion sentence.

_____

▶ Transfer your conclusion sentence to the end of your main idea paragraph in Exercise 2.

Unit 24 · Lesson 5

Exercise 4 · Challenge Writing: A Compare and Contrast Essay

Task: Think of two characters you have read about in one or two works of fiction. Write a compare and contrast essay in which you explain how the two characters are alike and how they are different. The conclusion of your essay should make clear whether you think the two characters are more alike, or more different. You should justify your conclusion with one or more clear reasons.

Note: In your essay, be sure to clearly identify the characters you are comparing, as well as give the name of the story or stories they are from.

Language to Compare and Contrast

Look at the words shown in boldface below. Using signal words such as those to compare and contrast will make your ideas clear for readers. Fill in the blanks with the names of the two characters you are comparing and the ways in which they are similar or different.

Ways in Which the Two Characters Are Alike

- _____ and _____ are very **similar** characters.

- The first **similarity** between _____ and _____ is that they **both**

  _____.

- The second thing that _____ and _____ **have in common** is that

  they _____.

- They **both** _____.

(continued)

Exercise 4 (continued) · Challenge Writing: A Compare and Contrast Essay

Ways in Which the Two Characters Are Different

- _____ and _____ are very **different** in some ways.

- The first **difference** between _____ and _____ is that

  _____.

- Another way that _____ and _____ are different is that

  _____, **but** _____.

- _____; **however,** _____.

- _____.

  In contrast, _____

  _____.

Planning a Compare and Contrast Essay

Look at the character descriptions and traits you listed in your Venn diagram. Use this planner to take notes about the similarities and differences between the two characters. This planner will help you organize your ideas when you are ready to write your first draft.

Main Idea: Introduce the two characters and tell whether they are quite similar, quite different, or have some similarities and some differences.

_____

_____

_____

(continued)

Exercise 4 *(continued)* · Challenge Writing: A Compare and Contrast Essay

List two ways that the characters are similar:

1. _____

_____

2. _____

_____

List two ways that the characters are different:

1. _____

_____

2. _____

_____

Conclusion: Restate the main idea. Then take a stand! Are the characters mostly similar or mostly different? Why?

_____

_____

_____

Exercise 1 • Spelling Pretest 2

▶ Write the word your teacher repeats.

1. _____

2. _____

3. _____

4. _____

5. _____

6. _____

7. _____

8. _____

9. _____

10. _____

11. _____

12. _____

13. _____

14. _____

15. _____

Unit 24 · Lesson 6

Exercise 2 · Word Line—Degrees of Meaning

▶ Read the words on the word line.

▶ Discuss the meaning of the words **unsatisfactory**, **satisfactory**, and **fabulous** with your teacher.

▶ Read the words in the **Word Bank**.

Word Bank

adequate	inadequate	wonderful	astounding	okay
awesome	passable	poor	dismal	marvelous

▶ Use a dictionary to determine the meanings of unfamiliar words.

▶ Sort and record each word under the word line according to its degree of meaning.

unsatisfactory   **satisfactory**   **fabulous**

_____   _____   _____

_____   _____   _____

_____   _____   _____

_____   _____   _____

_____   _____   _____

(continued)

Exercise 2 (continued) · Word Line—Degrees of Meaning

▶ Read the sentences below.

▶ Fill in the blank with the word from below the word line that makes the best sense. Words may be used more than once. There may be more than one correct answer.

1. My paper was barely _____. I'm glad that I did not do a

_____ job.

2. Her performance was _____. She did not feel _____ after the play.

3. I did _____ on the test, but my partner's performance was

_____!

4. My test results were so _____ that I earned a scholarship. I feel

_____!

5. Your work is _____, but you have a _____ attitude in class.

▶ Locate the words **unsatisfactory**, **satisfactory**, and **fabulous** in a thesaurus.

▶ Select another example for each word and add them to the columns on the previous page.

Exercise 3 · Identify It: Predicate Nominative or Predicate Adjective

▸ Do the first example with your teacher.

▸ Read each remaining sentence.

▸ Underline the main verb, which is a form of **be**.

▸ Find and label the predicate nominative (PN) or the predicate adjective (PA).

▸ Draw an arrow from the predicate nominative or predicate adjective to the subject.

1. Martin Luther King, Jr. was a powerful preacher.

2. Dr. King's speech, "I Have a Dream," is famous.

3. Dr. King was a follower of Mohandas Gandhi.

4. Nonviolent protest was a way to attack segregation.

5. Martin Luther King's movement was successful.

6. The crowd was enormous on the day of the speech.

7. Dr. King's hopeful words were uplifting.

8. Martin Luther King, Jr. is an inspiration for us all.

Exercise 1 · Build It: Words With Roots and Affixes

▸ Work with a partner to combine prefixes, roots, and suffixes to make as many words as you can in five minutes.
Example: re- + tract + -able = retractable

▸ Record each word in the chart below according to its root.

▸ After time is up, use a dictionary to check that you have built real words.

in-	ject	-able
re-	tract	-or
ex-	spect	-ate

ject	tract	spect

Exercise 1 · Fill In: Words With Roots and Affixes

▶ Read the words in the **Word Bank**.

Word Bank

inspect	inspector	respect	spectate	spectator
retract	extract	tractable	tractor	retractable
extractable	retractor	extractor	inject	injector
injectable	reject	rejected	rejectable	respectable

▶ Read each sentence below. Fill in the blank with a word from the **Word Bank** that makes sense.

1. The plane's _____ landing gear was repaired.

2. The fuel _____ pumps gas into the engine.

3. The coach will _____ the lockers after the game.

4. It is important to _____ your elders.

5. My uncle drove his _____ through the field.

6. The dentist will _____ my wisdom teeth in his office.

7. Their proposal was _____ because it was incomplete.

8. Cats can _____ their claws.

9. Clean this kitchen before the health _____ arrives.

10. Every _____ will need to purchase a ticket before entering the arena.

Exercise 2 · Diagram It: Predicate Nominative, Predicate Adjective, and Direct Object

▶ Read each sentence.

▶ Underline the verb in each sentence and code it **action verb** (V), **linking verb** (LV), or **helping verb** (HV).

▶ Identify what comes after the verb and label it **direct object** (DO), **predicate nominative** (PN), or **predicate adjective** (PA).

▶ Diagram each sentence.

    1. Millions of people heard Dr. King's speech.

    2. The speech is famous around the world.

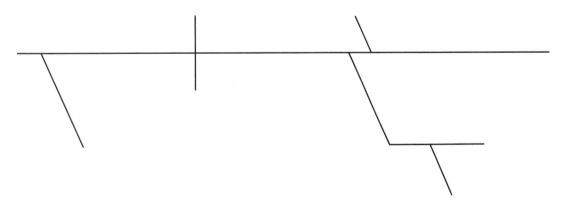

(continued)

Exercise 2 (continued) · **Diagram It: Predicate Nominative, Predicate Adjective, and Direct Object**

3. Martin Luther King, Jr. was an inspiration to everyone.

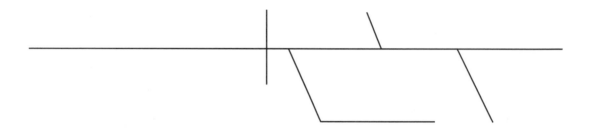

4. Dr. King practiced nonviolent protest.

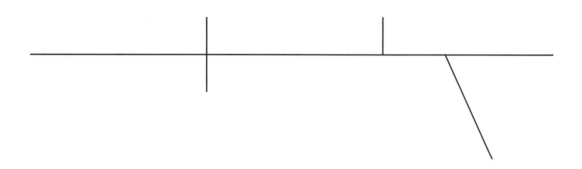

5. His leadership was inspirational.

Exercise 3 · Answer It: Multiple Choice

▶ Follow along as you discuss each question with your teacher.

▶ Underline the correct answer.

1. According to the coach, which of the following is one of the qualities that a "benny" possesses?

      A. a commitment to helping teammates

      B. a determination to be the best player of all

      C. the ability to be good without practicing

      D. the ability to make almost every shot

2. According to the coach, what was most important to students at Cubberly High School?

      A. playing basketball

      B. being successful

      C. learning a lot in school

      D. spending time with friends

3. The narrator of the story is _____.

      A. a basketball coach

      B. a high school student

      C. Huey

      D. Dave

(continued)

4. Huey can be described as _____.

    A. good-natured

    B. optimistic

    C. generous

    D. all of the above

5. Why did the basketball team forfeit their game?

    A. because Dave had died

    B. because they knew they would win anyway

    C. to protest the rule barring transfer students from playing

    D. to protest the decision to cancel the league championship

Exercise 4 · Write It: Character Summary

▸ Review the **Character Trait** chart you completed for **"Dream Team."**

▸ Use the chart and the text for **"Dream Team"** to write a summary about the character you selected.

_____

_____

_____

_____

_____

_____

_____

_____

_____

_____

_____

_____

_____

_____

Exercise 1 · Rewrite It: Predicate Nominative, Predicate Adjective, and Direct Object

▶ Read each diagram.

▶ Write the complete sentence for the diagram on line A.

▶ Expand either the subject or predicate part of the sentence.

▶ Write your expanded sentence on line B.

1.

| boycott | changed | law |

Dr. King's
the

A. _____

B. _____

_____

2.

| children | were | young |

Dr. King's
in
1963

A. _____

B. _____

_____

(continued)

3.

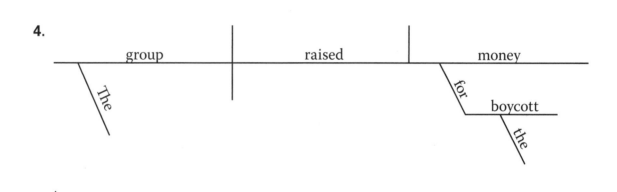

```
    Dr. King    |    was    \    follower
                               a \  of
                                     Gandhi
```

A. _____

B. _____

_____

4.

```
    group    |    raised    |    money
  The \                          for \
                                      boycott
                                        the \
```

A. _____

B. _____

_____

5.

```
    protest    |    was    \    successful
  The \  nonviolent \
```

A. _____

B. _____

_____

Text Connections

Text Connection 1

Fiber Optics: High-Speed Highways for Light

Faster than a bolt of lightning, able to carry billions of light pulses a second, yet thinner than a human hair, it's . . . optical fiber!

1   What happens when you download research from the Internet? What carries your messages when you chat online with a friend? You may be using fiber optics .[1] Fiber optic cables hide under streets. They are under many of our cities

5 and towns. These cables [2] carry all kinds of information.
    Fiber optic technology is being used more and more. It has been around since the 1930s, but, today, as much as 2,000 miles of fiber optic cable are being laid every hour. Why is the use of fiber optics increasing?

10   One reason to use fiber optics is the material. It's better. Electric signals [3] use wires. The wires carry electric pulses .[4] What is the problem? The electricity moves through the wires quickly. However, the metal in the wire can slow down the signal along the way. Fiber optics is different. It uses long

15 tubes. The tubes are thin. Instead of wires, these tubes are made from glass. The tubes don't carry electricity. They carry pulses of light. They send out light signals.

Identify It: Words in Text

Read the sentences that include highlighted words. Decide if each highlighted word is functioning as a noun or a verb.

Write **N** (noun) or **V** (verb) above the word.

---

[1] **optics:** science of light; vision; lenses

[2] **cables:** covered bundles of wire

[3] **signals:** sounds, images, or messages that are sent or received

[4] **pulses:** bursts of movement; vibrations

Take Note

Identify the topic, position statement, reasons, and details.

Topic:

_____

_____

Position Statement:

_____

_____

_____

_____

▲ ● ▲ ● ▲

Reason 1:

_____

_____

_____

Supporting Details:

_____

_____

_____

_____

_____

_____

_____

_____

_____

(continued)

Unit 19

Reason 2:

_____

_____

_____

Supporting Details:

_____

_____

_____

_____

_____

_____

_____

_____

▲ ● ▲ ● ▲

Reason 3:

_____

_____

_____

Supporting Details:

_____

_____

_____

_____

_____

_____

_____

_____

A second reason for using fiber optics is speed. Glass speeds up the light signals. The signals travel at almost the
20 speed of light. Light speeds millions of times faster than racing cars! The glass tubes can even be bent. Light moves at such quickness that some bending doesn't bother the signal.

A final reason for using fiber optics is space. The system uses less space. Glass fibers are thin. They are <u>thinner</u> than
25 wires. More fibers can fit into a cable. This means more signals can be sent.

Use the Clues A:

- Read lines 23–26.

- Reread the underlined word, **thinner**. The suffix **-er** signals a comparison between two things. Highlight the two things being compared here.

- Combine sentences to show the comparison.

_____

_____

The use of fiber optics has improved communications .[5] Light signals send huge amounts of information. Cable TV is <u>faster</u> because of fiber optics. Thanks to fiber optics, we have
30 high-speed Internet. Phone lines could never carry this much information this fast.

Use the Clues B:

- Read lines 27–31.

- Reread the underlined word, **faster**. The suffix **-er** signals a comparison between two things. Use inference to list the two things being compared.

_____

_____

[5] **communications:** ways of exchanging information

(continued)

Fiber optics has changed the way some people do their work. Doctors can now see into a person's body without doing major surgery. How? Doctors place special scopes

35 inside a person's body. Fiber optics is used to send a picture for the doctor to see. Astronomers use fiber optics to learn more about space. Special optic fibers receive and interpret [6] signals. The signals come from telescopes. They let scientists measure changes in light and temperature for

40 stars and planets. Fiber optics is also used by engineers. The technology is used for lighting homes and offices. It is even used to direct solar lighting into buildings.

The fiber optic age has just begun. As it develops, how will it affect your life?*

Adapted from "High-Speed Highways for Light" by Nancy Day

---

[6] **interpret:** translate; figure out

Take Note

Meet the Main Character:

Identify the main character and write about the main character on the lines below.

_____

_____

_____

_____

_____

Underline words or phrases as your teacher reads the story. Listen for information that describes Squeaky.

Setting:

Draw a box around words or phrases that describe the setting.

Time: _____

_____

_____

Place: _____

_____

_____

Raymond's Run

by Toni Cade Bambara

1   I don't have much work to do around the house like some girls. My mother does that. And I don't have to earn my pocket money by hustling; George runs errands for the big boys and sells Christmas cards. And anything else that's got
5 to get done, my father does. All I have to do in life is mind [1] my brother Raymond, which is enough.

    Sometimes I slip and say my little brother Raymond. But as any fool can see he's much bigger and he's older too. But a lot of people call him my little brother cause he needs
10 looking after cause he's not quite right. And a lot of smart mouths got lots to say about that too, especially when George was minding him. But now, if anybody has anything to say to Raymond, anything to say about his big head, they have to come by me. And I don't play the dozens or believe in
15 standing around with somebody in my face doing a lot of talking. I much rather just knock you down and take my chances even if I am a little girl with skinny arms and a squeaky voice, which is how I got the name Squeaky. And if things get too rough, I run. And as anybody can tell you, I
20 am the fastest thing on two feet.

Identify It: Words in Text

Read the sentences that include highlighted words. Decide if each highlighted word is functioning as a noun, verb, or adjective.

Write **N** (noun), **V** (verb), or **A** (adjective) above the word.

    There is no track meet that I don't win the first place medal. I used to win the twenty-yard dash when I was a little kid in kindergarten. Nowadays, it's the fifty-yard dash. And tomorrow I'm subject [2] to run the quarter-mile relay

---

[1] **mind:** take care of; look after

[2] **subject:** expected to

(continued)

Text Connection 2 (continued)

25 all by myself and come in first, second, and third. The big
kids call me Mercury cause I'm the swiftest thing in the
neighborhood. Everybody knows that—except two people
who know better, my father and me.

He can beat me to Amsterdam Avenue with me having a
30 two fire-hydrant head-start and him running with his hands
in his pockets and whistling. But that's private information.
Cause can you imagine some thirty-five-year-old man
stuffing himself into PAL shorts to race little kids? So as
far as everyone's concerned, I'm the fastest and that goes
35 for Gretchen, too, who has put out the tale that she is going
to win the first-place medal this year. Ridiculous. In the
second place, she's got short legs. In the third place, she's got
freckles. In the first place, no one can beat me and that's all
there is to it.

40 I'm standing on the corner admiring the weather and
about to take a stroll down Broadway so I can practice my
breathing exercises, and I've got Raymond walking on the
inside close to the buildings, cause he's subject [3] to fits of
fantasy and starts thinking he's a circus performer and that
45 the curb is a tightrope strung high in the air. And sometimes
after a rain he likes to step down off his tightrope right into
the gutter and slosh around getting his shoes and cuffs wet.
Then I get hit when I get home.

Use the Clues A:

- Read line 40–47.

- Use context clues to define the underlined phrase, **fits of fantasy**.

- Highlight examples that support your definition.

  Fits of fantasy _____

  _____

Or sometimes if you don't watch him, he'll dash across
traffic to the island in the middle of Broadway and give the

---

[3] **subject:** prone; having a tendency toward

(continued)

More About the Main Character:

Underline words or phrases as your teacher reads the story. Listen for information that describes Squeaky.

Setting:

Draw a box around words or phrases that describe the setting.

Time: _____

_____

_____

Place: _____

_____

_____

What other clues did you find about the location?

_____

_____

Where do you think Squeaky is?

_____

_____

Text Connection 2 (continued)

More About the Main Character:

Underline words or phrases as your teacher reads the story. Listen for information that describes Squeaky.

Setting:

Draw a box around words or phrases that describe the setting.

Time: _____

_____

_____

Place: _____

_____

_____

50 pigeons a fit. Then I have to go behind him apologizing to all the old people sitting around trying to get some sun and getting all upset with the pigeons fluttering around them, scattering their newspapers and upsetting the waxpaper lunches in their laps. So I keep Raymond on the inside of

55 me, and he plays like he's driving a stage coach which is o.k. by me so long as he doesn't run me over or interrupt my breathing exercises, which I have to do on account of I'm serious about my running and don't care who knows it.

Now some people like to act like things come easy to

60 them, won't let on that they practice. Not me. I'll high-prance down 34th Street like a rodeo pony to keep my knees strong even if it does get my mother uptight so that she walks ahead like she's not with me, don't know me, is all by herself on a shopping trip, and I am somebody else's crazy child.

65 Now you take Cynthia Procter for instance. She's just the opposite. If there's a test tomorrow, she'll say something like, "Oh, I guess I'll play handball this afternoon and watch television tonight," just to let you know she ain't thinking about the test. Or like last week when she won the spelling

70 bee for the millionth time, "A good thing you got 'receive,' Squeaky, cause I would have got it wrong. I completely forgot about the spelling bee." And she'll clutch the lace on her blouse like it was a narrow escape. Oh, brother.

But of course when I pass her house on my early morning

75 trots around the block, she is practicing the scales on the piano over and over and over and over. Then in music class

(continued)

she always lets herself get bumped around so she falls
<u>accidentally on purpose</u> onto the piano stool and is so
surprised to find herself sitting, and so decides just for

80 fun to try out the ole keys and what do you know—Chopin's
waltzes just spring out of her fingertips and she's the most
surprised thing in the world. A regular prodigy [4]. I could kill
people like that.

Use the Clues B:

- Read lines 74–83.

- Use context clues to define the underlined phrase,
  accidentally on purpose.

- Highlight examples that support your definition.

Accidentally on purpose _____

_____

I stay up all night studying the words for the spelling
85 bee. And you can see me anytime of day practicing running.
I never walk if I can trot and shame on Raymond if he
can't keep up. But of course he does, cause if he hangs back
someone's liable to walk up to him and get smart, or take his
allowance from him, or ask him where he got that great big
90 pumpkin head. People are so stupid sometimes.

▲ ● ▲ ● ⋏

**End of reading for lesson 7. Paraphrase and predict what
might happen next.**

_____

_____

_____

_____

_____

_____

[4] **prodigy:** genius; someone of great ability

(continued)

More About the Main Character:

Underline words or phrases as your teacher reads the story. Listen for information that describes Squeaky.

Setting:

Draw a box around words or phrases that describe the setting.

Time: _____

_____

_____

Place: _____

_____

_____

▲ ● ▲ ● ▲

So I'm strolling down Broadway breathing out and breathing in on counts of seven, which is my lucky number, and here comes Gretchen and her sidekicks—Mary Louise who used to be a friend of mine when she first moved to
95 Harlem from Baltimore and got beat up by everybody till I took up for her on account of her mother and my mother used to sing in the same choir when they were young girls, but people ain't grateful, so now she hangs out with the new girl Gretchen and talks about me like a dog, and Rosie, who
100 is as fat as I am skinny and has a big mouth where Raymond is concerned and is too stupid to know that there is not a big deal of difference between herself and Raymond and that she can't afford to throw stones. So they are steady coming up Broadway and I see right away that it's going to be one of
105 those Dodge City scenes cause the street ain't that big and they're close to the buildings just as we are. First I think I'll step into the candy store and look over the new comics and let them pass. But that's chicken and I've got a reputation to consider. So then I think I'll just walk straight on through
110 them or even over them if necessary. But as they get to me, they slow down. I'm ready to fight, cause like I said I don't feature a whole lot of chit-chat, I much prefer to just knock you down right from the jump and save everybody a lotta precious time.
115 "You signing up for the May Day races?" smiles Mary Louise, only it's not a smile at all.

A dumb question like that doesn't deserve an answer. Besides, there's just me and Gretchen standing there really, so no use wasting my breath talking to shadows.

(continued)

120   "I don't think you're going to win this time," says Rosie, trying to signify [5] with her hands on her hips all salty, completely forgetting that I have whupped her behind many times for less salt than that.

    "I always win cause I'm the best," I say straight at

125 Gretchen who is, as far as I'm concerned, the only one talking in this ventriloquist-dummy routine.

    Gretchen smiles but it's not a smile and I'm thinking that girls never really smile at each other because they don't know how and don't want to know how and there's probably no one

130 to teach us how cause grown-up girls don't know either. Then they all look at Raymond who has just brought his mule team to a standstill. And they're about to see what trouble they can get into through him.

    "What grade you in now, Raymond?"

135   "You got anything to say to my brother, you say it to me, Mary Louise Williams of Raggedy Town, Baltimore."

    "What are you, his mother?" sasses Rosie.

    "That's right, Fatso. And the next word out of anybody and I'll be their mother too." So they just stand there and

140 Gretchen shifts from one leg to the other and so do they. Then Gretchen puts her hands on her hips and is about to say something with her freckle-face self but doesn't. Then she walks around me looking me up and down but keeps walking up Broadway, and her sidekicks follow her. So me

145 and Raymond smile at each other and he says, "Gidyap" to his team and I continue with my breathing exercises, strolling down Broadway toward the icey man on 145th with not a care in the world cause I am Miss Quicksilver herself.

    I take my time getting to the park on May Day because

150 the track meet is the last thing on the program. The biggest thing on the program is the May Pole dancing which I can do without, thank you, even if my mother thinks it's a shame I don't take part and act like a girl for a change.

More About the Main Character:

Underline words or phrases as your teacher reads the story. Listen for information that describes Squeaky.

Setting:

Draw a box around words or phrases that describe the setting.

Time: _____

_____

_____

Place: _____

_____

_____

---

[5] **signify:** show; indicate

(continued)

Unit 19

More About the Main Character:

Underline words or phrases as your teacher reads the story. Listen for information that describes Squeaky.

Setting:

Draw a box around words or phrases that describe the setting.

Time: _____

_____

_____

Place: _____

_____

_____

You'd think my mother'd be grateful not to have to make
155 me a white organdy dress with a big satin sash and buy me
new white baby-doll shoes that can't be taken out of the
box till the big day. You'd think she'd be glad her daughter
ain't out there prancing around a May Pole getting the new
clothes all dirty and sweaty and trying to act like a fairy or
160 a flower or whatever you're supposed to be when you should
be trying to be yourself, whatever that is, which is, as far as
I'm concerned, a poor Black girl who really can't afford to
buy shoes and a new dress you can only wear once a lifetime
cause it won't fit next year.

165   I was once a strawberry in a Hansel and Gretel pageant
when I was in nursery school and didn't have no better sense
than to dance on tiptoe with my arms in a circle over my
head doing umbrella steps and being a perfect fool just so my
mother and father could come dressed up and clap. You'd
170 think they'd know better than to encourage that kind of
nonsense. I am not a strawberry. I do not dance on my toes. I
run. That is what I am all about. So I always come late to the
May Day program, just in time to get my number pinned on
and lay in the grass till they announce the fifty-yard dash.

175   I put Raymond in the little swings, which is a tight
squeeze this year and will be impossible next year. Then I
look around for Mr. Pearson who pins the numbers on. I'm
really looking for Gretchen if you want to know the truth,
but she's not around. The park is jam-packed. Parents in
180 hats and corsages and breast-pocket handkerchiefs peeking
up. Kids in white dresses and light-blue suits. The parkees
unfolding chairs and chasing the rowdy kids from Lenox as if
they had no right to be there. The big guys with their caps on
backwards, leaning against the fence swirling the basketballs
185 on the tips of their fingers waiting for all these crazy people
to clear out the park so they can play. Most of the kids in my
class are carrying bass drums and glockenspiels and flutes.
You'd think they'd put in a few bongos or something for real
like that.

(continued)

190   Then here comes Mr. Pearson with his clipboard and
his cards and pencils and whistles and safety pins and fifty
million other things he's always dropping all over the place
with his clumsy self. He sticks out in a crowd because he's on
stilts. We used to call him Jack and the Beanstalk to get him
195   mad. But I'm the only one that can outrun him and get away,
and I'm too grown for that silliness now.

"Well, Squeaky," he says, checking my name off the
list and handing me number seven and two pins. And I'm
thinking he's got no right to call me Squeaky, if I can't call
200   him Beanstalk.

"Hazel Elizabeth Deborah Parker," I correct him and tell
him to write it down on his board.

"Well, Hazel Elizabeth Deborah Parker, going to <u>give
someone else a break</u> this year?" I squint at him real hard
205   to see if he is seriously thinking I should lose the race on
purpose just to give someone else a break.

> **Use the Clues C:**
>
> - Read lines 203–206.
>
> - Use context clues to define the underlined phrase,
>   **give someone else a break**.
>
> - Highlight examples that support your definition.
>
>   **Give someone else a break** _____
>
>   _____

"Only six girls running this time," he continues, shaking
his head sadly like it's my fault all of New York didn't turn
out in sneakers. "That new girl should give you a run for
210   your money." He looks around the park for Gretchen like
a periscope in a submarine movie. "Wouldn't it be a nice
gesture [6] if you were . . . to ahhh . . ."

---

[6] **gesture:** thoughtful action

(continued)

I give him such a look he couldn't finish putting that idea into words. Grownups got a lot of nerve sometimes. I pin
215 number seven to myself and stomp away—I'm so burnt. And I go straight for the track and stretch out on the grass while the band winds up with "Oh the Monkey Wrapped His Tail Around the Flag Pole," which my teacher calls by some other name. The man on the loudspeaker is calling everyone over
220 to the track and I'm on my back looking at the sky trying to pretend I'm in the country, but I can't, because even grass in the city feels hard as sidewalk, and there's just no pretending you are anywhere but in a "concrete jungle" as my grandfather says.

▲ ● ▲ ● ▲

End of reading for lesson 8. Paraphrase and predict what might happen next.

_____

_____

_____

_____

_____

_____

_____

_____

▲ ● ▲ ● ▲

(continued)

225   The twenty-yard dash takes all of two minutes cause most of the little kids don't know no better than to run off the track or run the wrong way or run smack into the fence and fall down and cry. One little kid though has got the good sense to run straight for the white ribbon up ahead so

230 he wins. Then the second-graders line up for the thirty-yard dash and I don't even bother to turn my head to watch cause Raphael Perez always wins. He wins before he even begins by psyching the runners, telling them they're going to trip on their shoelaces and fall on their faces or lose their shorts or

235 something, which he doesn't really have to do since he is very fast, almost as fast as I am. After that is the forty-yard dash, which I used to run when I was in the first grade. Raymond is hollering from the swings cause he knows I'm about to do my thing cause the man on the loudspeaker has just announced

240 the fifty-yard dash, although he might just as well be giving a recipe for angel food cake cause you can hardly make out what he's saying for the static. I get up and slip off my sweat pants and then I see Gretchen standing at the starting line kicking her legs out like a pro. Then as I get into place I see

245 that ole Raymond is in line on the other side of the fence, bending down with his fingers on the ground just like he knew what he was doing. I was going to yell at him but then I didn't. It burns up your energy to holler.

    Every time, just before I take off in a race, I always feel

250 like I'm in a dream, the kind of dream you have when you're sick with fever and feel all hot and weightless. I dream I'm flying over a sandy beach in the early morning sun, kissing the leaves of the trees as I fly by. And there's always the smell of apples, just like in the country when I was little and

255 used to think I was a choo-choo train, running through the fields of corn and chugging up the hill to the orchard.

More About the Main Character:

Underline words or phrases as your teacher reads the story. Listen for information that describes Squeaky.

Setting:

Draw a box around words or phrases that describe the setting.

Time: _____

_____

_____

Place: _____

_____

_____

What are some clues that this part of the story is during the race?

_____

_____

_____

_____

(continued)

And all the time I'm dreaming this, I get lighter and lighter until I'm flying over the beach again, getting blown through the sky like a feather that weighs nothing at all. But once

260 I spread my fingers in the dirt and crouch over for the Get on Your Mark, the dream goes and I am solid again and am telling myself, Squeaky you must win, you must win, you are the fastest thing in the world, you can even beat your father up Amsterdam if you really try. And then I feel my weight

265 coming back just behind my knees then down to my feet then into the earth and the pistol shot explodes in my blood and I am off and weightless again, flying past the other runners, my arms pumping up and down and the whole world is quiet except for the crunch as I zoom over the gravel in the track. I

270 glance to my left and there is no one. To the right, a blurred [7] Gretchen, who's got her chin jutting out as if it would win the race all by itself. And on the other side of the fence is Raymond with his arms down to his side and the palms tucked up behind him, running in his very own style, and

275 it's the first time I ever saw that and I almost stop to watch my brother Raymond on his first run. But the white ribbon is bouncing toward me and I tear past it, racing into the distance till my feet with a mind of their own start digging up footfuls of dirt and brake me short. Then all the kids

280 standing on the side pile on me, banging me on the back and slapping my head with their May Day programs, for I have won again and everybody on 151st Street can walk tall for another year.

"In the first place . . ." the man on the loudspeaker is clear

285 as a bell now. But then he pauses and the loudspeaker starts to whine. Then static. And I lean down to catch my breath and here comes Gretchen walking back for she's overshot

---

[7] **blurred:** indistinct; unclear

(continued)

the finish line too, huffing and puffing with her hands on her hips taking it slow, breathing in steady time like a real

290 pro and I sort of like her a little for the first time. "In first place . . ." and then three or four voices get all mixed up on the loudspeaker and I dig my sneaker into the grass and stare at Gretchen who's staring back, we both wondering just who did win. I can hear old Beanstalk arguing with the man on

295 the loudspeaker and then a few others running their mouths about what the stop watches say.

Then I hear Raymond yanking at the fence to call me and I wave to shush him, but he keeps rattling the fence, but then like a dancer or something he starts climbing up nice

300 and easy but very fast. And it occurs to me, watching how smoothly he climbs hand over hand and remembering how he looked running with his arms down to his side and with the wind pulling his mouth back and his teeth showing and all, it occurred to me that Raymond would make a very fine

305 runner. Doesn't he always keep up with me on my trots? And he surely knows how to breathe in counts of seven cause he's always doing it at the dinner table, which drives my brother George up the wall. And I'm smiling to beat the band cause if I've lost this race, or if me and Gretchen tied, or even if I've

310 won, I can always retire as a runner and begin a whole new career as a coach with Raymond as my champion. After all, with a little more study I can beat Cynthia and her phony self at the spelling bee. And if I bugged my mother, I could get piano lessons and become a star. And I have a big rep as the

315 baddest thing around. And I've got a roomful of ribbons and medals and awards. But what has Raymond got to call his own?

So I stand there with my new plans, laughing out loud by this time as Raymond jumps down from the fence and

320 runs over with his teeth showing and his arms down to the side, which no one before him has quite mastered as a running style. And by the time he comes over I'm jumping up and down so glad to see him—my brother Raymond, a great runner in the family tradition. But of course everyone

(continued)

325 thinks I'm jumping up and down because the men on the loudspeaker have finally gotten themselves together and compared notes and are announcing "In first place—Miss Hazel Elizabeth Deborah Parker." (Dig that.) "In second place—Miss Gretchen P. Lewis." And I look over at Gretchen
330 wondering what the "P" stands for. And I smile. Cause she's good, no doubt about it. Maybe she'd like to help me coach Raymond; she obviously is serious about running, as any fool can see. And she nods to congratulate me and then she smiles. And I smile. We stand there with this big smile of
335 respect between us. It's about as real a smile as girls can do for each other, considering we don't practice real smiling every day you know, cause maybe we too busy being flowers or fairies or strawberries instead of something honest and worthy of respect . . . you know . . . like being people.

The Marble Champ

by Gary Soto

1   Lupe Medrano, a shy girl who spoke in whispers, was the school's spelling bee champion, winner of the reading contest at the public library three summers in a row, blue ribbon awardee in the science fair, the top student at her piano
5 recital, and the playground grand champion in chess. She was a straight-A student and—not counting kindergarten, when she had been stung by a wasp—never missed one day of elementary school. She had received a small trophy for this honor and had been congratulated by the mayor.

10   But though Lupe had a razor-sharp mind, she could not make her body, no matter how much she tried, run as fast as the other girls'. She begged her body to move faster, but could never best anyone in the fifty-yard dash.

    The truth was that Lupe was no good in sports. She could
15 not catch a pop-up or figure out in which direction to kick the soccer ball. One time she kicked the ball at her own goal and scored a point for the other team. She was no good at baseball or basketball either, and even had a hard time making a hula hoop stay on her hips.

20   It wasn't until last year, when she was eleven years old, that she learned how to ride a bike. And even then she had to use training wheels. She could walk in the swimming pool but couldn't swim, and chanced roller skating only when her father held her hand.

25   "I'll never be good at sports," she fumed one rainy day as she lay on her bed gazing at the shelf her father had made to hold her awards. "I wish I could win something, anything, even marbles."

    At the word "marbles," she sat up. "That's it. Maybe I
30 could be good at playing marbles." She hopped out of bed and rummaged [1] through the closet until she found a can full of

---

[1] **rummaged:** searched

In **The Marble Champ**, the main character, Lupe, displayed character traits that helped her become the champion. Those traits were: **persistence**, **willingness to train**, and a **willingness to accept support**.

As you read the story, underline details that provide evidence of each of these traits.

Write a 1, 2, or 3 next to the underlined evidence that Lupe's traits helped her become a champion.

1 - persistent
2 - willing to train
3 - willing to accept support

(continued)

her brother's marbles. She poured the rich glass treasure on her bed and picked five of the most beautiful marbles.

She smoothed her bedspread and practiced shooting,
35 softly at first so that her aim would be accurate [2]. The marble rolled from her thumb and clicked against the targeted marble. But the target wouldn't budge. She tried again and again. Her aim became accurate, but the power from her thumb made the marble move only an inch or two. Then she
40 realized that the bedspread was slowing the marbles. She also had to admit that her thumb was weaker than the neck of a newborn chick.

She looked out the window. The rain was letting up, but the ground was too muddy to play. She sat cross-legged on
45 the bed, rolling her five marbles between her palms. Yes, she thought, I could play marbles, and marbles is a sport. At that moment she realized that she had only two weeks to practice. The playground championship, the same one her brother had entered the previous year, was coming up. She had a lot to do.

50 To strengthen her wrists, she decided to do twenty push-ups on her fingertips, five at a time. "One, two, three . . ." she groaned. By the end of the <u>first set</u> she was breathing hard, and her muscles burned from exhaustion. She did <u>one more set</u> and decided that was enough push-ups for the first day.

Use the Clues A:

- Read lines 50–54

- Reread the underlined phrases, **first set** and **one more set**. Highlight the context clues that help you define the phrase.

- Define a **set**. How many push-ups did Lupe do in all? How many did she want to do?

_____

_____

_____

[2] **accurate:** precise; without error

(continued)

55   She squeezed a rubber eraser one hundred times, hoping
it would strengthen her thumb. This seemed to work because
the next day her thumb was sore. She could hardly hold a
marble in her hand, let alone send it flying with power. So
Lupe rested that day and listened to her brother, who gave
60   her tips on how to shoot: get low, aim with one eye, and place
one knuckle on the ground.

"Think 'eye and thumb'—and let it rip!" he said.

After school the next day she left her homework in her
backpack and practiced three hours straight, taking time
65   only to eat a candy bar for energy. With a popsicle stick, she
drew an odd-shaped circle and tossed in four marbles. She
used her shooter, <u>a milky agate</u> with hypnotic swirls, to blast
them. Her thumb had become stronger.

Use the Clues B:

- Read lines 63–68

- Reread the underlined phrase, **a milky agate**. Highlight
  the context clues that help you define the phrase.

- Define a **milky agate**.

  _____

  _____

After practice, she squeezed the eraser for an hour. She
70   ate dinner with her left hand to spare her shooting hand
and said nothing to her parents about her dreams of athletic
glory.

Practice, practice, practice. Squeeze, squeeze, squeeze.
Lupe got better and beat her brother and Alfonso, a neighbor
75   kid who was supposed to be a champ.

"Man, she's bad!" Alfonso said. "She can beat the other
girls for sure, I think."

The weeks passed quickly. Lupe worked so hard that one
day, while she was drying dishes, her mother asked why her
80   thumb was swollen.

"It's muscle," Lupe explained. "I've been practicing for the
marbles championship."

(continued)

"You, honey?" Her mother knew Lupe was no good at sports.

85 "Yeah. I beat Alfonso, and he's pretty good."

That night, over dinner, Mrs. Medrano said, "Honey, you should see Lupe's thumb."

"Huh?" Mr. Medrano said, wiping his mouth and looking at his daughter.

90 "Show your father."

"Do I have to?" an embarrassed Lupe asked.

"Go on, show your father."

Reluctantly [3], Lupe raised her hand and flexed her thumb. You could see the muscle.

95 The father put down his fork and asked, "What happened?"

"Dad, I've been working out. I've been squeezing an eraser."

"Why?"

100 "I'm going to enter the marbles championship."

Her father looked at her mother and then back at his daughter. "When is it, honey?"

"This Saturday. Can you come?"

The father had been planning to play racquetball with a
105 friend Saturday, but he said he would be there. He knew his daughter thought she was no good at sports and he wanted to encourage her. He even rigged some lights in the backyard so she could practice after dark. He squatted with one knee on the ground, entranced [4] by the sight of his daughter easily
110 beating her brother.

The day of the championship began with a cold blustery sky.

---

[3] **Reluctantly:** hesitantly; unwillingly

[4] **entranced:** enchanted; fascinated

(continued)

Identify It: Predicate Nominative or Direct Object

Read the underlined section of the numbered sentences.

Write PN over the Predicate Nominative, DO over the Direct Object.

There are five sentences.

1 The sun was a silvery light behind slate clouds.

"I hope it clears up," her father said, rubbing his hands together as he returned from getting the newspaper. 2 They
115 ate breakfast, paced nervously around the house waiting for 10:00 to arrive, and walked the two blocks to the playground (though Mr. Medrano wanted to drive so Lupe wouldn't get tired). She signed up and was assigned her first match on baseball diamond number three.

120 Lupe, walking between her brother and her father, shook from the cold, not nerves. 3 She took off her mittens, and everyone stared at her thumb. Someone asked, "How can you play with a broken thumb?" Lupe smiled and said nothing.

125 She beat her first opponent [5] easily, and felt sorry for the girl because she didn't have anyone to cheer for her. Except for her sack of marbles, she was all alone. Lupe invited the girl, whose name was Rachel, to stay with them. She smiled and said, "OK." The four of them walked to a card table in
130 the middle of the outfield, where Lupe was assigned another opponent.

She also beat this girl, a fifth-grader named Yolanda, and asked her to join their group. They proceeded to more matches and more wins, and soon there was a crowd of
135 people following Lupe to the finals to play a girl in a baseball cap. This girl seemed dead serious. She never even looked at Lupe.

"I don't know, Dad, she looks tough."

Rachel hugged Lupe and said, "Go get her."

---

[5] **opponent:** person who takes the other side in a game or contest

(continued)

140   "You can do it," her father encouraged. "Just think of the marbles, not the girl, and let your thumb do the work."

  The other girl broke first and earned one marble. She missed her next shot, and Lupe, one eye closed, her thumb quivering with energy, blasted two marbles out of the circle

145 but missed her next shot. Her opponent earned two more before missing. She stamped her foot and said "Shoot!" The score was three to two in favor of Miss Baseball Cap.

  4 <u>The referee stopped the game</u>. "Back up, please, give them room," he shouted. Onlookers had gathered too tightly

150 around the players.

  Lupe then earned three marbles and was set to get her fourth when a gust of wind blew dust in her eyes and she missed badly. Her opponent quickly scored two marbles, tying the game, and moved ahead six to five on a lucky shot.

155 Then she missed, and Lupe, whose eyes felt scratchy when she blinked, relied on instinct and thumb muscle to score the tying point. It was now six to six, with only three marbles left. Lupe blew her nose and studied the angles. She dropped to one knee, steadied her hand, and shot so hard she cracked

160 two marbles from the circle. **5** <u>She was the winner</u>!

  "I did it!" Lupe said under her breath. She rose from her knees, which hurt from bending all day, and hugged her father. He hugged her back and smiled.

  Everyone clapped, except Miss Baseball Cap, who made a

165 face and stared at the ground. Lupe told her she was a great player, and they shook hands. A newspaper photographer took pictures of the two girls standing shoulder-to-shoulder, with Lupe holding the bigger trophy.

  Lupe then played the winner of the boys' division, and

170 after a poor start beat him eleven to four. She blasted the marbles, shattering one into sparkling slivers of glass. Her opponent looked on glumly [6] as Lupe did what she did best—win!

  The head referee and the President of the Fresno Marble

175 Association stood with Lupe as she displayed her trophies for the newspaper photographer. Lupe shook hands with

---

[6] **glumly:** sadly; unhappily

(continued)

everyone, including a dog who had come over to see what the commotion was all about.

That night, the family went out for pizza and set the two
180 trophies on the table for everyone in the restaurant to see. People came up to congratulate Lupe, and she felt a little embarrassed, but her father said the trophies belonged there.

Back home, in the privacy of her bedroom, she placed the trophies on her shelf and was happy. She had always earned
185 honors because of her brains, but winning in sports was a new experience. She thanked her tired thumb. "You did it, thumb. You made me champion." As its reward, Lupe went to the bathroom, filled the bathroom sink with warm water, and let her thumb swim and splash as it pleased. Then she
190 climbed into bed and drifted into a hard-won sleep.

Meet the Main Character

_____

_____

_____

Underline words or phrases as your teacher reads the story. Listen for information that describes Scho.

Setting:

Time: _____

_____

_____

Place: _____

_____

_____

A Game of Catch
by Richard Wilbur

How could something as innocent as a game of catch result in such painful consequences?

1   Monk and Glennie were playing catch on the side lawn of the firehouse when Scho caught sight of them. They were good at it, for seventh-graders, as anyone could see right away. Monk, wearing a catcher's mitt, would lean easily
5 sidewise and back, with one leg lifted and his throwing hand almost down to the grass, and then lob the white ball straight up into the sunlight. Glennie would shield his eyes with his left hand and, just as the ball fell past him, snag it with a little dart of his glove. Then he would burn the ball straight
10 toward Monk, and it would spank into the round mitt and sit, like a still-life apple on a plate, until Monk flipped it over into his right hand and, with a negligent flick of his hanging arm, gave Glennie a fast grounder.

Then they were going on and on like that, in a kind of slow,
15 mannered, luxurious[1] dance in the sun, their faces perfectly blank and entranced, when Glennie noticed Scho dawdling along the other side of the street and called hello to him. Scho crossed over and stood at the front edge of the lawn, near an apple tree, watching.

20   "Got your glove?" asked Glennie after a time. Scho obviously hadn't.

"You could give me some easy grounders," said Scho. "But don't burn 'em."

"All right," Glennie said. He moved off a little, so the
25 three of them formed a triangle, and they passed the ball around for about five minutes, Monk tossing easy grounders to Scho, Scho throwing to Glennie, and Glennie burning them in to Monk. After a while, Monk began to throw them back to Glennie once or twice before he let Scho have
30 his grounder, and finally Monk gave Scho a fast, bumpy

---

[1] **luxurious:** extremely enjoyable; self-indulgent

(continued)

grounder that hopped over his shoulder and went <u>into the brake</u> on the other side of the street.

"Not so hard," called Scho as he ran across to get it.

"You should've had it," Monk shouted.

35   It took Scho a little while to find the ball among the <mark>ferns and dead leaves</mark>, and when he saw it, he grabbed it up and threw it toward Glennie. It struck the trunk of the apple tree, bounced back at an angle, and rolled steadily and stupidly <u>onto the</u> <mark>cement <u>apron</u></mark> in front of the firehouse, where one of the

40 <mark>trucks was parked</mark>. Scho ran hard and stopped it just before it rolled under the truck, and this time he carried it back to his former position on the lawn and threw it carefully to Glennie.

Use the Clues A:

- Read lines 24–42

- Reread the underlined phrases, **into the brake** and **onto the cement apron**. Highlight the context clues that help you define the phrases.

- Define **into the brake**. Hint: Where did the ball go?

  _____

- Define **onto a cement apron**. Where did the ball go next?

  _____

  _____

    "I got an idea," said Glennie. "Why don't Monk and I catch for five minutes more, and then you can borrow one of

45 our gloves?"

    "That's all right with me," said Monk. He socked his fist into his mitt, and Glennie burned one in.

    "All right," Scho said, and went over and sat under the tree. There in the shade he watched them resume their

50 skillful play. They threw lazily fast or lazily slow—high, low, or wide—and always handsomely, their expressions <mark>serene</mark>,[2] changeless, and forgetful. When Monk missed a

---

[2] **serene:** very calm; peaceful

(continued)

low backhand catch, he walked indolently[3] after the ball
and, hardly even looking, flung it sidearm for an imaginary
55 put-out. After a good while of this, Scho said, "Isn't it five
minutes yet?"

"One minute to go," said Monk, with a fraction of a grin.

Scho stood up and watched the ball slap back and forth
for several minutes more, and then he turned and pulled
60 himself up into the crotch of the tree.

"Where you going?" Monk asked.

"Just up the tree," Scho said.

"I guess he doesn't want to catch," said Monk.

Scho went up and up through the fat light-gray branches
65 until they grew slender and bright and gave under him. He
found a place where several supple branches were knit to
make a dangerous chair, and sat there with his head coming
out of the leaves into the sunlight. He could see the two other
boys down below, the ball going back and forth between
70 them as if they were bowling on the grass, and Glennie's
crew-cut head looking like a sea urchin.

▲●▲●▲

**End of reading for Lesson 7. Summarize and predict what
might happen next.**

_____

_____

_____

_____

_____

_____

_____

_____

▲●▲●▲

_____

[3] **indolently:** lazily

(continued)

"I found a wonderful seat up here," Scho said loudly. "If I don't fall out." Monk and Glennie didn't look up or comment, and so he began jouncing³ gently in his chair of branches
75 and singing "Yo-ho, heave ho" in an exaggerated way.

"Do you know what, Monk?" he announced in a few moments. "I can make you two guys do anything I want. Catch that ball, Monk! Now you catch it, Glennie!"

"I was going to catch it anyway," Monk suddenly said.
80 "You're not making anybody do anything when they're already going to do it anyway."

"I made you say what you just said," Scho replied joyfully.

"No, you didn't," said Monk, still throwing and catching but now less serenely absorbed in the game.
85 "That's what I wanted you to say," Scho said.

The ball bounded off the rim of Monk's mitt and plowed into a gladiolus bed beside the firehouse, and Monk ran to get it while Scho jounced in his treetop and sang, "I wanted you to miss that. Anything you do is what I wanted you to do."
90 "Let's quit for a minute," Glennie suggested.

"We might as well, until the peanut gallery shuts up," Monk said.

Meet the Main Character

_____

_____

_____

Underline words or phrases, as your teacher reads the story. Listen for information that describes Scho.

Setting:

Time: _____

_____

_____

Place: _____

_____

_____

> ### Use the Clues B:
>
> • Read lines 86–92
>
> • Reread the underlined phrase, **peanut gallery**. Highlight the context clues that help you understand the phrase.
>
> • Who represents the **peanut gallery**?
>
> _____
>
> _____
>
> _____

They went over and sat crosslegged in the shade of the tree. Scho looked down between his legs and saw them on
95 the dim, spotty ground, saying nothing to one another.

---

⁴ **jouncing:** bouncing; moving with bumps or jolts

(continued)

Glennie soon began abstractedly spinning his glove between his palms; Monk pulled his nose and stared out across the lawn.

"I want you to mess around with your nose, Monk," said
100 Scho, giggling. Monk withdrew his hand from his face.

"Do that with your glove, Glennie," Scho persisted. "Monk, I want you to pull up hunks of grass and chew on it."

Glennie looked up and saw a self-delighted, intense face staring down at him through the leaves. "Stop being a dope
105 and come down and we'll catch for a few minutes," he said.

Scho hesitated, and then said, in a tentatively [5] mocking voice, "That's what I wanted you to say."

"All right, then, nuts to you," said Glennie.

"Why don't you keep quiet and stop bothering people?"
110 Monk asked.

"I made you say that," Scho replied, softly.

"Shut up," Monk said.

"I made you say that, and I want you to be standing there looking sore. And I want you to climb up the tree. I'm
115 making you do it!"

Monk was scrambling up through the branches, awkward in his haste, and getting snagged on twigs. His face was furious and foolish, and he kept telling Scho to shut up, shut up, shut up, while the other's exuberant [6] and panicky voice
120 poured down upon his head.

"Now you shut up or you'll be sorry," Monk said, breathing hard as he reached up and threatened to shake the cradle of slight branches in which Scho was sitting.

"I want—" Scho screamed as he fell. Two lower branches
125 broke his rustling, crackling fall, but he landed on his back with a deep thud and lay still, with a strangled look on his face and his eyes clenched. Glennie knelt down and asked breathlessly, "Are you O.K., Scho? Are you O.K.?," while Monk swung down through the leaves crying that honestly
130 he hadn't even touched him, the crazy guy just let go. Scho doubled up and turned over on his right side, and now both

---

[5] **tentatively:** shyly; hesitantly

[6] **exuberant:** high-spirited; enthusiastic

(continued)

the other boys knelt beside him, pawing at his shoulder and begging to know how he was.

Then Scho rolled away from them and sat partly up, still
135 struggling to get his wind but forcing a species of smile onto his face.

"I'm sorry, Scho," Monk said. "I didn't mean to make you fall."

Scho's voice came out weak and gravelly, in gasps. "I
140 meant—you to do it. You—had to. You can't do—anything— unless I want—you to."

Glennie and Monk looked helplessly at him as he sat there, breathing a bit more easily and smiling fixedly, with tears in his eyes. Then they picked up their gloves and the
145 ball, walked over to the street, and went slowly away down the sidewalk, Monk punching his fist into the mitt, Glennie juggling the ball between glove and hand.

From under the apple tree, Scho, still bent over a little for lack of breath, croaked after them in triumph and misery, "I
150 want you to do whatever you're going to do for the whole rest of your life!"

▲ ◉ ▲ ◉ ▲

End of reading for Lesson 8.

Take Note

Underline information about Anne's feelings toward herself and others. Then paraphrase that information in the spaces provided.

A Family in Hiding: Anne Frank's Diary

1   Anne Frank was born on June 12, 1929, in Frankfurt, Germany. Anne's father, Otto Frank, was a respected businessman. For Anne and her older sister, Margot, the world of early childhood was a secure place inhabited by
5 loving parents and relatives. But beyond their family's comfortable environment, the world around them was not so pleasant. By 1933, the Nazi movement had gained control of the German government, and Adolf Hitler was made the chancellor of Germany. Freedom of speech and assembly
10 were suspended, and the Nazi government decreed a boycott of Jewish businesses.

Because of these increasing tensions in Germany and the fact that the Frank family was Jewish, her father decided it would be best to move his business and family to the
15 Netherlands. In 1939, Hitler invaded Poland and started World War II. By 1940, Nazi Germany conquered and controlled several other European countries including the Netherlands. The Nazi government made Jewish citizens wear yellow stars on their clothing. As the Holocaust gained
20 momentum, the Nazis began deporting Jewish citizens and others from these countries to German concentration camps*. The Frank family was no longer safe. In 1942,

Identify It: Words in Text

Read the sentences that include the highlighted words.

Decide if each highlighted word is functioning as a noun, verb, or adjective. Write **N** (noun), **V** (verb), or **A** (adjective) above the word.

* The word **Holocaust** comes from the Greek word, **holokauston**, meaning "a sacrifice burned by fire." It refers to the destruction of the Jews in Europe during the Nazi regime. Over 6 million Jewish people along with many others were killed during World War II.

(continued)

Use the Clues A:

- Read lines 12–22.

- Reread the underlined word, **Holocaust**.

- Check the box that best defines the underlined word. What does the word **Holocaust** mean in this context?

  ❏ Nazi persecution of Jews

  ❏ Nazi government

  ❏ concentration camp

- How did you choose this answer?

  _____

  _____

Anne celebrated her thirteenth birthday in Amsterdam with her family and received a diary as a birthday present.
25 A few weeks later, Anne, her parents, and her older sister were forced to go into hiding with four other people in a Secret Annex of a warehouse that was part of her father's factory.

While in hiding, Anne Frank wrote in her diary about
30 everything that happened to her and her family. She was a teenager who was experiencing all the emotions and conflicts that a typical teenager would, but she was doing so under extraordinarily difficult circumstances. Her family and the four others with them lived for 25 months in cramped
35 quarters, worrying every day about the progress of the war and about what would happen to them if they were discovered. These excerpts from her diary reveal some of Anne Frank's feelings about her family and about the events going on around her.

▲ ● ▲ ● ▲

Identify It: Perfect Tense

Read the underlined section of each numbered sentence. Circle the verb phrase. Decide whether it is a present perfect tense verb or a past perfect tense verb. There are four sentences.

(continued)

40 **Saturday, June 20, 1942**

Writing in a diary is a really strange experience for someone like me. 1 Not only because <u>I've never written anything before</u>, but also because it seems to me that later on neither I nor anyone else will be interested in the musings [1] 45 of a thirteen-year-old schoolgirl. Oh well, it doesn't matter. I feel like writing and I have an even greater need to <u>get things off my chest</u>. . . .

Use the Clues B:

- Read lines 41–47.
- Reread the underlined idiom, **get things off my chest**.
- Check the box that best defines the underlined words. What does the idiom **get things off my chest** mean in this context?

  ❏ remove clothing

  ❏ let go of feelings

  ❏ put things away

- How did you choose this answer?

  _____

  _____

Notes About Anne's Feelings:

_____

_____

_____

_____

My father, the most adorable father I've ever seen, didn't marry my mother until he was thirty-six and she was twenty- 50 five. My sister Margot was born in Frankfurt-am-Main in Germany in 1926. I was born on June 12, 1929. I lived in Frankfurt until I was four. Because we're Jewish, my father immigrated to Holland in 1933, when he became the Managing Director of the Dutch Opteka Company. . . .

---

[1] **musings:** deep thoughts

(continued)

55 Our lives were not without anxiety since our relatives in Germany were suffering under Hitler's anti-Jewish laws. . . . In 1938 my two uncles (my mother's brothers) fled Germany, finding <u>safe refuge</u> in North America. My elderly grandmother came to live with us. She was seventy-three

60 years old at the time. . . . Grandma died in January 1942. No one knows how often I think of her and still love her. . . .

Use the Clues C:

- Read lines 55–61.

- Reread the underlined phrase, **safe refuge**.

- Check the box that best defines the underlined words. What does the phrase **safe refuge** mean in this context?

  ❑ not so pleasant

  ❑ safe place

  ❑ locked up

- How did you choose this answer?

  _____

  _____

▲ ● ▲ ● ▲

On July 9, the Frank family went into hiding in the Secret Annex after Anne's sister, Margot, received a call-up to be sent to a labor camp. They were helped
65 by friends, who brought them food and news from the outside. On July 13, they were joined in hiding by another Jewish family, Mr. and Mrs. van Daan and their fifteen-year-old son, Peter. The seven of them, living so closely together, became an extended family.

▲ ● ▲ ● ▲

70 **Friday, August 21, 1942**

Now our Secret Annex has truly become secret. . . . Mr. Kugler thought it would be better to have a bookcase built in

(continued)

**Notes About Anne's
Feelings:**

_____

_____

_____

_____

front of the entrance to our hiding place. It swings out on its
hinges and opens like a door. . . .

75   There's little change in our lives here. Peter's hair was
washed today, but that's nothing special. Mr. van Daan and
I are always at loggerheads with each other. Mama always
treats me like a baby, which I can't stand. For the rest, things
are going better. I don't think Peter's gotten any nicer. He's

80   an obnoxious boy who lies around on his bed all day, only
rousing himself to do a little carpentry work before returning
to his nap. . . .

Mama gave me another one of her dreadful sermons
this morning. We take the opposite view of everything.

85   Daddy's a sweetheart. He may get mad at me, but it never
lasts longer than five minutes.

Friday, October 9, 1942

Today I have nothing but dismal and depressing news to
report. Our many Jewish friends and acquaintances are being

90   taken away in droves. The Gestapo is treating them very roughly
and transporting them in cattle cars to Westerbork. . . . It must
be terrible in Westerbork. The people get almost nothing to eat,
much less to drink, as water is available only one hour a
day, and there's only one toilet and sink for several thousand

95   people. Men and women sleep in the same room, and women
and children often have their heads shaved. Escape is almost
impossible. Many people look Jewish, and they're branded by
their shorn heads.

If it's that bad in Holland, what must it be like in those

100 faraway and uncivilized ² places where the Germans are
sending them. We assume that most of them are being
murdered. . . .

⚠ ● ⚠ ● ⚠

On November 17, Mr. Albert Dussel joined the others
in hiding in the Secret Annex and became a part of this

105 secret family.

⚠ ● ⚠ ● ⚠

_____

² **uncivilized:** primitive; barbarous, without basic services or
humanity

(continued)

Thursday, November 19, 1942

Just as we thought, Mr. Dussel is a very nice man. . . .
The first day Mr. Dussel was here he asked me all sorts of
questions—for example, what time the cleaning lady comes
110 to the office, how we've arranged to use the washroom,
and when we're allowed to go to the toilet. You may laugh,
but these things aren't so easy in a hiding place. During
the daytime we can't make any noise that might be heard
downstairs. And when someone else is there, like the
115 cleaning lady, we have to be extra careful. . . .

Saturday, November 28, 1942

Mr. Dussel, the man who was said to get along so
well with children and absolutely adore them, has turned
out to be an old-fashioned disciplinarian and preacher
120 of unbearably long sermons on manners. . . . Since I am
generally considered to be the worst behaved of the three
young people, it's all I can do to avoid having the same old
scoldings and admonitions repeatedly flung at my head and
pretend not to hear. This wouldn't be so bad if Mr. Dussel
125 weren't such a tattletale and hadn't singled out Mother to
be the recipient [3] of his reports. If Mr. Dussel's just read
me the riot act, Mother lectures me all over again, this time
throwing the whole book at me. And if I'm really lucky, Mrs.
van D. calls me to account five minutes later and lays down
130 the law as well!

Really, it is not easy being the badly brought-up center of
attention in a family of nit-pickers. . . .

Friday, February 5, 1943

. . . Margot and Peter aren't exactly what you'd call
135 "young"; they're both so quiet and boring. Next to them,
I stick out like a sore thumb and I am always being told,
"Margot and Peter don't act that way. Why don't you follow
your sister's example!" I hate that.

---

[3] **recipient:** one who receives

(continued)

**Notes About Anne's
Feelings:**

_____

_____

_____

_____

140　　　I confess that I have absolutely no desire to be like
Margot. She is too weak-willed and passive [4] to suit me;
she lets herself be swayed by others and always backs down
under pressure. I want to have more spunk! But I keep ideas
like these to myself. They'd only laugh at me if I offered this
in my defense.

145 **Monday Evening, November 8, 1943**
　　　I see the eight of us in the Annex as if we were a patch
of blue sky surrounded by menacing clouds. The perfectly
round spot on which we're standing is still safe, but the
clouds are moving in on us, and the ring between us and the
150 approaching danger is being pulled tighter and tighter. We're
surrounded by darkness and danger, and in our desperate
search for a way out, we keep bumping into each other. We
look at the fighting down below and the peace and beauty up
above. In the meantime, we've been cut off by the dark mass
155 of clouds, so that we can go neither up nor down. It looms
before us like an impenetrable wall, trying to crush us, but
not yet able to. I can only cry out and implore, "Oh ring, ring,
open wide and let us out!"

Friday, December 24, 1943
160　　　. . . Believe me, if you've been shut up for a year and a half,
it can get to be too much for you sometimes. But feelings
can't be ignored, no matter how unjust or ungrateful they
seem. I long to ride a bike, dance, whistle, look at the world,
feel young and know that I'm free, and yet I can't let it show.
165 Just imagine what would happen if all eight of us were to feel
sorry for ourselves or walk around with the discontent clearly
visible on our faces. Where would that get us? . . .

Sunday, January 2 , 1944
　　　This morning, when I had nothing to do, I leafed
170 through the pages of my diary and came across so many
letters dealing with the subject "Mother" in such strong

---

[4] **passive:** accepting without resistance or struggle

**Notes About Anne's
Feelings:**

_____

_____

_____

_____

_____

_____

(continued)

terms that I was shocked. I said to myself: "Anne, is that really you talking about hate? Oh, Anne, how could you?" . . .

Wednesday Evening, January 19, 1944

175   . . . You know that I always used to be jealous of Margot's relationship with Father. There's not a trace of my jealousy left now. I still feel hurt when Father's nerves cause him to be unreasonable toward me, but then I think, "I can't blame you for being the way you are. You talk so much about the minds

180 of children and adolescents but you don't know the first thing about them!". . .

Saturday, March 11, 1944

I haven't been able to sit still lately. I wander upstairs and down and then back again. I like talking to Peter, but I'm

185 always afraid of being a nuisance. He's told me a bit about the past, about his parents and about himself, but it's not enough, and every five minutes I wonder why I find myself longing for more. He used to think I was a real pain in the neck, and the feeling was mutual. [2] I've changed my mind, but how

190 do I know <u>he's changed his</u>? I think he has, but that doesn't necessarily mean we have to become the best of friends, although, as far as I am concerned, it would make the time here more bearable. But I won't let this drive me crazy. . . .

Notes About Anne's Feelings:

_____

_____

_____

Friday, March 17, 1944

195   . . . For both of us [Anne and Margot], it's been quite a blow to suddenly realize that very little remains of the close and harmonious [5] family we used to be at home! This is mostly because everything's out of kilter here. By that I mean that we're treated like children when it comes to external

200 matters, while, inwardly, we're much older than other girls our age. Even though I'm only fourteen, I know what I want. I know who's right and who's wrong. I have my own opinions, ideas, and principles. And though it may sound odd coming from a teenager, I feel I'm more of a person than a child—I

205 feel I'm completely independent of others. . . .

Notes About Anne's Feelings:

_____

_____

_____

_____

---

[5] **harmonious:** in agreement; working well together

(continued)

Friday, March 24, 1944

I often go up to Peter's room after dinner nowadays to breathe in the fresh evening air. You can get around to meaningful conversations more quickly in the dark than
210 with the sun tickling your face. It's cozy and snug sitting beside him on a chair and looking outside. The van Daans and Dussel make the silliest remarks when I disappear into his room. . . . "Is it proper for a gentleman to receive young girls in his room at night. . .?" Peter has amazing presence of
215 mind in the face of these so-called witticisms. My Mother, incidentally, is also bursting with curiosity and simply dying to ask what we talk about, only she's secretly afraid I'd refuse to answer. Peter says that grown-ups are just jealous because we're young and that we shouldn't take their obnoxious
220 comments to heart. . . .

Tuesday, April 11, 1944

. . . 3 <u>None of us have ever been in such danger</u> as we were that night. . . . 4 Just think—the police were right at the bookcase, the light was on, and still <u>no one had discovered</u>
225 <u>our hiding place</u>! "Now, we're done for!" I'd whispered at that moment, but once again we were spared. . . .

I'm becoming more and more independent of my parents. Young as I am, I face life with more courage and have a better and truer sense of justice than Mother. I know
230 what I want. I have a goal. I have opinions. . . . If only I can be myself, I'll be satisfied. I know that I'm a woman, a woman with inner strength and a great deal of courage.

Saturday, July 15, 1944

. . . So if you're wondering whether it's harder for the
235 adults here than for the children, the answer is no. It's certainly not. Older people have an opinion about everything and are sure of themselves and their actions. It's twice as hard for us young people to hold on to our opinions at a time when ideals are being shattered and destroyed, when the
240 worst side of human nature predominates [6]. . . .

---

[6] **predominates:** overshadows or overpowers others

(continued)

It's utterly impossible for me to build my life on a foundation of chaos, suffering, and death. I see the world being slowly transformed into a wilderness, I hear the approaching thunder that, one day, will destroy us too. I feel
245 the suffering of millions. And yet, when I look up at the sky, I somehow feel that everything will change for the better, that this cruelty too will end, that peace and tranquility will return once more. In the meantime, I must hold on to my ideals. Perhaps the day will come when I'll be able to realize them.

▲ ● ▲ ● ▲

250　Tuesday, August 1, 1944, is the date of the last entry in Anne Frank's diary. On August 4, 1944, Gestapo officers and Dutch members of the Security Police arrested the eight people hiding in the Secret Annex and brought them to a prison in Amsterdam. They were then transferred to
255 Westerbork, the transport camp for Jews in north Holland. They were deported on September 3, 1944, on the last transport to leave Westerbork, and arrived three days later in the Auschwitz concentration camp in Poland. The men and women were separated there. Margot and Anne were
260 transferred to Bergen-Belsen, another concentration camp in Germany. A typhus epidemic broke out there in the winter of 1944–45, and both Margot and Anne became ill and died. The camp was liberated by British troops on April 12, 1945.

All the others who had hidden in the Secret Annex died
265 in concentration camps as well, except for Anne's father, Otto Frank. One of the family's friends had saved Anne's diary and gave it to him. He published the first edition in 1947. Anne Frank's *The Diary of a Young Girl* has since been translated into 47 languages and is one of the most widely
270 read books in the world.

Excerpted from *The Diary of a Young Girl: Anne Frank, The Definitive Edition* edited by Otto H. Frank and Mirjam Dressler

Text Connection 6

Take Note

Underline information about the main character's feelings. Highlight or circle information about his actions. Then paraphrase his actions in the spaces provided.

My Side of the Story

by Adam Bagdasarian

1 I was sitting at my desk in my bedroom practicing my signature when my brother came in and asked me if I wanted to throw the ball around or shoot baskets.

"No," I said. So he looked over my shoulder at the

5 signatures, went into the bathroom for a few seconds, came out, went to his own desk, unraveled an entire roll of Scotch tape and stuck it on my head.

Naturally, I was outraged. "What did you do that for?" I asked. It was a stupid question because I knew very well why

10 he had done it. He had done it for the same reason he had stuffed me in the laundry <u>hamper</u> and tied me to a chair with my best ties.

Use the Clues A:

- Read lines 8–12.

- Reread the underlined word, **hamper**. Check the box that best defines the underlined word.
  What does the word **hamper** mean in this context?

  ❑ to hold you back

  ❑ appliance

  ❑ a container for dirty clothes

- How did you choose this answer?

  _____

  _____

He had done it because he was fourteen and had the great good fortune to be blessed with a little brother he could

15 bedevil [1] <u>at will</u>.

---

[1] **bedevil:** to annoy or harass; torment

(continued)

Use the Clues B:

- Read lines 13–15.

- Reread the underlined phrase, **at will**.

- Check the box that best defines the underlined words. What does the phrase **at will** mean in this context?

  ❑ a contract

  ❑ when he wishes

  ❑ a boy's name

- How did you choose this answer?

  _____

  _____

"Try to get it off," he said.

This I attempted to do, but he had rubbed the Scotch tape so hard into my scalp that it had become a part of my head.

"Let me try," he said.

20   So he tried, and I yowled, and he stopped. Then he gently pulled a piece of the Scotch tape off the side of my head, along with six or seven of my <u>temple</u> hairs.

Use the Clues C:

- Read lines 17–22.

- Reread the underlined word, **temple**.

- Check the box that best defines the underlined word. What does the word **temple** mean in this context?

  ❑ flat region on either side of the forehead

  ❑ a building for worship

  ❑ a device used while weaving

- How did you choose this answer?

  _____

(continued)

Unit 21

Action Taken by the Main Character:

_____

_____

_____

_____

Even at the age of nine I knew that I had been mightily wronged; even at nine I knew that this violated every code of
25 justice [2] and fair play that I had ever been taught. And so, my heart full of righteous [3] rage and indignation, I leaped out of my chair, past my brother, in search of justice.

In those days justice looked a good deal like my mother. It had lovely brown hair, a warm enchanting smile, and a soft,
30 understanding voice. It was comforting to know that in a matter of seconds my mother would hear the evidence, weigh the evidence, and punish my brother. Generally, things were murkier. Generally, I did something by accident, then my brother did something back, and I did something back, and
35 on and on until it was impossible to tell who was at fault. But this—this was the case of a lifetime. And the best part of all was that the evidence was stuck to my head.

When I reached my mother's room, I saw that the door was closed. For a moment I hesitated, wondering if she was
40 sleeping, but I was so sure of my case, so convinced of the general rightness of my mission that I threw open the door and burst into the room screaming, "Mom! Mom! Skip put—"

And then I realized that I was talking to my father, not my mother.

45 In order to understand the enormity [4] of the mistake I had made, you have to understand my father. My father was five feet seven and a half inches tall, stocky, powerfully built, and larger than life in laughter, strength, character, integrity,[5] humor, appetite, wit, intelligence, warmth, curiosity,
50 generosity, magnetism, insight, and rage. Consequently, he was not concerned with the little things in life, such as sibling shenanigans, rivalries, or disputes. His job, as he saw it, was to make us the best human beings we could possibly be—to guide us, love us, and teach us the large laws of honor,
55 courage, honesty, and self-reliance. He was the only man to

Action Taken by the Main Character:

_____

_____

_____

_____

---

[2] **justice:** fairness

[3] **righteous:** right; justified

[4] **enormity:** great evil; outrage

[5] **integrity:** strong morals; honesty

(continued)

turn to if you had a severed artery, broken ribs, or any serious disease or financial problems, but he was not the kind of man one would knowingly burst in upon screaming anything less than "The house is on fire!" or "Somebody stole your car!"

60 I knew this, of course, which is why I had run to my mother's room in the first place, and why, when I saw my father, most of the color drained from my face. My first impulse was to walk backward out of the room, closing the door gently before me as I did so, but I had shifted so

65 suddenly from offensive indignation to defensive fear and astonishment that I felt a little disoriented .[6] For a moment I considered telling him that I smelled smoke or saw someone stealing his car, but I couldn't lie. I couldn't tell the truth, either. In fact, for a moment, I couldn't speak.

70 "What on earth are you doing?" my father said.

I started to say, "I was sitting at my desk minding my own business, when—" and I stopped. I stopped because I knew instinctively that Scotch tape on my head was not enough, not nearly enough to warrant my wild, unannounced

75 entrance into this room.

"When what?"

"Nothing."

"You ran in here screaming about something. What happened?"

80 "I didn't..."

"You didn't what?"

"I didn't know you were here."

"So what! You knew someone was here! What did Skip do?"

85 "Skip...uh. I was sitting at my desk, and Skip..."

"Skip what? Tell me!"

"Put Scotch tape on my head."

Identify It: Quotations in Text

Reread lines 76–87. Decide who is speaking in each line of text. Write the person's name beside the words spoken.

---

[6] **disoriented:** confused

(continued)

This apparently was all my father needed to set the wheels of his anger in motion.

90 "You came running in here without knocking because Skip put Scotch tape on your head?"

"No, I—"

"You didn't care that the door was closed? You didn't care that your mother might have been sleeping?"

95 I wanted to explain to him that this had been going on for years, that Mom and Skip and I had an understanding, but I knew that we weren't having a discussion. I also knew that he was working himself into a rage and that anything I said would only make it worse.

100 "Is that what you do? You run into rooms screaming?" He was on his feet now and advancing toward me. "You don't knock?"

"No. Yes."

At this point my brother entered the room, saw what was 105 happening, and stood transfixed.

"Here!" my father said. "Here's what we do with Scotch tape!" And with that he pulled the whole wad off my head, along with fifty or sixty of my hairs.

I knew that he was only a few seconds away from his 110 closing arguments now, and my calculations were just about right.

"You don't *ever* come in here without knocking! Do you hear me?" my father bellowed. Silence. "Do you hear . . ."

At this point I heard a wheeze of escaping laughter where 115 my brother was standing, and saw him run out of the room.

"Do you?"

"Yes, Pop, yes. I hear you."

"Are you ever going to come in here without knocking again?"

120 "No, no."

"Ever!"

"No."

"Now get out of here!"

And I got out and heard the door slam behind me.

125 There was not much to do after that but sit at my desk and wonder what had happened. I had been signing my

(continued)

name, Skip put Scotch tape on my head, I ran to tell Mom, found Pop, and the lights went out. Where, I wondered, was the justice in that? Obviously, when I burst into my mother's

130 room, I had entered a larger world of justice, a world where screaming, whining, mother dependence, not knocking on closed doors, and startling one's father were serious crimes. That part I understood. The part I didn't understand was the part about why my brother, who had started the whole thing

135 by putting Scotch tape on my head, hadn't been punished. So, in the interest of a smaller justice, I went over to his trophy shelf, picked up one of his baseball trophies, and gradually wrested the little gold-plated athlete off its mount.

With a little luck, my brother would want to tell Pop

140 about it.

Action Taken by the Main Character

_____

_____

_____

_____

Take Note

Identify the characters, setting and problem in each of the folktales. Use the spaces provided on the pages that follow.

A Collection of Puzzling Tales

1   Around the world, people like to tell and hear stories. We especially like stories that give us puzzles to solve. Puzzling stories satisfy our natural curiosity .[1] For centuries, in many different cultures such tales have been told. Often, these
5   stories become <u>folktales</u>. Folktales are stories that usually have a message. They appeal to young and old alike. They are passed down orally from one generation to the next.

Use the Clues A:

- Read lines 1–7.

- Reread the underlined word, **folktales**.

- Check the boxes that define the underlined word. What does the word **folktales** mean in this context?

    ❏ a tale told by folks

    ❏ a true story about people

    ❏ a legend or story forming part of an oral tradition

- Highlight the context clues that helped you choose your answer(s).

Today, modern mystery writers <u>puzzle</u> us with their stories. A mystery story presents us with some kind of
10 confusing event. At the beginning of the mystery, we don't know what made the event happen. We read the mystery for clues. The clues often reveal the truth. From ancient times until today, we love stories that puzzle us.

Four <u>puzzling</u> tales follow. The challenge is to figure
15 out what happened and how it happened. Each story is different. Visualize [2] the characters. Imagine the settings.

---

[1] **curiosity:** desire to know or learn

[2] **Visualize:** to imagine

(continued)

Text Connection 7 (continued)

Think about the events. Listen and read each story carefully. Look for the clues that will help you solve each puzzle!
3

> **Use the Clues B:**
>
> • Read lines 8–19. Think about the function of the underlined words.
>
> • Reread the underlined words: 1) **puzzle**, 2) **puzzling**, and 3) **puzzle**.
>
> • Use context clues to match each word with its definition.
>
> | | |
> |---|---|
> | 1) puzzle | a) a game or problem to solve |
> | 2) puzzling | b) to confuse or baffle |
> | 3) puzzle | c) confusing or baffling |

20 **1. THE STICKS OF TRUTH—A Tale From India**

Long ago in India, judges traveled from village to village. One day, a judge stopped at an inn to rest. The innkeeper who greeted the judge was very upset. Someone had just that day stolen his daughter's gold ring. The judge told the
25 innkeeper not to worry because he would find out who the thief was. The judge had all the guests gather in one room so that he could question them. Their answers to his questions did not reveal the thief, so the judge decided to use some old magic. He told all the guests he was going to give them the
30 sticks of truth.

"These are magic sticks," he explained, "that will catch the thief."

He kept a stick for himself and gave each guest a stick to keep under the bed during the night.
35 "The stick belonging to the thief will grow two inches during the night. At breakfast we will compare sticks, and the longest stick will be the thief's."

The next morning the judge had the guests assemble at his table and hold their sticks up to his to see if the sticks
40 had increased in length. But one after another, the sticks were the same length.

Setting:

_____
_____
_____
_____

Characters:

_____
_____
_____
_____

Problem:

_____
_____
_____
_____

(continued)

Unit 22

Setting:

_____

_____

_____

_____

Characters:

_____

_____

_____

_____

Problem:

_____

_____

_____

_____

At last, there was only one woman left to show her magic stick. She held her stick carefully up to the judge's stick. The judge looked at it and then called out, "This is the thief! Her
45 stick is shorter than all the rest."

Once caught, the woman confessed ³ she was the thief and returned the ring. But all the guests were confused about the sticks of truth. The judge had said the longest stick would belong to the thief, but instead she had the shortest stick.
50 Why?

Solution: The thief, worried about being caught, cut off two inches of her stick during the night in an effort to hide its growth. But since the sticks were not magical, her stick was the only short one.

Find It: Prepositional Phrases in Text

Locate the numbered sentences. Find and underline the prepositional phrases and circle the prepositions in each sentence.

55 2. **THE CLEVEREST SON—A Tale From Ethiopia**

Once there lived an old man who had three sons.
1 When he grew old and ill and knew that he soon would die, he gathered his three sons in his room.

"There is no way I can divide the house and farm to
60 support all three of you. The one who proves himself the cleverest will inherit ⁴ the house and farm. 2 There is a coin on the table for each of you. The one who can buy something that will fill this room will inherit all I own."

3 The eldest son took his coin, went straight to the
65 marketplace, and filled his wagon full of straw. 4 The second son thought a bit longer and then also went to the marketplace, where he bought sacks and sacks of feathers. 5 The youngest son thought and then quietly went to a little shop. 6 He bought two small things and tucked them into his pocket.

---

³ **confessed:** admitted; disclosed

⁴ **inherit:** to receive something from an ancestor

(continued)

70   That night the father asked his sons to show him what they had bought. **7** The eldest son spread his straw on the floor, but it filled only a portion of the room. The second son dumped out his sacks of feathers, but they filled only two corners of the room. **8** Then the youngest son smiled, pulled

75 the two small things out of his pocket and filled the room with them from corner to corner.

    "Yes," said the father, "you are indeed the cleverest and have filled my room when the others could not. You shall inherit my house and farm."

80   What had the youngest son bought and with what did he fill the room?

Solution: He bought a match and a candle and filled the room with light.

3. WHICH FLOWER?—A Tale From the Middle East

85   Once long ago there lived two rulers named the Queen of Sheba and King Solomon. They were from different lands and were both famed for their wisdom. King Solomon paid a visit to the Queen of Sheba, and she decided to test King Solomon's wisdom by a series of tests and riddles. He passed

90 each one with ease until she led him to a room filled with flowers of every shape and color. The queen had directed the finest craftsmen and magicians in her land to construct [5] the flowers so that they looked exactly like the real flowers from her garden.

95   "The test," she told King Solomon, "is to find the one real flower among all the artificial [6] ones."

    King Solomon carefully looked from flower to flower and back again, searching for even the smallest of differences. He looked for any sign of wilted leaves or petals but found

100 lifelike leaves and petals on every flower. And fragrance was no help, because the room was filled with fragrances.

Setting:

_____

_____

_____

Characters:

_____

_____

_____

Problem:

_____

_____

_____

---

[5] **construct:** to put together; assemble

[6] **artificial:** man-made; not natural

(continued)

Unit 22

Setting:

_____

_____

_____

_____

Characters:

_____

_____

_____

_____

_____

Problem:

_____

_____

_____

_____

"Please," said King Solomon. "This room is so warm. Could we open the curtains and let in the breeze? The fresh air will help me think more clearly."

105   The Queen of Sheba agreed. Within minutes after the curtains were opened, King Solomon leaned over, picked the one real flower, and handed it to the queen.

How did he discover it?

110   **Solution:** A bee flew in the window and immediately went to the real flower.

4. **LOVE AND PUMPKINS—A Tale From the Philippines**

When the king announced he was going to marry, stories of the bride quickly spread through the palace.

"She's beautiful," said one servant.

115   "With the voice of a bird," said another.

"More than that," said the third. "She can do anything! When the king dared her to get a large pumpkin inside a narrow-necked jar without cutting the pumpkin or breaking the jar, she did it. My cousin was there when the king broke

120 open the jar."

"That's impossible. Your cousin tells lies," said a servant just joining the group.

"No, it's true," said another. "I heard the king announce it myself."

125   How did the bride do it?

Solution: Since the king did not say she had to start with a large pumpkin, the bride placed a tiny pumpkin inside the jar, then let it grow while it was attached to the vine.

Tales reprinted from *Stories to Solve: Folktales from Around the World* by George Shannon.

The Disappearing Man

by Isaac Asimov

Take Note

Underline clues that helped Larry identify the thief. Paraphrase those clues in the spaces provided.

1 I'm not often on the spot when Dad's on one of his cases, but I couldn't help it this time.

I was coming home from the library that afternoon, when a man dashed by me and ran full speed into an alley between
5 two buildings. It was rather late, and I figured the best thing to do was to keep on moving toward home. Dad says a nosy fourteen-year-old isn't likely to make it to fifteen.

But in less than a minute, two policemen came running. I didn't wait for them to ask. "He went in there," I said.

10 One of them rushed in, came out, and shouted, "There's a door open. He went inside. Go 'round to the front."

They must have given the alarm, because in a few minutes, three police cars drove up, there were <u>plainclothesmen</u> on the scene, and the building was surrounded.

Use the Clues A:

- Read lines 12–14

- Reread the underlined word, **plainclothesmen**.

- Check the box that best defines the underlined word. What does the word **plainclothesmen** mean in this context?

  ❏ civilians in plain clothes

  ❏ police officers in street clothes

  ❏ off-duty police officers

- How did you choose this answer?

  _____

  _____

  _____

15 I knew I shouldn't be hanging around. Innocent bystanders get in the way of the police. Just the same, I was

(continued)

there when it started and, from what I heard the police saying, I knew they were after this man, Stockton. He was a loner [1] who'd pulled off some pretty spectacular jewel
20 robberies over the last few months. I knew about it because Dad is a detective on the force, and he was on the case.

"Slippery fellow," he said, "but when you work alone, there's no one to double-cross you."

I said, "Doesn't he have to work with someone, Dad? He's
25 got to have a <u>fence</u>—someone to peddle [2] the jewels."

Use the Clues B:

- Read lines 22–25
- Reread the underlined word, **fence**.
- Check the box that best defines the underlined word. What does the word **fence** mean in this context?
  - ❏ to defend
  - ❏ a barrier to mark boundaries
  - ❏ someone who buys and sells stolen goods
- How did you choose this answer?

_____

_____

_____

"If he has," said Dad, "we haven't located him. And why don't you get on with your homework?" (He always says that when he thinks I'm getting too interested in his cases.)

Well, they had him now. Some jeweler must have pushed
30 the alarm button.

The alley he ran into was closed on all sides but the street, and he hadn't come out. There was a door there that was open, so he must have gone in. The police had the possible exits guarded. They even had a couple of men on the roof.

Clue:

_____

_____

_____

_____

---

[1] **loner:** a person who prefers to be alone

[2] **peddle:** to sell things

(continued)

Text Connection 8 (continued)

35   I was just beginning to wonder if Dad would be involved, when another car came up, and he got out. First thing he saw me and stopped dead. "Larry! What are you doing here?"

    "I was on the spot, Dad. Stockton ran past me into the alley."

40   "Well, get out of here. There's liable [3] to be shooting."

    I backed away, but I didn't back off all the way. Once my father went into the building, I got into his car. The driver knew me, and he said, "You better go home, Larry. I'm going to have to help with the search, so I can't stay here to keep an 45 eye on you."

    "Sure, you go on," I said. "I'll be leaving in a minute." But I didn't. I wanted to do some thinking first.

    Nobody leaves doors open in New York City. If that door into the alley was open, Stockton must have opened it. That 50 meant he had to have a key; there wasn't time to pick the lock. That must mean he worked out of that building.

Clue:

_____

_____

_____

_____

Identify It: Predicate Nominative, Predicate Adjective, or Direct Object

Read the underlined sections of each numbered sentences.

Identify the verb.

Label the words that come after the verb as predicate nominative (PN), predicate adjective (PA), or direct object (DO).

    I looked at the building. 1 <u>It was an old one</u>, four stories high. 2 <u>It had small businesses in it</u>, and you could still see the painted signs in the windows in the fading light.

55   On the second-floor window, it said, "Klein and Levy, Tailors." Above that was a theatrical costumer ,[4] and on the top floor was a jeweler's. That jeweler's made sense out of it.

    If Stockton had a key to the building, he probably worked with that jeweler. Dad would figure all that out.

Clue:

_____

_____

_____

_____

---

[3] **liable:** likely; probably going to

[4] **costumer:** a person who makes costumes

(continued)

60   I waited for the sound of shots, pretty scared Dad might get hurt. But nothing happened. Maybe Stockton would see he was cornered and just give in. I hoped so. At least they didn't have to evacuate the building. Late on Saturday, I supposed it would be deserted .[5]

65   After a while, I got tired of waiting. <u>3</u> <u>I chose a moment</u> when no policemen were looking and moved quickly to the building entrance. <u>4</u> Dad would be hopping mad when he saw me, but <u>I was curious</u>. I figured they had Stockton, and I wanted to see him.

70   They didn't have him.

    There was a fat man in a vest in the lobby. He looked scared, and I guess he was the watchman. He kept saying, "I didn't see *anybody*."

    Policemen were coming down the stairs and out of the
75 old elevator, all shaking their heads.

    <u>5</u> <u>My father was pretty angry</u>. He said, "No one has anything?"

    A police sergeant said, "Donovan said no one got out on the roof. All the doors and windows are covered."

80   "If he didn't get out," said my father, in a low voice that carried, "then he's in the building."

    "We can't find him," said the sergeant. "He's nowhere inside."

    My father said, "It isn't a big building—"

    "We had the watchman's keys. We've looked everywhere."

85   "Then how do we know he went into the building in the first place? Who saw him go in?"

    There was a silence. A lot of policemen were milling [6] about the lobby now, but no one said anything. So I spoke up. "I did, Dad."

90   Dad whirled and looked at me and made a funny sound in the back of his throat that meant I was in for it for still being there. "You said you saw him run into the alley," he said. "That's not the same thing."

    "He didn't come out, Dad. There was no place else for him
95 to go."

---

[5] **deserted:** left empty; abandoned

[6] **milling:** moving around randomly; wandering

(continued)

"But you didn't actually see him go in, did you?"

"He couldn't go up the side of the buildings. There wouldn't have been time for him to reach the roof before the police—"

But Dad wasn't listening. "Did *anyone* actually see him
100 go in?"

Of course no one said anything, and I could see my father was going to call the whole thing off, and then when he got me home I was going to get the talking-to of my life.

The thought of that talking-to must have stimulated
105 my brain, I guess. I looked about the lobby desperately, and said, "But, Dad, he *did* go into the building, and he didn't disappear. There he is right now. That man there." I pointed, and then I dropped down and rolled out of the way.

There wasn't any shooting. The man I pointed to was
110 close to the door—he must have been edging toward it— and now he made a dash for it. He almost made it, but a policeman who had been knocked down grabbed his leg and then everyone piled on him. Later they had the jeweler, too.

I went home after Stockton was caught, and when my
115 father got home much later, he did have some things to say about my risking my life. But he also said, "You got onto that theatrical costume bit very nicely, Larry."

I said, "Well, I was sure he went into the building and was familiar with it. He could get into the costumer's if he had to,
120 and they would be bound to have policemen's uniforms. I figured if he could dump his jacket and pants and get into a policeman's uniform quickly, he could just walk out of the building."

Dad said, "You're right. Even after he got outside, he could pretend he was dealing with the crowd and then just walk away."

125 Mom said, "But how did you know which policeman it was, Larry? Don't tell me you know every policeman by sight."

"I didn't have to, Mom," I said. "I figured if he got a policeman's uniform at the costumer's, he had to work fast and grab any one he saw. And they wouldn't have much of
130 an assortment of sizes anyway. So I just looked around for a policeman whose uniform didn't fit, and when I saw one with trouser legs stopping above his ankles, I knew he was Stockton."

Clue:

_____

_____

_____

_____

Text Connection 9

Take Note

Underline words and sentences that describe the setting. Summarize the setting and identify the characters in the spaces provided.

Zaaaaaaaap!

Prologue

1   *The year is 2160. Thirteen-year old Maitn and her family are living at the end of "*<u>The Dark</u>*," a period of history when the world faced a serious energy* crisis *.[1] Many factors contributed to this dark period. Fossil fuel supplies on Earth*
5   *suddenly ran out in 2080. At the turn of the century, a severe drought in the Northern Hemisphere limited the use of hydroelectric power. Alternative energy sources—such as solar, wind, and ocean wave power—were in development but not ready for powering whole cities.*

> **Use the Clues A:**
>
> • Read lines 1–9.
>
> • Use context clues to define the underlined phrase "The Dark."
>
> • Highlight the context clues that helped you learn more about this dark period.
>
> • Describe the period called "The Dark" in your own words:
>
> _____
>
> _____
>
> _____

Setting:

_____

_____

_____

10   *To respond to the crisis, many nuclear power plants were built as quickly as possible. A massive earthquake in the Pacific Ocean in 2152 damaged nuclear power plants in several countries and exposed thousands of people to unhealthy doses of radiation. Maitn's best friend, Josha, suffers from radiation*
15   *exposure.*

_____

[1] **crisis:** an emergency

(continued)

Text Connection 9 (continued)

However, this time period has not been all dark. Scientists
have made advances in medical research as a result of a
whole new field of study called "organic engineering." Organic [2]
engineering of some kinds of fruit has raised the hope of
20 finding a cure for radiation sickness and some types of cancer.
This cure is still being tested, however, and is not ready for
public use.

A major breakthrough in energy generation has also
made it possible to harness the power of lightning. The
25 system isn't perfect, but, overall, it seems to be much safer
than nuclear power. But watch out when a lightning storm
comes!

Use the Clues B:

- Read lines 23–27.

- Reread the underlined word **harness**.

- Check the box that best defines the underlined
  word in this context.

  ❏ to make use of

  ❏ leather straps

  ❏ to avoid

---

[2] **organic:** produced from living things

(continued)

Text Connection 9 (continued)

Characters:

_____

_____

_____

Zaaaaaaaap!

Maitn shimmied up the branches of the pear tree, her
feet feeling for a firm hold. She saw what she was looking for
30 almost ten feet farther above. The fruit glimmered huge and
welcoming, a feat of organic engineering, and the world's
next miracle cure.

The pear was for Josha, so the fact that picking it from the
tree was illegal meant little to her. Josha was close enough
35 to be family. He had been getting weaker. On his last trip to
the clinic, the doctor had told his family that his exposure to
radiation eight years earlier was slowly killing him. Josha had
been visiting a friend near the Powell Nuclear Power Plant
when the accident happened. The earthquake damaged the
40 plant's cooling system, and the radiation leak made many
people in the area sick, including Josha. Ironically, both of
his parents now worked at the same plant although no power
had been produced by it since the accident. Josha's parents
were part of a team responsible for assisting in the cleanup
45 after the nuclear accident.

Lost in thought, Maitn didn't see the cracked branch
above her. As her left hand went to grasp it, the branch split,
and she skittered almost halfway down the trunk. Intent
on her goal, Maitn deftly [3] climbed back up to the pear. She
50 picked the ripened fruit off the branch and dropped it into
the duffel bag that hung at her side.

The task complete, she sighed and looked off to the west.
There was a storm brewing; the clouds on the horizon hung
dark and heavy. In the distance, she could see the flashes that
55 could only be lightning. The lightning meant that her Mom
would be working this evening. Her Mom had a job at the
new Lightning Power Corral.

Maitn looked toward the lightning corral that was right
next to the experimental orchard. It consisted of a huge web
60 of thin metal wires. Thousands of thin metal wires connected

---

[3] **deftly:** skillfully; quickly

(continued)

to the web were lifted into the sky. The wires were held up by small weather balloons that sent meteorological data to the power plant operators on the ground. Just before the lightning was right above the <u>corral</u>, Maitn's mother would
65 flip the vacuum switch. The energy from the lightning bolts would funnel down the wires to be stored in giant batteries, and then doled out and shipped to the surrounding counties.

Use the Clues C:

- Read lines 52–67.

- Reread the underlined word **corral**.

- Check the box that best defines the underlined word in this context.

  ❏ a fenced-in place for animals

  ❏ a web of wires designed to capture energy from lightning

  ❏ a container

"Hey!" a voice yelled.

Maitn glanced down. It was her brother, Mriel.
70 "Get down from there! A storm is coming!"

Maitn let gravity take her down the branches until she hung just five feet above the ground. Then she dropped and dusted off her pants.

"What're you doing? Trying to get killed?"
75 Maitn pointed to the duffel bag. "For Josha."

Mriel let out a sound that was half smug, half aggravated .[4]

"That won't do him any good. Don't you know that radiation poisoning is irreversible [5]?"

"I know that," Maitn said, shuffling her feet. "But at least
80 he'll have some hope. At least that's something he can hold on to."

---

[4] **aggravated:** irritated; annoyed

[5] **irreversible:** not able to be changed; permanent

(continued)

"You're a saint, you know that? Come on, Mom's getting ready to go to work, and she said she has permission for us to go with her and watch."

85 They made it home just before the warning siren sounded. It reverberated [6] off the buildings surrounding the corral. A friendly voice advised them, "Stay indoors or don a rubber suit. Leave all electrical appliances on standby for the duration of the storm."

90 Mom was leaving the house. Maitn and Mriel ran after her. The three of them mounted the four-seater trike and pedaled to the corral. The wind started picking up as they neared Demante Avenue, and now it blew dust in their eyes and rustled in their jackets.

95 Her mother used a key card to get into power plant next to the corral. Mriel followed closely behind her, but Maitn stopped and turned. Her eyes fell on a same pear tree she had climbed earlier that bordered the station. As they were pedaling, she thought she had seen someone in that tree.

100 "Mom!" she shouted, above the wind.

But Mom and Mriel were now locked inside the power plant. As a safety precaution, the doors locked automatically when a storm was very close.

The flashes of lightning grew brighter. The clouds loomed 105 darker overhead. It wouldn't be long before her Mom had to activate the switch so that the storm's energy was sucked down into the power corral.

Maitn ran over to the tree and strained to see through the wind-whipped branches. There was someone up there, 110 all right, and it didn't take long to see who it was. Quickly, Maitn climbed up the tree.

"My sleeve is stuck!" Josha yelled when he saw her.

Identify It: Quotations in Text

- Reread the text, lines 68–112.
- Decide who is speaking in each line where there is dialogue.
- Write the speaker's name beside the line.

[6] **reverberated:** echoed

(continued)

His eyes were sunken and his face was pale, but in his hands he held a pear even larger than the one Maitn had picked.

115 "Great minds think alike," she muttered.

Josha started to speak, but she waved him to be quiet. She had heard a sound that made her stomach lurch. It was the loud hum of the vacuum switching on. In less than a minute, more than a billion volts of electricity would be spewing

120 through the atmosphere, striking the spider web's wires helter-skelter. Though not many volts would stray, some would, and a tree 40 feet tall would be a great bull's-eye.

Maitn climbed above Josha and ripped his jacket loose from the branch that held it tight.

125 "Hurry up!" she screamed, pulling at him as she went down. Another flash of lightning lit up the sky and painted spots in front of her eyes. As her heart pounded in her throat, she jumped from the tree, pulling Josha with her.

Their landing was rough, but necessity jerked them

130 instantly to their feet. Suddenly, the air changed texture. The hairs on the back of Maitn's neck stood on end. It was coming. The incredible power was coming.

The pair ran as fast as they could, the sound of crackling electricity filling their ears. They spotted a concrete drainage

135 pipe 20 yards from the tree, and dived into it. They lay there while the storm crashed around them, breathing heavily and watching the spectacular fireworks as the corral collected the lightning's power.

Then, after what seemed like an eternity, the storm

140 moved on, and the hum of the wires died down. The plant's workers emerged to inspect the corral. The captured energy would soon be transported to the hundreds of thousands of people in the state who needed it.

Josha took a huge bite from his prize pear, and offered one

145 to Maitn, his way of thanking her for his rescue. She took the bite willingly, and tucked her smaller pear into his pocket for later. Energized by the power of hope, the two headed home.

Adapted from "Zaaaaaaaap!" By Jennifer A. Ratliff

Problem:

_____

_____

_____

Unit 23

Take Note

Summarize the important events of the story in the spaces provided.

Satyagraha: Power for Change

by Alden R. Carter

1   Ramdas Bahave met me at the sidelines. "In what part of the body are you wounded, Kenneth?" he asked.

"Hand," I gritted.

"The smallest finger again?"

5   "Yeah."

"Let me see it, please."

I held out my right hand, the <u>dislocated</u> little finger already twice normal size and rapidly turning purple.

Rollin Acres, my best buddy and the team's fullback,
10 made a barfing sound. "Jeez, I wish you'd stop messing up that finger, Ken. It's disgusting."

Use the Clues A:

- Read lines 7–11.

- Reread the underlined word **dislocated**.

- Use the context and what you know about the meaning of the prefix to determine its meaning.

- Check the box that best defines the underlined word. What does the word **dislocated** mean in this context?

  ❑ lost

  ❑ put out of position or location

  ❑ broken

(continued)

"Just watch the game, Rollin."

"Sure. But, you know, if you had a little more <u>vertical</u> you could catch a pass like that."

15   "I've got more <u>vertical</u> than you do."

"You're supposed to. You're a tight end. Who ever heard of a fullback with vertical leap?"

Use the Clues B:

- Read lines 12–17.

- Reread the underlined word **vertical**.

- Check the box that best defines the underlined word in this context.
  What does Rollin wish that Ken could do?

  ❑ grow taller

  ❑ throw better

  ❑ jump higher

Ramdas interrupted. "Would you like me to correct this problem now?"

20   "Yeah, do it," I said.

Ramdas took my pinkie in his strong, slender fingers and pulled. Pain shot up my arm and my eyes teared. Dang! This time he really was going to pull it out by the roots. Then there was a pop and sudden easing of the pain. He felt gently

25 along the joint. "It is back in place. Are you all right? Feel faint, perhaps?"

"I'm okay. Just tape me up and get me back in."

He made a disapproving sound but started buddy-taping my pinkie and ring fingers. Out on the field we'd covered the

30 punt and held Gentry High to four yards on two running plays. Still time to win if we could hold them on third down. "Come on, Patch," I yelled. "Now's the time."

"Please hold your hand still, Kenneth," Ramdas said.

(continued)

The Gentry quarterback dropped back to pass as Bill
35 Patchett, our all-conference defensive end, bull-rushed their
left tackle. Bill slung the kid aside, leaped a shot at his ankles
by the fullback, and buried the quarterback. The ball popped
loose and Bill dove on it, but the ref signaled no fumble,
down by contact. Bill jumped up and started yelling at the
40 ref, but a couple of the other seniors pulled him away before
he got a flag.

Ramdas handed me a bag of ice. "Here. Sit down. Rest."

"I can't sit down. We're getting the ball back."

While Gentry set up to punt, Coach Carlson strolled
45 down the line to me. "Finger again?"

"Yes, sir."

"Can you play?"

"Yes, sir."

Coach looked at Ramdas, who shrugged. "It is a dislocation
50 like the other times. I think he should keep ice on it."

Coach looked at me. "Right hand?"

I nodded.

"Hard for you to hold on to a football, then. I'll put in
Masanz."

55 So that was it for me for that game. We got the ball back
on our thirty with two minutes to go. Marvin Katt, our
quarterback, got two quick completions against their prevent
defense but couldn't connect on the big pass downfield. Final
score: 16–10. Yet another loss for ol' Argyle High.

60 . Bill Patchett spent his usual five minutes bashing his fists,
forearms, and head into lockers. At six four, 240, that's a lot
of frustration on the loose, and the rest of us stayed out of his
way. "Hey, Bauer," he yelled at me. "Where were you on that
last series?"

65 I held up my bandaged hand. "Dislocated a finger."

"And so little doc Ramdas wouldn't let you play, huh?"

"It wasn't like that, Bill."

Event:

_____

_____

_____

_____

_____

Event:

_____

_____

_____

_____

_____

(continued)

He didn't listen. Instead he grabbed a roll of tape and
fired it at Ramdas, who was straightening up the training
70 room, his back to us. The roll of tape flew through the open
door and did a three-cushion bank shot around the room.
Ramdas jumped out of the way and looked at us in confusion.

"Hey, Ramboy!" Bill yelled. "Your job is to get people back
in, not keep them out!"

75 Ramdas didn't answer, only stared. That just made Bill
madder, and he started for the door, fists balled. "The idea is
to win. No matter what it costs. So unless a guy's got an arm
ripped off, you get him back in!"

Rollin stepped in front of him. "Come on, Bill. We all feel
80 terrible about losing. You played—"

"He doesn't feel terrible! He doesn't care one way or the
other as long as he gets to play with his bandages and his ice
packs."

"Yeah, yeah, sure, Bill," Rollin said. "Just let it alone now.
85 Go take a shower. You'll feel better."

Bill stalked [1] back to his corner, smashing another locker
door, and started pulling off his uniform.

I got into the passenger seat of the Toyota pickup piloted
by my liberated ,[2] non-committed, female friend, Sarah
90 Landwehr. (You can call her my girlfriend if you've got the
guts. I don't.) "Tough loss," Sarah said.

"Aren't they all? A couple more, and we'll have to start
replacing lockers."

"Billy Patchett took it out on poor, defenseless inanimate [3]
95 objects again, huh?"

"Yep. He got after Ramdas too. Rollin broke it up."

"What's with Bill, anyway? It's not Ramdas's fault you
guys lost."

---

[1] **stalked:** walked in an angry way

[2] **liberated:** independent; freed from influence or control by others

[3] **inanimate:** lifeless; nonliving

(continued)

Event:

_____

_____

_____

_____

_____

"Well, Ramdas would rather sit a guy down than risk
100 making an injury worse. Bill doesn't think that's the way to
win football games."

Sarah snorted. "So he thinks you should risk permanent
injury just to win a stupid game?"

"Something like that. Let's go to Mac's. I'm hungry." I
105 started fiddling with the radio dial, hoping she'd let the
subject drop.

She didn't, which is pretty typical of her. "I still don't get
it. There's got to be more to it than that."

I sighed. How to explain? "Ramdas doesn't seem to care
110 if we win or lose. And that drives Bill nuts. I mean, look at
it from his standpoint. Here he is, the best player on a lousy
team. He's been all-conference, but he could have been all-
state if he'd played in a winning program. And all-state
means a scholarship and the chance to play for a Division
115 One or a Division Two school. All-conference doesn't
guarantee anything."

"None of that justifies [4] being mean to Ramdas."

"No, but it explains it a little."

She harrumphed, unimpressed. "So what's going to
120 happen next? Is Bill going to start punching him?"

"I don't think it'll come to that."

"Well, I think it might! And I think you'd better do
something about it, *team captain*."

"Only one of four."
125 "Still—"

"I know, I know. I'll keep an eye on things."

She glared at me. "You should do a heck of a lot more
than that, Kenny."

Maybe she was right, but I didn't plan on doing anything.
130 If Ramdas felt there was a big problem, he should go to
Coach Carlson. Me, I was going to ignore the whole thing as
long as possible.

---

[4] **justifies:** explains; gives reasons for

(continued)

We didn't have practice Monday, and I didn't see anything of Ramdas or Bill until Tuesday morning. Rollin and I were
135 coming down the east corridor maybe twenty feet behind Bill when Ramdas turned the corner. Bill took a step to his left and put a shoulder into him. Ramdas bounced off the lockers, skidded on the slippery floor, and only just managed to keep his balance. Bill didn't even look back.

140   "Oh-oh," I said. "I hope Bill doesn't make a habit of that."

    "He already has," Rollin said. "Started yesterday morning. Every time he sees Ramdas, *wham*, into the lockers."

    "Wow, did you say anything to him?"

    "To Bill?"

145   "Yeah."

    "I said something. Asked him why. He says he's gonna get Ramdas's attention one way or another."

    "I don't think getting his attention is the problem."

    "Neither do I, but are you going to argue with someone as
150 big and ornery as Billy Patch?"

    No, and it wouldn't do any good if I did. Besides, I had a couple questions of my own for Ramdas.

    At noon I found him sitting by himself in the cafeteria, a textbook open beside his tray. I sat down across from him.
155 "Hey, Ram," I said.

    "Hello, Kenneth." He marked his place, closed the book, and looked at me expectantly.

    "Why do you always use people's full names?"

    He smiled, shrugged slightly. "I like their sound. I do not
160 like to use contractions either. I like the full words."

    "It makes you sound like a professor or something."

Event:

_____

_____

_____

_____

_____

(continued)

"Sorry."

"Uh, well, not a problem. But, look, you've got to do something about this thing between you and Bill Patchett."

Identify It: Quotations in Text

- Reread the text, lines 140–164.
- Determine who is speaking in each line where there is dialogue.
- Write the speaker's name beside the line.

---

165   "What would you suggest?"

"For starters you could act like you care if the team wins or loses."

"But I do not care. Football is a lot of pointless violence as far as I can see."

170   "Then why'd you volunteer to be a trainer?"

"To help with the wounded."

I shook my head. "Well, maybe you could at least stop being so passive about everything."

He laughed. "You would have me fight William 175 Patchett?"

"Well, not exactly, but—"

"Because I will not fight. It goes against everything I believe."

"I don't expect you to fight him, but you can stand up to 180 him in other ways."

"But I am."

"How's that?"

"By not reacting with force. Force is never justified."

"Well, maybe not in this case, but—"

185   "No, Kenneth, in all cases. Never, no matter how good the cause."

"Oh, come on. How else are we supposed to keep other people or other countries from taking what's ours? Sometimes you've got to use force."

(continued)

190   He sighed. "I guess that is what a lot of you Americans believe. But I believe that you can resist [5] in another way. Mahatma Gandhi called it *satyagraha*, to stand firmly for truth and love without ever resorting to force."

Use the Clues C:

- Read lines 174–193.
- Reread the underlined word **satyagraha**.
- Use meaning signals to define the underlined word, **satyagraha**.
- Circle the meaning signal and underline the context clues.
- Define **satyagraha** in your own words:

    _____

    _____

    _____

    I stared at him in disbelief. I mean, Bill was about to turn
195 him into a smear of jelly and Ramdas was talking about some dead holy man! "Well, that may be very cool, Ram, but—"

    "You have heard of Gandhi, have you not?"

    "Sure. I mean, the name, anyway. And I'd love to hear more. But right now I think you'd better tell me what you're
200 planning to do about Bill Patchett."

    "I am telling you. The Mahatma used *satyagraha* to free all of India from the British. I think I can use it to control Mr. William Patchett."

    Oh, sure. But I bet Gandhi never had to face down six foot
205 four, 240 pounds of crazed defensive end. "Ram, listen—"

    He interrupted gently. "Let me tell you a story. Under British rule it was illegal for Indians to make their own salt. Everyone had to buy expensive government salt, and that was very hard on the poor. Three thousand of the

Event:

_____

_____

_____

_____

_____

---

[5] **resist:** oppose; be against

(continued)

210 Mahatma's followers went to protest the law at a place called the Dharasana Salt Works. They stepped four at a time up to a line of soldiers, never lifting a hand to defend themselves, and let the soldiers beat them down with bamboo clubs. Those who could got up and went to the back of the line. All

215 day they marched up to the soldiers until the soldiers were so tired they could not lift their arms."

"What did that prove?"

"It proved that the Mahatma's followers were willing to suffer for what they believed without doing hurt to others.

220 Their example brought hundreds of thousands of new recruits to the struggle for independence. Eventually, the jails were full and the country did not work anymore and the British had to leave."

It was my turn to sigh, because this had gotten a long

225 way from football or figuring out a way to keep Bill from turning Ramdas into an ooze of pink on a locker door. "Look, Ramdas, that might have worked in India, but in this country—"

"Your Martin Luther King made it work in this country."

230 "Okay, point taken, but what are you going to do about Bill?"

"Just what I am doing. I am going to answer his violence with *satyagraha*. Someday, his arms will get tired."

"If he doesn't kill you first."

235 Ramdas smiled faintly. "There is always a risk."

Ramdas didn't get it. OK, he was Indian, had moved here with his family only a couple of years ago. But somehow he must have gotten this *satyagraha* thing wrong. No way could it work. During study hall I went to the library, figuring I

240 could find something that would prove it to him. All the Internet computers were busy, so I went to the shelves. I found a thick book with a lot of photographs of Gandhi and sat down to page through it. And . . . it . . . blew . . . me . . .

(continued)

Event:

away. Here was this skinny little guy with thick glasses and
245 big ears wandering around in sandals and a loincloth, and
he'd won! And I mean big time: freed his country without
ever lifting his hand against anybody. Incredible.

Now, I'm not the kind who tosses and turns half the night
worrying about things. I'm a jock. I need my sleep. When I
250 hit the pillow, bam, I'm gone. But that night I lay thinking
until well past midnight. Hadn't Jesus said to turn the other
cheek? Ramdas was living that, and he was a Hindu or
something, while most of the guys I saw in church on Sunday
would prefer to beat the other guy to a pulp. Man, oh, man,
255 I didn't need this. Let Sarah and Ramdas talk philosophy; I
was just a jock. But like it or not, I was going to have to do
something or feel like a hypocrite [6] forever.

Wednesday morning I went to see Coach Carlson with
my plan. He didn't like it. "Look, I'll get Patchett's attention,"
260 he said. "I'll tell him to quit giving Ramdas a hard time."
"Coach, I really want to do this. For a lot of reasons."
We talked some more and he finally agreed, though he
still didn't like it much.
Next I talked to Rollin. He shook his head. "Man, you
265 could get hurt. And I mean *bad*."
"I'll take that chance. Just tell the other guys not to step
in. And if Ramdas starts, you stop him."
Finally, I told Sarah. She studied me for a long minute.
"You're not really doing this for Ramdas, are you?"
270 "I'm not sure."
"Can I shoot Bill with a tranquilizer dart if things get out
of hand?"
"I guess that wouldn't be too bad an idea. But I don't
think they will. He's big, but I'm pretty big too."

275 Bill Patchett takes everything seriously, which makes it
all the scarier practicing against him. Bill is, by the way, not a

---

[6] **hypocrite:** a person who claims to believe one way, but acts
differently

(continued)

Event:

_____

_____

_____

_____

_____

moron. He maintains a 4.0 in a full load of honors classes and is the only kid in school with the guts to carry a briefcase. On the football field, he studies an opponent, figures out his
280 moves, and then pancakes him or blows by him. Believe me, I know; I've been practicing against him for years. But as I'd reminded Sarah, I'm big too, and I'd seen all his moves.

We lined up for pass rushing/blocking drill. The center hiked the ball to Marvin Katt, who was back in the shotgun.
285 Billy Patch hit me with a straight bull rush. I took it, letting him run over me. When I got up and took my stance for the next play, he gave me a funny look. "Ready this time?"

"Yep," I said, and set my feet to make it just as hard as possible for him.
290 Cat Man yelled, "Hut, Hut, HUT!" and there was the familiar crash of helmets and shoulder pads. Bill hit me so hard my teeth rattled. Every instinct told me to bring up my arms to defend myself, but I just took the hit. I landed flat on my back, the air whooshing out of my lungs.
295 He glared down at me. "C'mon, Bauer. Get with the program, huh?"

He must have figured I was trying to sucker him, because the third time he took a step to the right, as if he expected me to come at him hard. Instead, I took a step to my left to
300 get in front of him and let him run me down.

After that play he didn't talk and he didn't try to go around me. He just came at me as hard as he could. After a while the other players stopped practicing and just watched. Cat Man would yell, "Hut, Hut, HUT!" and the same thing
305 would happen again. I lost count how many times Bill decked me. Finally, he hit me so hard my ears rang and the back of my helmet bounced two or three times on the turf. I just lay there, almost too stunned to move, as he stalked off toward the locker room. But it wasn't quite enough. Not yet.

(continued)

310 Somehow I managed to stumble to my feet. "Hey, Bill
I can still stand, Bill. Can still stand up to you." He turned
and came at me with a roar. And it was the hardest thing I'd
ever done in my life to take that hit without trying to protect
myself. He hit me with every ounce of his 240, drove me into
315 the turf, and the world flashed black and then back to light.

We lay a yard apart, panting. "Okay," he gasped. "I give
up. What's this all about?"

"It's about standing up without fighting back."

"Don't give me puzzles, man. I'm too tired."

320 "It's about Ramdas. He doesn't want to fight."

"The little weasel should stand up for himself."

"He is, just like I did now. He calls it *satyagraha*. I don't
know if I'm even pronouncing it right, but it means standing
firm without using force. He won't fight no matter what you
325 do."

"That's dumb."

"It's what he believes. I think he's got a right to that."

We sat up, still breathing hard. Bill took off his helmet
and wiped sweat from his face. "You were driving me crazy.
330 This was harder than a game. I'm whipped."

I took a breath. "Ramdas told me a story." I told him
about the three thousand guys who'd walked up to the
soldiers at the Dharasana Salt Works and let themselves get
beaten down with clubs.

335 Bill listened. "And that worked, huh?"

"Yeah, it did."

He shook his head. "I couldn't do that. I don't have the
guts." He struggled to his feet and plodded toward the
sidelines where Sarah, Ramdas, Coach Carlson, and most
340 of the team were watching. Passing Ramdas, he laid a hand
briefly on his shoulder. It wasn't much, but a start maybe.

Ramdas met me halfway to the sideline. "In what part of
the body are you wounded this time, Kenneth?"

(continued)

"All over, but nothing special."

345 "Your hand. It is all right?"

"Fine."

He hesitated. "And your spirit? How is it?"

I looked at him, saw his eyes shining with something that might have been laughter or maybe a joy I didn't quite 350 understand but thought I recognized from the old black-and-white pictures of Gandhi and his followers.

"Feeling not too bad," I said. "Not bad at all."

Dreaming the Night Away

by Judith Herbst

Take Note

Identify the main idea and supporting details of sections of the text where indicated.

1   You have been asleep for perhaps an hour. Your muscles are relaxed. Your chest rises and falls with the slow, even rhythm of your breathing. There is a calm, almost angelic expression on your face. Silence and peace surround you.
5 The clock on your dresser ticks out the minutes to showtime. Four . . . three . . . two . . . one . . .

     And suddenly the curtain is up! Your eyes are rolling back and forth, back and forth, back and forth behind your closed lids. This is it! This is REM, the amazing,
10 mysterious Rapid Eye Movement that signals a dream is in progress. You appear to be watching something, but your eyes are not looking at anything at all. Blind people also display REM.

     REM begins quite early in our development as human
15 beings. It seems to be controlled by a part of the brain called the "<u>pons</u>," which is located in the brain stem. Research has shown that as soon as the brain stem develops in the fetus, there are signs of REM.

Use the Clues A:

- Read lines 14–18.

- Reread the underlined word, **pons**. Put a box around the meaning signal. Highlight the context clues that help you define the phrase.

- Define **pons**.

_____

_____

     So it looks as though we all start dreaming even before we're
20 born, but what fetal dreams are like is anybody's guess.

     . . .back and forth, back and forth, back and forth . . .

(continued)

Unit 24

Take Note

Identify the topic, main idea, and supporting details.

Topic:

_____

_____

Main Idea:

_____

_____

_____

Supporting Details:

_____

_____

_____

_____

_____

_____

_____

Main Idea:

_____

_____

_____

_____

Supporting Details:

_____

_____

_____

_____

_____

_____

_____

        This is the dance of REM. Somewhere deep inside your mind you are <u>creating</u> a little drama for an audience of one. Your story, though, can hardly be called one of the year's
25 ten best. It's almost impossible to follow. The events are confusing and disconnected. The characters come and go for no apparent reason. The dialogue [1] doesn't make any sense. It's a mess, all right, but you don't seem to notice it. On and on you dream, accepting even the most <u>ridiculous</u>
30 situations without question, thoroughly convinced that it's all really <u>happening</u>. Furthermore, you are not just a <u>sleepy</u> member of the audience, you're a participant, and you react to everything that goes on. A <u>frightening</u> dream in particular catches you like a hook, and you actually experience fear.

Identify It: Noun, Verb, or Adjective

Read the text, beginning with line 22.

Decide if each underlined word is functioning as a noun, verb, or adjective.

Write **N** (noun), **V** (verb), or **ADJ** (adjective) above the word.

35   **OH MY GOSH!** *You're in the back of a <u>speeding</u> car and there's no <u>driver</u>! You try desperately to reach the steering wheel, but you can't move. Crazily, the car swerves off the road. The brake! You've got to reach the brake!*
        Meanwhile, back in your bedroom, your heart is
40 thundering. Your breath is <u>coming</u> in quick, shallow bursts. Beads of perspiration break out, soaking your pajamas and pasting your hair to your forehead. Your blood pressure has shot up, and the adrenaline [2] is pumping, pumping, pumping.
        Suddenly the car is on a high cliff. The speedometer
45 *needle is climbing . . . 90 . . . 100 . . . 110 . . . You can see the edge of the cliff just ahead. It's an endless drop to nowhere. Do something! DO SOMETHING!*

---

[1] **dialogue:** a conversation between two or more people

[2] **adrenaline:** the hormone produced by the body when frightened, angry, or excited

(continued)

Text Connection 11 (continued)

Your terror in this dream is very real. You are not pretending to be scared; you are scared, and all the readouts
50 in the sleep laboratories prove it. The readouts also show something else. You are almost completely paralyzed. With a few exceptions, your muscles have lost so much tone, they are literally immovable. We do indeed toss and turn and roll around quite a bit while we're sleeping but not during a
55 dream. During a dream we have about as much ability to get up and walk around as our pillow does. Scientists believe the purpose of this strange paralysis is to prevent us from acting out our dreams.

Although sleepwalkers appear to be giving a dream
60 performance, they are not. In fact, sleepwalkers are in an entirely different level of sleep. They are sound asleep but strangely mobile.[3] No one knows why some people—several million in North America alone—sleepwalk. This bizarre activity may begin at any time in a person's life and without
65 any apparent cause. Sleepwalkers are completely unaware of what they are doing and usually remain ignorant unless they are told about it. And even then, they will strenuously deny it. They'll insist they've been asleep all night, as, of course, they have. But while they've been snoozing upright, they have
70 been involved in some very strange activities.

Like fleshy robots, they will suddenly open their eyes, swing their legs over the side of the bed, and head off on some mysterious midnight errand. Talk to them and they won't answer. Wiggle your fingers in front of their eyes and
75 they won't see you. They will, however, steer their way around furniture, take the dog for a walk, do their grocery shopping, and even drive a car.

But sleepwalking is only funny in the cartoons. Some people have been injured during a walk because they
80 managed to climb out onto window ledges thinking they were stepping onto the front porch. Members of the family have been taken for intruders and attacked. It is a ridiculous myth that if you awaken a sleepwalker he or she

Main Idea:

_____

_____

_____

_____

Supporting Details:

_____

_____

_____

_____

_____

_____

_____

_____

_____

_____

---

[3] **mobile:** capable of going from one place to another

(continued)

will get lockjaw, die of a heart attack, or become paralyzed.
85 The danger, instead, lies in what the sleepwalker is doing, since these people have been known to get themselves into some pretty scary situations. Unfortunately, sleepwalking is as mysterious as dreaming, and science has not yet come up with a way to prevent a person from going on midnight
90 strolls.

Of course, sleepwalkers dream, just like everybody else, which makes for a pretty active night. They can return to bed, settle in, and slip easily into the next level of sleep. Before long, they are involved in more excitement, but this
95 time their muscles are holding them prisoner. Now they have to be content to stay put while a whole series of strange events unfolds before them in their dreams.

Sleep researcher Stephen La Berge has identified something about our dreams that most of us experience but
100 few of us are aware of. La Berge calls the phenomenon⁴ "lucid dreams." A lucid dream is one that you recognize as a dream. You almost say to yourself, "Hey! Hold on, here. This is a dream. All this stuff is fake. I'm dreaming!"

Use the Clues B:

- Read lines 98–103.

- Reread the underlined phrase **lucid dreams**. Highlight the context clues that help you define the phrase.

- Define the phrase **lucid dream**.

_____

_____

_____

La Berge believes that once we know we are dreaming,
105 we have the ability to control the outcome of the dream on a conscious⁵ level. We can change whatever we don't like. He says he has learned to alter his dreams while he's asleep,

---

⁴ **phenomenon:** a highly unusual event

⁵ **conscious:** awake; alert; aware

(continued)

110 and he can teach others to do the same. But if dreams, as they unfold naturally, are important in some way, perhaps we shouldn't be fiddling with them. Perhaps we should let nature take its course. Who knows? Maybe dreams are serving a very definite purpose, whether we remember them or not.

115 Dreams seem to be speeded-up versions of events, like a movie run in fast forward, but actually, dreamtime often parallels real time quite closely. If it takes you three seconds to open a door in real time, that's how long it will take you to open a door in your dream. The speed at which you do things in a dream is only an illusion [6] because you edit the scene. If you begin to walk across a bridge in your dream, each

120 step will match your waking steps, but you get to the other side faster than normal because you have edited out most of the steps. They are not necessary to the plot, so to speak. That's why you are able to be in a wheat field one minute and standing on a street corner the next. You simply eliminate

125 the travel time for the sake of the "real" action.

You are also able to put your dream into slow motion. You can slow down an attacking tiger to keep him from grabbing you. If you're running through deep snow, you can slow down the steps to make the event very frustrating. Why

130 you do this, however, is unclear, although it may have to do with the purpose of the dream itself.

In our lifetime we will crank out about 125,000 dreams. No one knows why. . . . Most scientists today admit that dreams are far more complex bits of mind stuff than we ever,

135 well . . . than we ever dreamed. Nature has provided us with a truly bio amazing mechanism. Now, if we could just figure out what it's for. . . .

---

[6] **illusion:** a false thought or idea

Unit 24

Take Note

In this unit you will be writing a character summary about a main character in "**Dream Team**." Use this **Text Connection** to gather the information you will need to write your character summary. Follow these steps.

1. Choose a main character to focus on. Write the character's name here:

_____

2. Underline important information about that character and his traits.

3. Summarize the information you find. Do this on the pages where you find the information.

_____

_____

_____

_____

_____

_____

_____

_____

_____

_____

_____

_____

_____

Dream Team
by Ron Jones

1   Every basketball coach hopes to encounter a "<u>benny</u>" somewhere in their coaching career. A benny is one of those special kids that come along once in a lifetime. A kid that won't leave the gym until you've turned out the lights and
5   locked the door. And after it's locked will have fourteen ways and nine friends ready to re-enter. They possess all the natural skills and instincts of a great player. A desire to work hard perfecting the most elementary moves. And work even harder to help their teammates experience success. Perhaps
10 that's the invisible quality that makes a benny. The unselfish willingness to share the art of basketball with anyone that cares to listen or participate in the game. Whatever that spirit is, it's the quality each coach looks for. It's the thing to build around and learn from. It's a winning season and
15 perhaps a lot more.

Use the Clues A:

- Read lines 1–15.

- Reread the underlined word, **benny**. Highlight the context clues that help you define the word.

- Define the word **benny**. Why is it important for a coach to have a "benny" on the team?

  _____

  _____

  _____

  _____

  _____

    At Cubberly High School in Palo Alto, where I was basketball coach, the presence of a benny was extremely unlikely. The students at Cubberly were white middle-class children of professionally oriented parents. For the most
20 part, these kids mirrored their parents. They were striving to

(continued)

become successful at something; what that something might be was never made clear. Without an objective in mind, the striving became all important. At Cubberly it meant getting in "advanced ability" groups, getting good grades, getting

25 accepted into a good university. Getting ahead. Getting through school. Getting. There was little time for intensity or giving to any one thing, especially a sport.

By a strange series of events it turned out I was wrong about ever finding a benny at Cubberly. It started when school

30 integration came to Palo Alto*. Black students volunteered to be bused across the freeway tracks. Cubberly High School as "host" school received its allotment of twenty-three "guest" students. As the basketball coach I waited anxiously to see if any athletes might be a part of this transfer. Of course I was

35 looking for a benny. Three days after the transfer students arrived I called the first basketball practice.

The turnout was excellent. Our basketball program had been successful during the past few years and it gradually became known that if you turned out, you would get a

40 chance to play. The prospect of gaining some new players from Ravenswood High School in East Palo Alto added to the tension and excitement of the first practice.

As the players came out onto the floor for the first time I noted some familiar kids that had started on last year's team.

45 In fluid movement they began the slow and graceful art of shooting their favorite shot. Dribbling a few steps and rearing up to take another shot. Rebounding and passing out to a fellow player. Reliving past plays. Moving to the fantasy of future game-winning shots. Eyeing the new players.

50 At the baskets on each side of the central court the new players are assembled. They dribble the available basketballs in place and watch the players moving on the center court. They don't talk much and look a little frightened. Then as if on cue they begin to turn and shoot at the available baskets.

55 They too have a private shot and a move to the basket. Soon the entire gym is alive with players outwitting invisible foes

* Until the 1960s, schools in many cities were segregated. In the early years of integration, students were often bused into different neighborhoods to achieve a better racial balance.

(continued)

Notes About Your Character's Traits:

Notes About Your Character's Traits:

_____

_____

_____

_____

_____

_____

_____

_____

_____

_____

_____

_____

_____

_____

_____

_____

_____

_____

_____

_____

_____

_____

and arcing up game winning shots. Another season is beginning.

60 Midway into this first practice Cubberly High School basketball met Huey Williams. He came rushing into the gym. In fact he ran around the entire court three times. He didn't have a basketball. He was just running. And smiling. Nodding his head to the dumbstruck players. He didn't speak a word. Just smiled and nodded hello. By his third lap,
65 everyone knew we had our first black athlete.

Identify It: Predicate Nominative, Predicate Adjective, or Direct Object

Read the underlined sections of the numbered sentences.

Write PN over the Predicate Nominative, PA over the Predicate Adjective, and DO over the Direct Object.

There are five sentences.

Huey Williams wasn't exactly the transfer student coaches dream about. 1 <u>He was short</u>, about the shortest player on the club. With stocky frame and bowed legs and radar-like hair, he seemed like a bottle of soda water, always about to
70 pop. 2 <u>His shots were explosions</u> of energy that pushed the ball like a pellet. When he ran, he couldn't stop. He'd race in for a layup and instead of gathering his momentum and softly placing the ball against the backboard, he raced straight ahead, full speed, ejecting the ball in midair flight
75 like a plane letting go a rocket. The ball usually slammed against the backboard or rim and careened across the gym. To say it simply, 3 <u>Huey was not a basketball player</u>. He was something else.

Every player carries to the game a personality. That's part
80 of what makes basketball so interesting. That personality is directly reflected in the way a person plays. Now, Huey brought with him a personality I had never quite seen before. 4 <u>He loved life</u>, people, school, anything and everything. "Mr. Jones, how are you today?" he'd say. "Fine I hope." You
85 would have to agree with Huey. 5 <u>His view of the world was contagious</u>. He always had a smile that burst out when you

(continued)

least expected. "Mr. Jones, I didn't shoot too well did I?" He'd be smiling, getting ready to shoot again.

90　　As the first black player on our team, Huey was well received. After all he didn't represent a threat to any of the white players. If anything he was a puzzlement. How could anyone try so hard, smile so much, and play so bad? Weren't all blacks supposed to be super athletes? How come he doesn't know his place, isn't solemn, and I like him?

95　You couldn't help but root for Huey and want to be around him. Carnegie and the make-you-feel-good folks could take lessons from Huey. He was a good human being that shared his optimism about life with anyone that ventured in his path. With a smile Huey started every practice with "We're
100　going to win this whole thing, Mr. Jones. Just watch!"

　　I didn't share Huey's enthusiasm. It was the most unusual group of kids I had ever coached. In fact the team really constituted three distinct groups. Huey represented one of these groups. This was a collection of five kids who had never
105　played before. They couldn't shoot or dribble, let alone jump. Passing was iffy. When they were on the court my greatest fear was that they might run into each other. Although lacking skill, they personified [1] Huey's faith and willingness to work hard. My gosh how they tried.

110　　A second group of kids on the team had all played together the past year. They were typical Palo Alto kids. I guess Chris Martin most exemplified the personality of this group. Chris was a class officer, good student, achievement oriented and serious about winning and of course playing.
115　Chris just tolerated Huey and most everything else. His attention was on the future. Basketball at Cubberly was like the Pony League, Little League and Junior League he had participated in so well. It was one more right step to some mythical big league called Hilton, or perhaps Standard Oil.

120　　Chris knew all the lessons and skills of basketball. His jump shot was a picturebook example of perfection. He released the ball at the peak of his jump and followed

---

[1] **personified:** described an object or idea as having human characteristics

(continued)

Notes About Your Character's Traits:

_____

_____

_____

_____

_____

_____

_____

_____

_____

_____

_____

_____

_____

_____

_____

_____

_____

_____

Unit 24

Notes About Your Character's Traits:

_____

_____

_____

_____

_____

_____

_____

_____

_____

_____

_____

_____

_____

_____

_____

_____

_____

_____

_____

_____

_____

_____

_____

_____

125 through with his hands guiding the path of the ball as it slid into the basket. The closest parallel to Chris' behavior might be described as that of a little old man. He was "finicky" at the age of sixteen. If things weren't just right, his voice would stretch several octaves and literally squeak. For Chris things going just right meant a championship and of course a star role. I liked and felt sorry for Chris all at the same time. He

130 reminded me of myself. A little selfish and awfully conceited. Extremely insulated from feelings.

A third group of kids making up the team can best be described as outlaws. Dave Warnock characterized this group. Whereas Huey had a reverence [2] for life and Chris

135 was busy controlling life, Dave seemed always on guard and challenging hell out of it. He was always in trouble. Usually a team is composed of kids like Huey who can't play and kids like Chris who have played throughout childhood. Kids like Dave rarely show up on a team. To have five kids like him on

140 the same team was most unusual. If not intolerable.

Dave's style of life and play was outside prediction. Dave reminded me of a stork trying to play basketball. His arms and legs flayed at the air as he stormed up and down the court. His shots were what players call "watch shots." He

145 would crank up the ball without facing the basket from some unexpected place and yet it would go right in. Prompting the defensive player to say, "Look in the other hand . . . you might find a watch." Dave was always a surprise. A surprise if he showed up for practice and a surprise that he stayed

150 with it. In a strange way he was also a breath of fresh air. He lived to the fullest. He didn't stop to explain his actions. He just acted.

---

[2] **reverence:** great admiration: respect

(continued)

Notes About Your Character's Traits:

Use the Clues B:

- Read lines 141–152.

- Reread the underlined phrase, **watch shots**. Highlight the context clues that help you define the phrase.

- Define a **watch shot**.

_____

_____

_____

So there you have it. Not exactly a dream team. Five kids charging around looking for the pass they just dropped. Five
155 kids straining for an expected championship. And five kids who might not even show up for the game. The entire team tilted on the verge of combustion. The kids that centered around Chris and Dave openly hated each other. Huey and his troop of warriors became the grease that kept the team
160 moving together. Happy and delighted to be playing they were oblivious [3] to the conflict. In their constant attempt to mimic a Warnock pass or a Chris jump shot they inevitably made the originals look ridiculous. Huey with his intensity and honesty put everything in perspective. It was simply
165 impossible to get angry or serious about yourself with Huey around. He had girlfriends to tell you about, a cheer for a good play, a hand for someone who had fallen, and a smile for everything. And if all that failed, he always had his "new shot" to show you.
170 It wasn't long before everyone was working to help Huey and the other inexperienced players. Chris was telling players about the right way to shoot. Dave was displaying one of his new trick passes. I was working hard to teach defense. If you don't have the ball, go get it. Don't wait for someone to put it
175 through the basket or even start a play. Go get the ball. Chase it. Surround it. Take it.

---

[3] **oblivious:** unaware; not noticing

(continued)

Unit 24

**Notes About Your
Character's Traits:**

_____

_____

_____

_____

_____

_____

_____

_____

_____

_____

_____

_____

_____

_____

_____

_____

_____

_____

_____

_____

_____

_____

We worked on how to press and trap a player with the ball. How to contest the inbound pass. Double team. Use the full court. Cut off the passing lane. Work together with
180 teammates to break over screens and sag into a help position. Work to keep midpoint vision. Block out. Experience the feeling of achievement without having the ball or scoring the winning point. Take pride in defense.

The intensity and intricate working of defense was
185 something everyone on the team could do, and something new for everyone to learn. Defense is something most basketball teams just do not concentrate on. It's the unseen part of the game. Working hard on the techniques of team defense began to slowly draw the team together with a
190 common experience. As for offense, well, I taught the basic passing pattern, but the shooting was up to whoever was on the court. Chris and his group ran intricate patterns for the layup or percentage shot. Dave with his team took the ball to the hoop usually after three dribbles and a confederate yell.
195 Huey's team did their best just to get the ball up the court.

By the start of the season we had one spectacular defense and three offenses. In fact I divided the team into the three distinct groups. In this way everyone could play. It confused the heck out of opponents. According to basketball etiquette
200 you're supposed to play your best five players. We played our best fifteen. You are also supposed to concentrate on scoring. We emphasized defense. Finally a good team has a mark of consistency. We were the most inconsistent team you could imagine.
205 We would start each game with Huey's bunch. They called themselves "the Reverends." With their tenacity [4] for losing the ball and swarming after it plus their complete inability to shoot, they immobilized their opponents. The starting fives they encountered couldn't believe the intensity
210 and madcaps of Huey's Reverends. By the time they realized they were playing against all heart and very little scoring potential, it was time to send in Chris' group. Chris' team called themselves the "A Train." That they were. They

[4] **tenacity:** determination; persistence

(continued)

Unit 24

methodically moved down the floor, executed a series of
215 crisp passes, and scored. By this time in the game Huey was
smiling his all-knowing smile, and the coach from the other
team was usually looking over at our bench in a state of
confusion. Just as the other team adjusted to systematic and
disciplined play, we sent in Dave's "G Strings." Dave's team
220 played with reckless abandon. They were always in places
they weren't supposed to be. Doing things that weren't in the
book. Playing their game.

By the middle of the season we were undefeated. Oh, I
had to suspend Dave for breaking rules in the locker room
225 and once for smuggling a girl onto the travel bus. And on
occasion I had to remind Chris that I was the coach, not
him. But all in all the team was actually becoming friends. It
was a joy to witness this chemistry. Huey's group gradually
improved. They started believing they could beat anyone. The
230 basketball still didn't go in the basket, but in their minds and
actions they were "starters." As for Chris, he was actually
beginning to yell for someone besides himself. And Dave,
well he didn't change much in an outward way. He was still
frantic on the basketball court. It was off the court that he
235 was becoming a little less defensive. He started telling me of
things he wanted in life. Things not that much different than
those securities and accomplishments sought by others. In
fact it was something as simple as friendship.

Our first defeat of the year came not on the basketball
240 court but at the hands of the school superintendent. With
twelve games already played, the superintendent declared
that all transfer students were ineligible [5] for interscholastic
sports. It was a knee-jerk reaction to other coaches in the
league who feared we might "raid" Ravenswood High School
245 of its top black athletes. No one worried about us stealing
away their intelligent students or class leaders, yet that's just
what we did. No one thought to ask the students and parents
how they felt. This was a coaches' decision. Coaches who
thought only about winning.

[5] **ineligible:** disqualified; cannot participate

(continued)

Notes About Your Character's Traits:

Unit 24

Notes About Your Character's Traits:

_____

_____

_____

_____

_____

_____

_____

_____

_____

_____

_____

_____

_____

_____

_____

_____

_____

_____

_____

250　　The superintendent ordered Huey off the team immediately. The announcement of this decision came not in a telephone call or personal visit, but in a ten word directive. "No transfer students will be eligible for interscholastic athletic teams."

255　　The announcement came on a game day. The team was already suited up waiting for the last minute game plan. I read the superintendent's decision to the team. They were stunned. And angry. Ideas and plots for Huey's survival rang out against the white-tiled dressing room walls. Dave

260　slammed his shoe against a locker. "It's a bad decision." Chris agreed. "We can appeal . . . let's go to the board of education." Dave snapped. "When—in three weeks?" Everyone joined the argument. "Let's give Huey a new number." Yeah, but can we also change his color?" "We can play against ourself . . .

265　can't we." "Let's make up our own league." In the din my own thoughts were welling up.

　　I didn't know when I started verbalizing my feelings, but I became aware of it as my whispers all of a sudden were audible in the now silent locker room. As my personal

270　decision became clearer so did my pronouncement of it. "Huey's dismissal is wrong. It's unfair to defer the decision or obey it. I think we should forfeit all our remaining games. Huey is a part of this team. If you are willing to give other teams an automatic win over us in exchange for having Huey

275　play . . . raise your hand." Fifteen players leaped to their feet. Dave was yelling, "Well, all right then, we've got a game to play!" It was unanimous.

　　The players streamed onto the floor to begin their warm up. I could hear a few rebel yells and even that high pitched

280　squeak of Chris'. Huey still brought gasps of surprise with his high velocity layup. When he did his latest new shot, a sweeping, running hook, the assembled fans roared approval. Huey grinned and promised more. As the players finished their warmup, the school principal came by to remind me of

285　the superintendent's decision. "Ron," he said, "I'm sorry about Huey, but he hasn't scored many points for you has he?" "No," I replied, "Huey hasn't scored a point." "Things will be different next year," he confided. I agreed.

(continued)

As the game was about to start they huddled for final
290 instructions. "Any after-thoughts?" I asked. "There is still
time." We were all bundled together in a knot. Hands thrust
together in a tight clasp. Everyone looked up. Eyes all met.
Every single kid was smiling. My gosh, I've got fifteen Hueys.

The horn sounded calling for the game to start. I took
295 the entire team to the scoring desk and informed the league
official. "We formally forfeit this game." The opposing
coach from Gunn High School rushed over to see what the
commotion was about. "What are you doing?" he asked. I
told him of our decision. "That doesn't make sense. You guys
300 are undefeated," he stammered. "We let two of *our* players
go today." "It's our decision," I explained. "We're here to play
basketball, all of us."

And we did. All of us. Huey did his patented dash.
Chris his jump shot while Dave relied on surprise. It was a
305 combination hard to beat. We poured in twenty more points
than Gunn and, more importantly, displayed a constant hustle.
Players ran to shoot free throws. Ran to take a place in the
game. Ran off the floor on being replaced. It reminded me of
that first practice with this strange kid running around the
310 gym. Perhaps we had learned more from Huey than we taught.
At the close of the game the Gunn coach stopped to comment,
"Congratulations, you've got quite a team there." I reminded
him that we had forfeited the game, that his team had won. He
turned, "No, your kids won. They're a bunch of bennys."

315 Dave Warmock was dead. Chris brought the message to
me. His father was a school official and he heard of the news
from the police. Dave had been at a party and suffocated
inhaling hair spray. Like a tape recorder erasing its content
I couldn't think or act. Then in forced flashes I began to
320 retread the past days. Searching for glimpses of Dave. His
face. His antics. Was there something there? A warning? A
plea? What did I miss?

The school community for the most part remained
ignorant of Dave's death and its self-destructive cause.
325 There were faculty murmurs, "That crazy kid." Other than
side glances at what had happened there was no marking of
Dave's death. Drugs and death are not part of the curriculum.

(continued)

**Notes About Your
Character's Traits:**

_____
_____
_____
_____
_____
_____
_____
_____
_____
_____
_____
_____
_____
_____
_____
_____
_____
_____
_____
_____
_____
_____
_____
_____
_____
_____
_____

Text Connection 12 (continued)

It was improper to alarm parents. The school didn't stop its parade. Even for a moment of respect or some such other
330 platitude. Nothing. Everything as usual. Including basketball.

The team gathered for practice out of habit. The season actually had only a few days left. It had been a corrugated course. Our protest to allow Huey the right to play had sparked a boycott of all team sports. The boycott led to
335 a change in the rules allowing transfer students to play with the condition that "due to the disruptions" no league championship would be awarded. It was ok with us. We declared ourselves champions. Actually it was Dave's idea. Oh man, it didn't seem fair. Dave was a storm. He kicked and
340 dared the world. And lost. Or did he? I don't know.

One good thing about sports is that you can lose yourself in physical exertion. Push yourself into fatigue. Let the body take over the crying in the brain. I informed the team that this would be our last practice. We would have a game, full
345 court scrimmage.

It was then that I realized Dave wasn't there. It's funny, Dave was dead yet I expected him to come prancing into the gym, the final trick on death itself.

Being short one player I joined in the scrimmage. First
350 Chris' bunch against Huey's team and then Dave's group to play Chris'. I stood in for Dave. The play was strangely conservative and sluggish. Perhaps this measured play was in deference to Dave. Were we all letting our thoughts wander? Just doing mechanical steps? Or was it a subconscious
355 statement that Dave's life was errant and not to be emulated?[6] Whatever, the play moved from one end of the gym to the other like the arm of a ticking clock. Up and down the floor.

It was Chris that broke the rhythm and silence. Without warning he sliced across the floor, stole a pass, dribbled the
360 length of the court and slam dunked. Then in an unexpected leap he stole the inbound pass. Taking the ball in one hand he pivoted up a crazy sweeping hook shot. It was a "watch shot" if I'd ever seen one. Out of the blue as the ball cut through the net Chris erupted with a shrill guttural yell that

---

[6] **emulated:** imitated

(continued)

Text Connection 12 (continued)

365 pierced the stillness. It was a signal. The game tempo picked
up, and became frantic. Everyone pushed to their maximum.
Straining for that extra effort. Hawking the ball. Diving for a
loose ball. Blowing tension. Playing with relaxed abandon.

It felt wonderful. The game was fierce. Everything learned
370 in years of play was used. New moves were tried. I crashed
for a rebound, dived, elbows flying after a loose ball and got
it. Sprinted full tilt on a fast break. Yelled full voice as I fed
Huey with a behind-the-back pass that he laid up for two.
Everyone is moving as if driven by some accelerating spell of
375 power and will. Everything goes in. We can play forever. Play
Forever.

The scrimmage raged on. The afternoon became evening
and still we played. The gym glowed in the yellow light, warm
and wet. We were racing now back and forth. Exploding for
380 shots. Playing the toughest defense. Jumping over a screen.
Blocking out. Back for one more sensation of excellence.

My chest heaved for relief. Body throbbed. I couldn't
stop playing. And didn't want to. Didn't Want To. Down the
court. Set up. That's it. Feed the cutter. Fantastic. Now the
385 defense. Keep low. No. Take it away. That's it. Steal the ball.
Now go. Fly.

In a heap I collapsed. Legs simply buckled. I was shaking.
Head not able to move. In slow motion the team centered
around my crumpled form. I'm all right. The air is rushing
390 back into an empty body. Giving life and movement. "I'm all
right." Everyone is breathing hard, pushing out air and taking
it back in. Grabbing their knees and doubling over. Letting
the body know it can rest.

Without any words everyone gathered themselves, then
395 silently headed for the locker room and home. It's over.
The scrimmage was ended. Practice finished. The season
complete.

I slowly shower and dress, waiting for the locker room to
empty. Walking through the silenced place I stop to look and
400 say goodbye. There is Chris' locker. A good kid. Hope his life
goes well. He has changed and matured. Been a part of other
lives. Huey's locker is still open. God, even his locker has a

Notes About Your Character's Traits:

_____

_____

_____

_____

_____

_____

_____

_____

_____

_____

_____

_____

_____

_____

_____

_____

_____

_____

_____

_____

_____

_____

_____

_____

(continued)

Unit 24

Notes About Your Character's Traits:

_____

_____

_____

_____

_____

_____

_____

_____

_____

_____

_____

_____

_____

_____

_____

_____

_____

_____

_____

_____

_____

_____

smile. What a person. I'll never forget. Dave's place. Empty. I hate you for leaving us. I love you.

405   I push up a twenty-five foot jump shot that is five feet beyond my range. It goes in. Rush to chase the ball. Try again. Seek the magnificent feeling of doing the undone. The unplanned. The unexpected.

    There is a sign that hangs over the exit from the locker 410 room. It reads, "There Is No Substitute For Winning." Someone scratched out the word winning and replaced it. "There Is No Substitute For Madness."

Resources

Resources

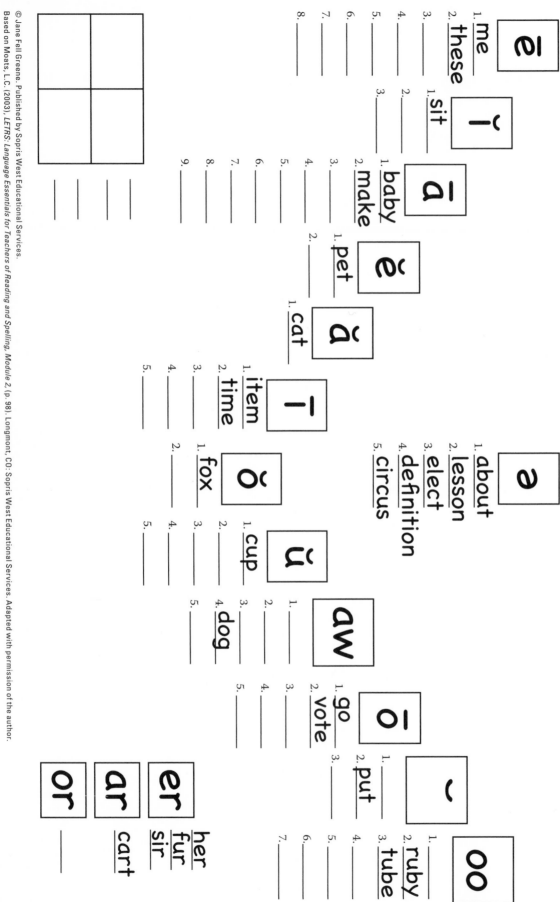

ē
1. me
2. these
3. _____
4. _____
5. _____
6. _____
7. _____
8. _____

ĭ
1. sit
2. _____
3. _____

ā
1. baby
2. make
3. _____
4. _____
5. _____
6. _____
7. _____
8. _____
9. _____

ĕ
1. pet
2. _____

ă
1. cat

ī
1. item
2. time
3. _____
4. _____
5. _____

ə
1. about
2. lesson
3. elect
4. definition
5. circus

ŏ
1. fox
2. _____
3. _____
4. _____
5. _____

ŭ
1. cup
2. _____
3. _____
4. dog
5. _____

aw
1. _____
2. _____
3. _____
4. _____
5. _____

ō
1. go
2. vote
3. _____
4. _____
5. _____
6. _____
7. _____

ˇ
1. put
2. ruby
3. tube
4. _____
5. _____
6. _____
7. _____

oo
1. _____

er
her
fur
sir

ar
cart

or
_____

Consonant Chart

Mouth Position

Type of Consonant Sound	Lips	Lips/Teeth	Tongue Between Teeth	Tongue Behind Teeth	Roof of Mouth	Back of Mouth	Throat
Stops	/ b / / p /			/ t / / d /		/ k / / g /	
Fricatives		/ f / / v /	/ th / / th /	/ s / / z /	/ sh /		/ h /
Affricatives					/ j / / ch /		
Nasals	/ m /			/ n /		/ ng /	
Lateral				/ l /			
Semivowels	/ w / / hw /			/ r /	/ y /		

© Jane Fell Greene. Published by Sopris West Educational Services.
Adapted with permission from Bolinger, D. (1975). *Aspects of Language* (2nd ed.) (p. 41). New York: Harcourt Brace Jovanovich.

Divide It Checklist

Steps for Syllable Division	Example: disconnected
First, check the word for prefixes and suffixes. Circle them. Next, look at the rest of the word:	(dis)connect(ed)
1. Underline the **first** vowel. Write a **v** under it.	(dis)connect(ed)
2. Underline the **next** vowel. Write a **v** under it.	(dis)connect(ed)
3. Look at the letters **between** the vowels. Mark them with a **c** for consonant.	(dis)connect(ed)
4. Look at the pattern and divide according to the pattern.	(dis)con/nect(ed)
5. Place a diacritical mark over the vowels. Cross out the **e** at the end of final silent **e** syllables. Listen for schwa in the unaccented syllable, cross out the vowel, and place a ə symbol above it.	(dis)con/nect(ed)
Finally, blend each syllable and read the word.	disconnected

Diacritical Marks and Symbols

Diacritical marks and **symbols** are used to indicate the correct sound for the vowel graphemes.

breve / brĕv /	ă	short vowel phonemes
macron	ā	long vowel phonemes
circumflex	âr	**r**-controlled phonemes
schwa	ə	schwa phoneme

Syllable Division Patterns

Pattern	How to Divide	Examples
vccv	vc / cv • Divide between the consonants. • The first syllable is closed. • The vowel sound is short.	nap/kin VCCV
vcv	v/cv • **Usually**, divide after the first vowel. • The first syllable is open. • The vowel sound is long. **Note:** If the first vowel is followed by an **r**, the syllable is **r**-controlled. or vc/v • If the first division does not result in a recognizable word, divide after the consonant. • The first syllable is closed. • The vowel sound is short.	si/lent VCV mar/ket V CV nev/er VCV
vcccv	• vc/ccv or vcc/cv • Divide before or after the blend or digraph. • Do not split the blend or digraph.	ath/lete VCCCV
vv	• v/v • Divide between the vowels if they are not a vowel team or diphthong. • The first syllable is open. • The vowel sound is long.	ne/on V V
c + le	• /cle • Count back three and divide.	cra/dle 321

Check It: Reasons/Examples Checklist

IDEAS AND CONTENT

☐ Is my position clearly stated?

☐ Did I give three reasons for evidence?

☐ Did I tell how the reasons support my topic?

ORGANIZATION

☐ Did I stick to the topic?

☐ Did I sequence my ideas?

☐ Did I end with a conclusion sentence?

Conventions

☐ Did I punctuate correctly?

☐ Did I capitalize correctly?

☐ Did I spell correctly?

☐ Did I use complete sentences?

Writer's Checklist

1. PRE-WRITING

Did I: ☐ Identify what kind of writing I am doing?

☐ Think about who my audience is?

☐ Generate a list of words and ideas to get me started?

☐ Determine what I need to know and gather the resources I need?

☐ Decide how my writing should be organized?

☐ Create an outline or other framework to organize my ideas?

2. WRITING A FIRST DRAFT

Did I: ☐ Write in pencil to make revising easier?

☐ Write from my notes or outline?

☐ Let my thoughts roll, without getting hung up on details?

☐ Keep my audience and purpose in mind as I wrote?

3. REVISING

I Used (check one):

☐ the **Checklist for Revising** (if I am revising my work independently)

☐ the **Peer Writing Review** (if I am revising with a peer)

4. PROOFREADING AND PUBLISHING

Did I: • Punctuate sentences correctly?

☐ capitalize first word

☐ capitalize proper nouns

☐ use correct end marks

• Check my spelling?

☐ words with endings (doubling, drop *e*, change *y*, advanced doubling)

☐ easily confused words (*there, their*)

☐ place names

☐ longer words

• Check sentence structure?

☐ run-ons and fragments

☐ verb tense

• Make a clean, correct, final copy of my work?

Checklist for Revising

Read your writing with a critical eye. Check to make sure you have done each thing below. Make any necessary revisions.

IDEAS AND DEVELOPMENT: *My writing has...*

- ☐ an introduction, body, and conclusion
- ☐ clear main ideas or clear story events
- ☐ enough details or facts to make my ideas interesting and well supported

ORGANIZATION: *My writing has...*

- ☐ a strong beginning that will grab my readers' interest
- ☐ an ending that won't leave my readers hanging
- ☐ a logical flow of ideas
- ☐ transition and signal words
- ☐ no repeated ideas
- ☐ no sentences that are off the topic

VOICE: *I have used...*

- ☐ language that fits my audience
- ☐ my personal voice

SENTENCE FLUENCY: *I have included...*

- ☐ a variety of sentence lengths
- ☐ different kinds of sentence types

WORD CHOICE: *I have made sure to use...*

- ☐ colorful adjectives
- ☐ specific nouns and verbs
- ☐ phrases that create pictures in readers' minds

IDEAS AND DEVELOPMENT

- Is the draft focused on the assigned topic?
- Does the draft include an introduction, body paragraphs, and a conclusion?
- Are the main ideas or main events easy to understand?
- Are there enough details to make the ideas clear and well supported?

Things That Work Well:

_____

_____

_____

Things You Might Improve:

_____

_____

_____

ORGANIZATION AND FLOW

- Does the beginning catch your interest? How can it be improved?
- Do the ideas flow in an order that makes sense?
- Has the writer used transition words to help make the flow of ideas clear? Give examples.
- Does the writing have a strong ending? How could the ending be stronger?

Things That Work Well:

_____

_____

_____

Things You Might Improve:

_____

_____

_____

STRONG SENTENCES

- Has the writer used a variety of sentence types? Give examples.
- If any sentences seem unclear, how can they be improved?
- Has the writer used specific verbs and nouns? What are some examples of these?
- Has the writer used colorful adjectives to create pictures in readers' minds? Can any be added or changed?

Things That Work Well:

_____

_____

_____

Things You Might Improve:

_____

_____

_____

Word Fluency 1

	Correct	Errors
1st Try		
2nd Try		

curtain	against	captain	abroad	nuisance	language	captain	curtain	abroad	language	10
captain	curtain	nuisance	against	language	abroad	against	language	captain	curtain	20
against	language	abroad	curtain	nuisance	captain	nuisance	captain	curtain	language	30
abroad	nuisance	captain	language	against	curtain	abroad	curtain	language	against	40
language	captain	abroad	nuisance	curtain	against	curtain	language	abroad	captain	50
captain	language	curtain	against	abroad	nuisance	abroad	captain	curtain	against	60
curtain	against	nuisance	captain	language	abroad	captain	language	nuisance	curtain	70
language	nuisance	curtain	abroad	against	captain	abroad	against	captain	language	80
abroad	language	captain	nuisance	curtain	against	language	curtain	abroad	captain	90
captain	nuisance	curtain	against	abroad	nuisance	abroad	language	curtain	against	100

	Correct	Errors
1st Try		
2nd Try		

pain	paint	rain	load	rail	speed	boat	free	keep	free	10
rain	boat	pain	paint	speed	keep	rail	load	load	road	20
boat	rail	rain	pain	paint	road	speed	keep	keep	free	30
paint	load	boat	rain	rail	pain	road	boat	road	speed	40
speed	keep	load	boat	rain	paint	load	pain	pain	free	50
rail	road	keep	load	speed	free	boat	paint	rain	pain	60
load	speed	keep	keep	road	rain	pain	boat	free	paint	70
road	boat	rail	free	rain	pain	boat	rail	keep	speed	80
boat	pain	load	speed	rain	keep	paint	road	free	rail	90
keep	load	boat	road	pain	rail	speed	free	paint	rain	100

Word Fluency 3

	Correct	Errors
1st Try		
2nd Try		

asleep	between	fifteen	entertain	explain	remain	constrain	contain	10
fifteen	restrain	asleep	constrain	between	complain	entertain	remain	20
restrain	entertain	fifteen	between	asleep	explain	remain	contain	30
between	explain	restrain	entertain	fifteen	asleep	complain	constrain	40
constrain	complain	explain	remain	contain	asleep	entertain	contain	50
entertain	remain	complain	restrain	fifteen	between	asleep	contain	60
explain	constrain	entertain	remain	complain	fifteen	restrain	between	70
remain	restrain	explain	fifteen	contain	asleep	between	constrain	80
restrain	asleep	between	constrain	explain	complain	fifteen	entertain	90
complain	explain	restrain	asleep	remain	entertain	contain	constrain	between	fifteen	100

Word Fluency 4

	Correct	Errors
1st Try		
2nd Try		

artist	artful	greener	greenness	plainer	plainness	sweeten	sweetness	steeper	steepness	**10**
greener	sweeten	artist	sweetness	artful	steeper	greenness	plainer	steepness	plainness	**20**
sweeten	greenness	greener	artful	artist	plainer	sweetness	plainer	steeper	steepness	**30**
artful	plainer	sweeten	greenness	artist	steeper	plainness	steeper	steepness	sweetness	**40**
sweetness	steeper	plainer	artful	greener	greenness	artist	steeper	plainness	steepness	**50**
greenness	plainness	steeper	plainer	sweeten	artful	greener	sweetness	artist	artist	**60**
plainer	sweetness	greenness	plainness	steeper	artist	sweeten	artist	steepness	artful	**70**
plainness	sweeten	greener	artful	artist	greener	artful	artist	steeper	sweetness	**80**
sweeten	artist	artful	sweetness	plainer	steeper	greener	artist	steepness	greenness	**90**
steeper	plainer	sweeten	artist	plainness	greenness	steepness	sweetness	artful	greener	**100**

Passage Fluency 1

	Errors	Correct
1st Try		
2nd Try		

Speed matters in some sports. Runners and speed skaters race with amazing speed. Let's look at the speeds of these two sports in the early days. — 8 / 17 / 26

In 1928, an unknown 16-year-old girl won gold. She was a high school junior. She took first place. The event itself was a first. Women's track and field was new. The sport had just been added to the Olympic Games. — 34 / 44 / 53 / 63 / 66

Betty Robinson was that girl. She won the women's 100-meter dash. Robinson had never thought of an Olympic race. One afternoon, she was running to catch a train. A track coach spotted her. Four months later, she won a college championship. Next, she finished second at the Olympic trials. Then, she won the 100-meter run at the Amsterdam games. She set a record at 12.2 seconds. — 74 / 80 / 88 / 97 / 106 / 113 / 121 / 131 / 132

In 1931, Robinson survived a plane crash. They thought she wouldn't walk again. She recovered and trained hard. She ran in the 1936 Olympics. She was on the women's relay team. — 140 / 147 / 156 / 163

They called Clas Thunberg the "king of speed skating." In 1924, he won three gold medals. He also won a silver and a bronze. Four years later, he continued his Olympic success. He won two more gold medals. Thunberg set the 1500-meter record. His time was 2:20.8. — 171 / 180 / 190 / 198 / 205 / 210

Thunberg was a master bricklayer from Helsinki, Finland. He won his last Olympic gold at age 34. He was the oldest Olympic champion in speed skating. He continued skating until he was 42. — 217 / 227 / 235 / 244

Word Fluency 1

	Correct	Errors
1st Try		
2nd Try		

course	friend	guarantee	guess	guard	course	guest	guard	guest	10
guarantee	course	guess	guest	friend	guest	friend	guarantee	course	20
friend	guest	guard	guess	guess	guarantee	guard	course	guest	30
guard	guess	guarantee	friend	friend	guest	course	course	friend	40
guest	guarantee	guard	guess	course	course	guard	guarantee	guarantee	50
guarantee	guest	course	friend	guard	friend	guard	guarantee	friend	60
course	friend	guess	guest	guard	guarantee	guess	course	course	70
guest	guard	course	friend	guard	friend	guard	guarantee	guest	80
guard	guest	guarantee	guess	course	guest	friend	guard	guarantee	90
guarantee	guess	course	guard	friend	guard	guest	course	friend	100

Unit 20 • Fluency   R17

Fluency

Word Fluency 2

	Correct	Errors
1st Try		
2nd Try		

hollow	shallow	increase	decrease	great	break	tie	lie	field	10
increase	lie	hollow	tie	shallow	feast	field	decrease	break	20
lie	decrease	increase	shallow	hollow	great	break	tie	field	30
shallow	great	lie	decrease	increase	field	hollow	feast	tie	40
tie	feast	great	break	lie	shallow	increase	decrease	field	50
decrease	break	feast	lie	great	field	tie	shallow	hollow	60
great	tie	decrease	break	feast	increase	hollow	lie	shallow	70
break	lie	great	increase	field	hollow	shallow	decrease	tie	80
lie	hollow	shallow	tie	great	feast	break	increase	decrease	90
feast	great	lie	break	decrease	field	tie	field	increase	100

Word Fluency 3

	Correct	Errors
1st Try		
2nd Try		

donkey	monkey	relieve	believe	steam	stream	valley	value	window	yellow	10
relieve	valley	donkey	value	monkey	window	believe	yellow	steam	stream	20
valley	believe	relieve	monkey	donkey	steam	value	stream	window	yellow	30
monkey	steam	valley	believe	relieve	yellow	donkey	window	stream	value	40
value	window	steam	stream	valley	monkey	relieve	believe	donkey	yellow	50
believe	stream	window	valley	steam	yellow	value	monkey	relieve	donkey	60
steam	value	believe	window	relieve	valley	donkey	yellow	monkey	monkey	70
stream	valley	relieve	stream	yellow	donkey	monkey	believe	window	value	80
valley	donkey	monkey	value	steam	window	stream	relieve	yellow	believe	90
window	steam	valley	donkey	stream	believe	yellow	value	monkey	relieve	100

Word Fluency 4

	Correct	Errors
1st Try		
2nd Try		

#										
10	sneaky	squeaky	export	extract	detract	deport	deform	reform	informal	formula
20	export	deform	sneaky	reform	squeaky	informal	formula	extract	detract	deport
30	deform	extract	export	squeaky	sneaky	detract	reform	deport	informal	formula
40	squeaky	detract	deform	extract	export	formula	sneaky	informal	deport	reform
50	reform	informal	detract	deport	deform	squeaky	export	extract	sneaky	formula
60	extract	informal	deport	detract	deform	formula	reform	squeaky	export	sneaky
70	detract	reform	extract	deport	informal	detract	deform	sneaky	formula	squeaky
80	deport	detract	deport	formula	export	informal	squeaky	extract	informal	reform
90	deform	sneaky	squeaky	reform	detract	informal	deport	export	formula	extract
100	informal	detract	deform	sneaky	deport	extract	formula	reform	squeaky	export

	Correct	Errors
1st Try		
2nd Try		

Ogden Nash became famous. He was known for playing. But his kind of play was unique. He was a 20th century poet. He became famous for playing with words. | 8
| 18
| 26
| 29

The times were bleak. His career was young. Life offered few opportunities for play. *The New Yorker* magazine was a prominent publication. It was first to publish his poetry. The year was 1930. The Great Depression had begun. The stock market had crashed in 1929. Banks and businesses closed. Investors lost vast sums of money. Unemployment was common. By 1930, it hit one person in five. People suffered. | 38
| 45
| 52
| 62
| 69
| 77
| 84
| 92
| 97

Nash knew he could help people. He understood words. He knew they were a great source of laughter. He knew something else. Humor could relieve despair. Humor could decrease hopelessness. He knew, too, that words held power. And he knew that words were *free.* | 105
| 114
| 121
| 126
| 133
| 141

It's his word play that stops us. It makes us pay attention. It is funny. It makes us think. It's humor for people who like having fun with words. | 152
| 162
| 170

Often, Nash plays with sounds in words. This helps create his word play. He knew what word repetition could do. He knew what rhythm could do. He knew what rhyme could do. They all triggered memory. They all helped him celebrate language. A celebration is a *bash.* Nash had a bash with words. We can have fun with him. Let's enjoy his word play. A few of Nash's bashes follow. | 178
| 187
| 195
| 204
| 211
| 220
| 230
| 239
| 240

Word Fluency 1

	Correct	Errors
1st Try		
2nd Try		

#										
10	beautiful	beauty	business	women	leopard	busy	business	beautiful	busy	women
20	business	beautiful	leopard	busy	women	beauty	women	business	beautiful	busy
30	beauty	women	busy	business	leopard	beautiful	business	leopard	beautiful	women
40	busy	leopard	business	women	beauty	beautiful	busy	beautiful	women	beauty
50	women	business	busy	beautiful	leopard	beauty	women	beautiful	business	busy
60	business	women	beautiful	beauty	busy	leopard	business	beautiful	busy	beauty
70	beautiful	beauty	leopard	business	women	business	leopard	women	leopard	beautiful
80	women	leopard	beautiful	busy	beauty	business	busy	business	women	women
90	busy	women	business	leopard	beautiful	busy	beauty	beautiful	busy	business
100	business	beautiful	busy	beauty	leopard	busy	beautiful	women	beautiful	beauty

	Correct	Errors
1st Try		
2nd Try		

10	modest	metal	moral	formal	road	industry	mystery	history	among	amongst
20	road	industry	modest	mystery	metal	among	moral	formal	amongst	history
30	modest	metal	road	moral	industry	amongst	history	mystery	among	formal
40	moral	road	metal	amongst	modest	history	formal	industry	moral	among
50	modest	amongst	metal	history	among	mystery	road	industry	road	moral
60	amongst	history	among	modest	moral	metal	formal	road	metal	mystery
70	among	modest	amongst	formal	history	metal	formal	history	mystery	road
80	moral	metal	mystery	among	modest	history	amongst	modest	industry	formal
90	mystery	modest	history	road	industry	metal	road	industry	among	amongst
100	history	among	moral	modest	mystery	road	amongst	formal	industry	metal

Word Fluency 3

	Correct	Errors
1st Try		
2nd Try		

10	separate	several	particular	practical	regular	regret	difficult	different	attract	attend
20	regular	regret	separate	difficult	several	attract	particular	practical	attend	different
30	separate	several	regular	particular	regret	attend	attract	difficult	different	practical
40	particular	regular	several	attend	separate	different	difficult	practical	regret	attract
50	separate	attend	difficult	different	practical	attract	regular	several	particular	difficult
60	attend	different	attract	particular	regret	separate	different	practical	several	regular
70	attract	separate	attend	practical	several	different	regular	difficult	particular	regret
80	particular	several	difficult	attract	separate	difficult	different	attract	regret	practical
90	difficult	separate	different	regular	several	regret	separate	particular	attract	attend
100	different	attract	particular	separate	regular	difficult	attend	practical	regret	several

Correct	Errors
1st Try	
2nd Try	

infinite	infinity	intensive	inventive	congregate	conductor	consider	sweetness	incomplete	inconsistent	10
intensive	consider	infinite	sweetness	infinity	incomplete	inventive	inconsistent	congregate	conductor	20
consider	inventive	intensive	infinity	infinite	congregate	sweetness	conductor	incomplete	inconsistent	30
infinity	congregate	consider	inventive	intensive	inconsistent	infinite	incomplete	conductor	sweetness	40
sweetness	incomplete	congregate	conductor	consider	infinity	intensive	inventive	infinite	inconsistent	50
inventive	conductor	incomplete	consider	congregate	inconsistent	sweetness	infinity	intensive	infinite	60
congregate	sweetness	inventive	conductor	incomplete	intensive	consider	infinite	inconsistent	infinity	70
conductor	consider	congregate	intensive	inconsistent	infinite	infinity	inventive	incomplete	sweetness	80
consider	infinite	infinity	sweetness	congregate	incomplete	conductor	intensive	inconsistent	inventive	90
incomplete	congregate	consider	infinite	conductor	inventive	inconsistent	sweetness	infinity	intensive	100

Passage Fluency 1

	Correct	Errors
1st Try		
2nd Try		

You know what cousins are. Imagine a tomato. | 8
Now, imagine a potato. Did you know that | 16
tomatoes and potatoes are cousins? Does that | 23
sound weird? It's true. Plants have families, too. | 31
They're placed in families according to a | 38
"taxonomy." Taxonomy is a method. It organizes | 45
things. It classifies. It categorizes. It helps | 52
scientists in their work. | 56

Scientists called botanists study plants. They | 62
consider all parts. They examine the stem. They | 70
study the seeds and the flowers. They inspect the | 79
roots. They decide which plants belong in the | 87
same families. They study plant parts that can be | 96
seen. They also study plants' genes. They search | 104
for similar features. Then, they group similar | 111
plants. Plants fit into families. | 116

A plant's flower is important. It often gives the | 125
best clue to its family. Flowers that are shaped | 134
like crosses indicate the *Cruciferae* or Cabbage | 141
family. The scientific name comes from a word | 149
that means "cross." | 152

Can you tell what plants are related? It isn't | 161
always easy to spot relatives. As in human | 169
families, they don't always look alike. Think of a | 178
rose and an apple. They don't look alike. But | 187
roses and apple trees are in the same family. Now, | 197
picture that potato again. Next, picture a chili | 205
pepper. The potato grows below ground. Its taste | 213
is mild. The pepper grows above ground. It tastes | 222
spicy. But, you guessed it. Both belong to same | 231
family. | 232

Word Fluency 1

	Correct	Errors
1st Try		
2nd Try		

colleague	extraordinary	iron	journal	peculiar	journey	iron	colleague	journal	peculiar	10
iron	colleague	journey	extraordinary	peculiar	journal	extraordinary	peculiar	iron	colleague	20
extraordinary	peculiar	journal	colleague	iron	iron	journey	iron	colleague	peculiar	30
journal	journey	iron	peculiar	extraordinary	colleague	journal	journal	peculiar	extraordinary	40
peculiar	iron	journal	journey	colleague	extraordinary	colleague	peculiar	journal	iron	50
iron	peculiar	colleague	extraordinary	journal	journey	journal	iron	colleague	extraordinary	60
colleague	extraordinary	journey	iron	peculiar	journal	iron	peculiar	journey	colleague	70
peculiar	journey	colleague	journal	iron	extraordinary	iron	journal	iron	peculiar	80
journal	peculiar	iron	journey	journal	colleague	iron	peculiar	journal	iron	90
iron	journey	colleague	extraordinary	peculiar	journey	journal	peculiar	colleague	extraordinary	100

Word Fluency 2

	Correct	Errors
1st Try		
2nd Try		

Words										#
humble	handle	double	trouble	title	little	angle	ankle	bottle	battle	10
double	angle	humble	ankle	handle	bottle	trouble	battle	title	little	20
angle	trouble	double	handle	humble	title	ankle	little	bottle	battle	30
handle	title	angle	trouble	double	battle	humble	bottle	little	ankle	40
ankle	bottle	title	little	angle	handle	double	trouble	humble	battle	50
trouble	little	bottle	angle	title	battle	ankle	handle	double	humble	60
title	ankle	trouble	little	bottle	double	angle	humble	battle	handle	70
little	angle	title	double	battle	humble	handle	trouble	bottle	ankle	80
angle	humble	handle	ankle	title	bottle	little	double	battle	trouble	90
bottle	title	angle	humble	little	trouble	battle	ankle	handle	double	100

	Correct	Errors
1st Try		
2nd Try		

threaten	between	guilt	guilty	build	built	death	cousin	country	10
guilt	deaf	threaten	death	between	cousin	country	build	built	20
deaf	guilty	guilt	between	threaten	build	built	cousin	country	30
between	build	deaf	guilty	guilt	country	threaten	built	death	40
death	cousin	build	built	deaf	between	guilt	threaten	country	50
guilty	built	cousin	deaf	build	country	death	guilt	threaten	60
build	death	guilty	built	cousin	guilt	deaf	threaten	country	between	70
built	deaf	build	guilt	country	threaten	between	guilty	cousin	death	80
deaf	threaten	between	death	build	cousin	guilt	country	guilty	90
cousin	build	deaf	threaten	built	guilty	country	between	guilt	100

Word Fluency 4

	Correct	Errors
1st Try		
2nd Try		

probable	portable	valuable	progress	vulnerable	hazardous	humorous	different	program	difficult	10
valuable	humorous	probable	different	portable	program	progress	difficult	vulnerable	hazardous	20
humorous	progress	valuable	portable	probable	vulnerable	different	hazardous	program	difficult	30
portable	vulnerable	humorous	progress	valuable	difficult	probable	program	hazardous	different	40
different	program	vulnerable	hazardous	humorous	portable	valuable	progress	probable	difficult	50
progress	hazardous	program	humorous	vulnerable	difficult	different	portable	valuable	probable	60
vulnerable	different	progress	hazardous	program	valuable	humorous	probable	difficult	portable	70
hazardous	humorous	vulnerable	difficult	probable	valuable	probable	portable	program	different	80
humorous	probable	portable	different	vulnerable	program	hazardous	valuable	difficult	progress	90
program	vulnerable	humorous	probable	hazardous	progress	difficult	different	portable	valuable	100

In step one, choose the words and write the clues. | 10
Pick six to eight words. Include a mix of shorter | 20
and longer words. Write a simple clue for each | 29
word. | 30

In step two, "cross" the words. Use grid paper to | 40
figure out how the words will fit together. Start by | 50
writing one word that goes across the grid. Then | 59
write another word that goes down. One letter in | 68
the second word should cross a letter in the first | 78
word. Add the remaining words, one at a time. | 87
Each word should cross at least one letter in | 96
another word. | 98

In step three, number the words. After all of the | 108
words are in place, number them. Start with the | 117
word at the top. Number the words from top to | 127
bottom and from left to right. | 133

In step four, number and sort the clues. Number | 142
the clues the same way you numbered the words. | 151
For example, let's say that the word "triangle" is | 160
number 1 in the puzzle. The clue for "triangle" | 169
should also be number 1. Then sort the clues into | 179
two groups: "Across" and "Down." | 184

In step five, make a blank puzzle. Draw a dark | 194
outline around the shape of your puzzle. Then | 202
make a blank version of it. Be sure to include the | 213
numbers. | 214

In step six, finish the puzzle. Write the clues | 223
under the puzzle. Then give your crossword to | 231
someone else to solve. | 235

Word Fluency 1

	Correct	Errors
1st Try		
2nd Try		

#									
10	hour	honest	honor	herb	courage	debt	courage	herb	courage
20	courage	herb	debt	honor	hour	courage	honor	debt	herb
30	hour	courage	honor	herb	debt	honest	honor	courage	debt
40	debt	hour	debt	honor	courage	hour	herb	honor	honest
50	herb	honest	honor	courage	hour	honest	honest	courage	hour
60	debt	herb	courage	honor	courage	debt	honest	courage	herb
70	courage	honor	hour	herb	honest	hour	herb	honor	courage
80	hour	herb	debt	honest	herb	debt	honest	courage	debt
90	herb	courage	honor	honest	courage	honor	hour	herb	honest
100	debt	courage	honor	honest	hour	honor	honest	courage	herb

	Correct	Errors
1st Try		
2nd Try		

boy	boil	soy	soil	joy	join	allow	aloud	sour	shower	10
soy	allow	boy	aloud	boil	sour	soil	shower	joy	join	20
allow	soil	soy	boil	boy	joy	aloud	join	sour	shower	30
boil	joy	allow	soil	soy	shower	boy	sour	join	aloud	40
aloud	sour	joy	join	allow	boil	soy	soil	boy	shower	50
soil	join	sour	allow	joy	shower	aloud	boil	soy	boy	60
joy	aloud	soil	join	shower	sour	allow	boy	shower	boil	70
join	allow	joy	soy	aloud	boy	boil	soil	sour	aloud	80
allow	boy	boil	aloud	joy	sour	join	soy	shower	soil	90
sour	joy	allow	boy	join	soil	shower	aloud	boil	soy	100

Fluency

Word Fluency 3

	Correct	Errors
1st Try		
2nd Try		

disappoint	exploit	annoy	enjoy	mouse	anyhow	mouth	shower	however	tower	10
annoy	mouth	disappoint	shower	exploit	however	enjoy	tower	mouse	anyhow	20
mouth	enjoy	annoy	exploit	disappoint	mouse	shower	anyhow	however	tower	30
exploit	mouse	mouth	enjoy	annoy	tower	disappoint	however	anyhow	shower	40
shower	however	mouse	anyhow	mouth	exploit	annoy	enjoy	disappoint	tower	50
enjoy	anyhow	however	mouth	mouse	tower	shower	exploit	annoy	disappoint	60
mouse	shower	enjoy	anyhow	however	annoy	mouth	disappoint	tower	exploit	70
anyhow	mouth	mouse	tower	disappoint	exploit	disappoint	enjoy	however	shower	80
mouth	disappoint	exploit	shower	mouse	however	anyhow	annoy	tower	enjoy	90
however	mouse	mouth	disappoint	anyhow	enjoy	tower	shower	exploit	annoy	100

Word Fluency 4

	Correct	Errors
1st Try		
2nd Try		

perform	perfect	prefer	difficult	defector	disinfect	reject	object	memorize	legalize	10
prefer	reject	perform	object	perfect	memorize	difficult	legalize	defector	disinfect	20
reject	difficult	prefer	perfect	perform	defector	object	disinfect	memorize	legalize	30
perfect	defector	reject	difficult	prefer	legalize	perform	memorize	disinfect	object	40
object	memorize	defector	disinfect	reject	prefer	difficult	perform	prefer	legalize	50
difficult	disinfect	memorize	reject	defector	legalize	object	perfect	prefer	perform	60
defector	object	difficult	disinfect	memorize	prefer	reject	perform	legalize	perfect	70
disinfect	reject	defector	prefer	difficult	perform	perfect	legalize	memorize	object	80
reject	perform	perfect	object	defector	memorize	disinfect	prefer	difficult	legalize	90
memorize	defector	reject	perform	disinfect	difficult	legalize	object	perfect	prefer	100

	Errors	
Correct		
1st Try	2nd Try	

We can measure length by using a ruler. We can | 10
measure heat and cold with a thermometer. We | 18
can measure how fast a car is going with a | 28
speedometer. But what if we want to measure a | 37
car's power? What would we use? Believe it or | 46
not, we would use horses. | 51

Cars are often described as having "horsepower." | 59
Why do we compare the power of cars to the | 68
power of horses? The rise of many civilizations | 76
throughout the world has happened with the help | 84
of horses. Approximately 50,000 years ago, some | 91
of the earliest people kept horses for food. When | 100
early humans started farming, they tamed the | 107
horse. For centuries, people have used horses to | 115
move things. | 117

James Watt was the first person to coin the term | 127
"horsepower." He invented a new kind of steam | 135
engine in the 18th century. When he was ready to | 145
sell it, he wanted a way to say how much power | 156
the engine had. He wanted to say that the engine | 166
could do the work of so many horses. To do this, | 177
he had to figure out the power of one horse doing | 188
a task. By watching a horse pull a mill, Watt | 198
calculated that one horse could pull 33,000 | 205
pounds, one foot, in one minute. This became the | 214
definition for "horsepower." | 217

We now measure the power of cars, lawn mowers, | 226
vacuums, and many other machines using | 232
horsepower. | 233

	Correct	Errors
1st Try		
2nd Try		

Words										Count
listen	villain	pour	half	limousine	tambourine	pour	listen	half	tambourine	10
pour	listen	limousine	villain	tambourine	half	listen	villain	tambourine	listen	20
villain	tambourine	half	listen	limousine	tambourine	limousine	pour	tambourine	limousine	30
half	limousine	pour	tambourine	villain	listen	pour	villain	villain	tambourine	40
tambourine	pour	half	limousine	villain	pour	half	listen	half	villain	50
pour	tambourine	listen	half	limousine	villain	listen	half	pour	listen	60
listen	villain	limousine	half	pour	tambourine	limousine	listen	tambourine	limousine	70
tambourine	limousine	villain	pour	half	villain	pour	villain	tambourine	pour	80
half	tambourine	pour	listen	villain	tambourine	half	pour	half	tambourine	90
pour	limousine	listen	villain	half	tambourine	listen	villain	limousine	villain	100

Fluency

Word Fluency 2

Correct	Errors
1st Try	
2nd Try	

tidy	tied	coil	cried	shout	shown	dream	beagle	grader	griddle	10
coil	dream	tidy	beagle	tied	grader	cried	griddle	shout	shown	20
dream	cried	coil	tied	tidy	shout	beagle	shown	grader	griddle	30
tied	shout	dream	cried	coil	griddle	tidy	grader	shown	beagle	40
beagle	grader	shout	shown	dream	tied	coil	cried	tidy	griddle	50
cried	shown	grader	dream	shout	griddle	beagle	tied	coil	tidy	60
shout	beagle	cried	shown	grader	coil	dream	tidy	griddle	tied	70
shown	dream	shout	coil	griddle	tidy	tied	cried	grader	beagle	80
dream	tidy	tied	beagle	shout	grader	shown	coil	griddle	cried	90
grader	shout	dream	tidy	shown	cried	griddle	beagle	tied	coil	100

	Correct	Errors
1st Try		
2nd Try		

excuse	expense	integrate	integrity	implicate	indicate	nuclear	abound	unclear	bounty	10
integrate	nuclear	excuse	abound	expense	unclear	integrity	bounty	implicate	indicate	20
nuclear	integrity	integrate	expense	excuse	implicate	abound	indicate	unclear	bounty	30
expense	implicate	nuclear	integrity	integrate	bounty	excuse	unclear	indicate	abound	40
abound	unclear	implicate	indicate	nuclear	excuse	unclear	integrity	excuse	bounty	50
integrity	indicate	unclear	nuclear	implicate	bounty	abound	expense	integrate	excuse	60
implicate	abound	integrity	unclear	integrate	nuclear	excuse	bounty	expense	expense	70
indicate	nuclear	implicate	integrate	bounty	excuse	expense	integrity	unclear	abound	80
nuclear	excuse	expense	abound	implicate	unclear	indicate	integrate	bounty	integrity	90
unclear	implicate	nuclear	excuse	indicate	integrity	bounty	abound	expense	integrate	100

Word Fluency 4

	Correct	Errors
1st Try		
2nd Try		

painful	playful	conductor	contractor	optimize	winterize	overhear	overload	disagree	disarray	10
conductor	overhear	painful	playful	overload	disagree	contractor	disarray	optimize	winterize	20
overhear	contractor	conductor	playful	painful	optimize	overload	winterize	disagree	disarray	30
playful	optimize	overhear	contractor	conductor	disarray	painful	disagree	winterize	overload	40
overload	disagree	winterize	overhear	contractor	conductor	disarray	painful	disagree	disarray	50
contractor	winterize	disagree	overhear	optimize	winterize	overhear	playful	conductor	painful	60
optimize	overload	contractor	winterize	disagree	overhear	disarray	overload	playful	conductor	70
winterize	overhear	optimize	conductor	disarray	conductor	overhear	painful	disarray	playful	80
overhear	painful	playful	overload	optimize	disagree	playful	contractor	disagree	overload	90
disagree	optimize	overhear	painful	winterize	contractor	disarray	overload	playful	conductor	100

	Correct	Errors
1st Try		
2nd Try		

Sleep. Benjamin Franklin warned it could be a   8
waste of time. Shakespeare disagreed. He called   15
sleep the bath that heals the pains of work. He   25
said that sleep soothes troubled minds. He called   33
it the most nourishing food in life's feast.   41

It looks like Shakespeare was on the right track.   50
Sleep is definitely not a waste of time. It's   59
essential. We can't live without it. But it's not just 69
the body that needs it. It's the brain!   77

During sleep, something fantastic happens. We   83
dream. Some people remember their dreams.   89
Others say they never dream. But everybody does.   97
We just don't always remember our dreams.   104
Before we begin to understand dreams, though,   111
we have to understand sleep.   116

What happens when we sleep? Our brains take a   125
roller-coaster ride. Sleep has five stages. It spikes 133
up and down. We drift. We dream. We wake. The   143
pattern repeats several times each night.   149

Dreams can happen during any stage. But REM   157
sleep is prime time for dreaming. During REM,   165
the brain's nerve impulses increase. The brain's   172
logic centers take a nap. The limbic system gets   181
involved. Emotion and memory become active.   187
The "big sleep" of dreamtime happens in part of   196
the brain's cortex. The cortex controls logic.   203
Maybe that's why dreams don't make sense. And   211
it's probably why our dreaming brains don't care.   219

Adapted from "The Brain Never Sleeps" by Faith Hickman Brynie

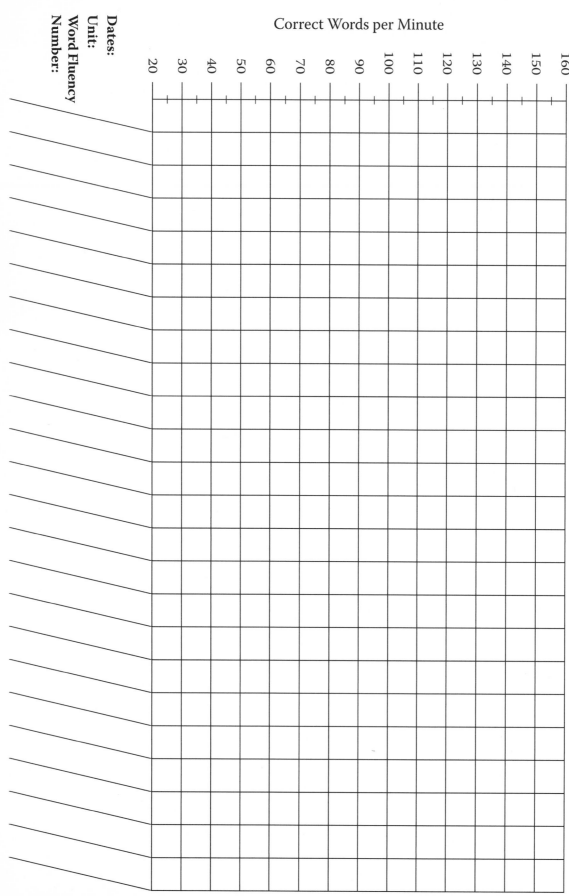

Correct Words per Minute

Dates:
Unit:
Word Fluency
Number:

Word Fluency Chart

160
150
140
130
120
110
100
90
80
70
60
50
40
30
20

Word Fluency Chart

Dates:
Unit:
Word Fluency
Number:

Fluency Charts

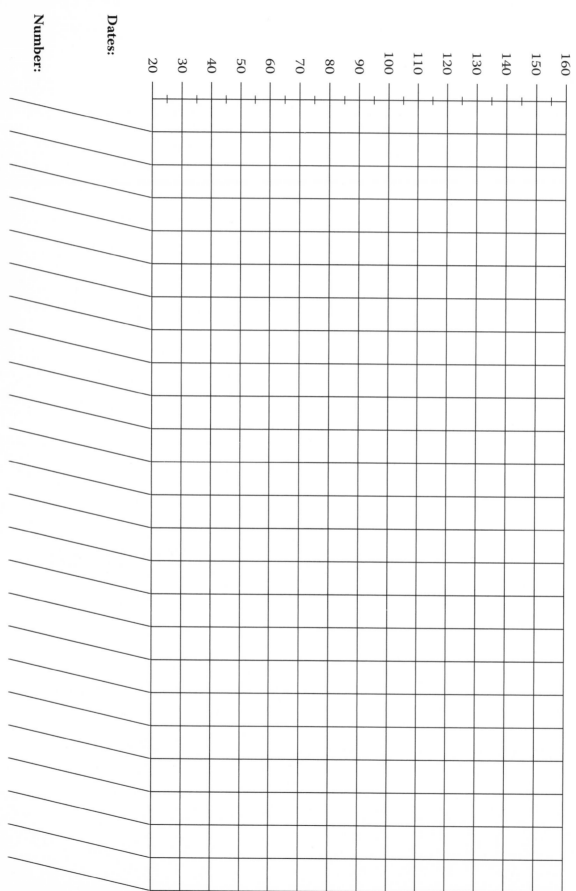

Correct Phrases Per _____

160
150
140
130
120
110
100
90
80
70
60
50
40
30
20

Dates:

Number:

Unit 19

abroad	against	captain
curtain	language	nuisance

Unit 20

course	friend	guarantee
guard	guess	guest

Unit 21

beautiful	beauty	business
busy	leopard	women

Unit 22

colleague	extraordinary	iron
journal	journey	peculiar

Unit 23

courage	debt	herb
honest	honor	hour

Unit 24

half	limousine	listen
pour	tambourine	villain

Word Building Letter Cards

Unit 19

| ai | ai | oa | oa | ee | ee | |

Unit 20

| ay | ay | ea | ea | ie | ie | |
| ey | ey | ow | ow | oe | oe | |

Unit 22

| ui | ui | ou | ou | ea | ea | |

Unit 23

| oi | oi | oy | oy | ow | ow | |
| ou | ou | | | | | |

Unit 19	Unit 19	Unit 19
mid-	mis-	fore-
Unit 19	Unit 19	Unit 19
over-	-ness	-ist
Unit 19	Unit 19	Unit 19
-ment	-less	-en
Unit 19	Unit 19	Unit 19
-ness	-ful	-dom

Unit 19 **-some**		
Unit 20 **ex-**	Unit 20 **de-**	Unit 20 **re-**
Unit 20 **pre-**	Unit 20 **un-**	Unit 20 **-y**
Unit 20 **-er**	Unit 20 **-est**	Unit 20 **-ing**

Unit 20	Unit 20	Unit 20
-ed	**-en**	**-ly**
Unit 20	Unit 20	Unit 20
port	**form**	**tract**
Unit 20	Unit 20	
pend	**pens**	
Unit 21	Unit 21	Unit 21
con-	**col-**	**com-**

Unit 21	Unit 21	Unit 21
cor-	in-	il-
Unit 21	Unit 21	Unit 21
im-	ir-	in-
Unit 21	Unit 21	Unit 21
il-	im-	ir-
Unit 21	Unit 21	Unit 21
-or	duc	duce

Unit 21	Unit 21	Unit 21
duct	**scrib**	**script**

Unit 21	Unit 21	
rect	**reg**	

Unit 22	Unit 22	Unit 22
dis-	**dif-**	**di-**

Unit 22	Unit 22	Unit 22
pro-	**-able**	**-ous**

Unit 22	Unit 22	Unit 22
dic	dict	spect

Unit 22	Unit 22	
puls	pel	

Unit 23	Unit 23	Unit 23
per-	e-	ef-

Unit 23	Unit 23	Unit 23
-ate	-ize	fac

Unit 23	Unit 23	Unit 23
fec	fic	fact
Unit 23	Unit 23	
ject	lumen	

Bank It

Student _____ Date_____

Syllable Types

Student _____ Date_____

Syllable Types

Student _____ Date _____

Syllable Types

Bank It

Student _____ Date _____

Prefixes

Bank It

Student _____ Date_____

Prefixes

Bank It

Student _____ Date_____

Prefixes

Bank It

Student _____ Date _____

Roots

Bank It

Student _____ Date _____

Roots

Bank It

Student _____ Date _____

Roots

Student _____ Date _____

Suffixes

Bank It

Student _____ Date_____

Suffixes

Student _____ Date_____

Suffixes

Sources

Unit 19

Fiber Optics: High Speed Highways for Light

Day, Nancy. 1996. "High-Speed Highways for Light: Optical Fibers," from *Odyssey* (February), vol. 5, no. 2. Carus Publishing, 315 Fifth St., Peru, IL 61354. All rights reserved. Adapted with permission.

Korenic, Eileen. 1994. "Zooming In on Light Speed," from *Odyssey*, vol. 3, no. 4. Carus Publishing, 315 Fifth St., Peru, IL 61354. All rights reserved. Adapted with permission.

O'Meara, Stephen James. 1996. "Space-Time and the 'Ether' Bunny," from *Odyssey*. Carus Publishing, 315 Fifth St., Peru, IL 61354. All rights reserved. Adapted with permission.

Raymond's Run

Bambara, Toni Cade. 1971. "Raymond's Run," from *Gorilla, My Love*. New York: Random House. Copyright 1971 by Toni Cade Bambara. Used with permission.

Unit 20

A Game of Catch

Wilbur, Richard. 1953. "A Game of Catch," from *The Sea-Green Horse: A Collection of Short Stories*. New York: Macmillan. Copyright 1953 by Richard Wilbur. Reprinted by permission of Harcourt. Originally appeared in *The New Yorker*, 1953.

The Marble Champ

"The Marble Champ" from *Baseball in April and Other Stories*, copyright 1990 by Gary Soto, reprinted by permission of Harcourt. This material may not be reproduced in any form or by any means without prior written permission of the publisher.

Unit 21

A Family in Hiding: Anne Frank's Diary

Frank, Anne. 1995. *The Definitive Edition: Anne Frank: The Diary of a Young Girl*. Edited by Otto H. Frank and Mirjam Pressler. Translated by Susan Massotty. New York: Bantam Books. Copyright 1995 by Doubleday, a division of Random House. Used by permission of the publisher.

The Anne Frank Center USA. 2003. "Anne Frank: Life and Times," from the Anne Frank Center USA website. http://www.annefrank.com/0_home.htm (accessed November 19, 2004).

My Side of the Story

Bagdasarian, Adam. 2002. "My Side of the Story," from *First French Kiss and Other Traumas*. New York: Melanie Kroupa, Farrar, Strauss, and Giroux. Copyright 2002 by Adam Bagdasarian. Reprinted by permission of Farrar, Straus, and Giroux.

Unit 22

A Collection of Puzzling Tales

Shannon, George. 1985. *Stories to Solve: Folktales From Around the World*. New York: Harper Collins. Text copyright 1985 by George Shannon. Used by permission of HarperCollins Publishers.

The Disappearing Man

Asimov, Isaac. 1985. "The Disappearing Man," from *The Disappearing Man and Other Mysteries*. New York: Walker. Reprinted by permission of the Estate of Isaac Asimov c/o Ralph M. Vicinanza, Ltd.

The Dust Bowl

Roop, Peter. 1983. "Living in the Dust Bowl," from *Cobblestone* (December), vol. 4, no. 12. Carus Publishing, 315 Fifth St., Peru, IL 61354. All rights reserved. Used with permission.

Sources

Unit 23

Zaaaaaaap!

Ratliff, Jennifer A. 2004. "Zaaaaaaap!" from *Odyssey* (April), vol. 13, no. 4. Carus Publishing, 315 Fifth St., Peru, IL 61354. All rights reserved. Adapted with permission.

Satyagraha

Carter, Alden R. 2001. "Satyagraha," from *On the Fringe*, edited by Donald R. Gallo. Copyright 2001 by Alden R. Carter. Used by permission of Dial Books for Young Readers, A Division of Penguin Young Readers Group, A member of Penguin Group (USA) Inc., 345 Hudson Street, New York, NY 10014. All rights reserved.

Unit 24

Dream Team

Jones, Ron. 1976. "Winning," from *The Co-Evolution Quarterly* (Summer). By permission of the author. Copyright 1976 by Ron Jones.

Dreaming the Night Away

Herbst, Judith. 1985. "The Great Shut-Eye Mystery," from *Bio Amazing: A Casebook of Unsolved Human Mysteries*. New York: Antheum Publishers. Reprinted with the permission of Atheneum Books for Young Readers, an imprint of Simon & Schuster's Children's Publishing Division. Copyright 1985 by Judith Herbst.